ENGLISH DENTIST

Happy reading.
Michael Sydney.

Jiesh

Michael Sydney

Published by Puppy Doom Publishing, 2017.

ISBN 978-1-912145-24-9

PUPPY DOOM PUBLISHING

HangoutWithMikey.com

To my beautiful A
With thanks to N, R and M

CONTENTS

PROLOGUE 7
1. EXILED 9
2. PRISON 11
3. CII 19
4. FIRED UP 24
5. BLAGGING THE JOB 36
6. I JUST LOVE TEETH 40
7. HIGH HATS 49
8. A BAD FIT 57
9. TIESHA 66
10. THE SACK RACE 74
11. BACK IN – FOR A BIT 80
12. UNFINISHED BUSINESS 92
13. JACK 98
14. THE DEAL 104
15. DAY ONE: GROUND ZERO 112
16. THE MADNESS CONTINUES 118
17. TITS VS MASH 125
18. CHAOS 137
19. PROGRESS 147
20. IT'S ALL ABOUT TRUST 155
21. DODGY DEALINGS 165
22. CLAWS IN 172

23. WHEN PUSH COMES TO SHOVE 179
24. THE MAKING OF A NARWHAL 187
25. BOILING POINT 197
26. THE FIGHT 209
27. HAMMER TIME 214
28. PAYING FOR IT 222
29. WAR BREAKS OUT 233
30. THE MASTERPLAN 236
31. THE MASTERPLAN: PART TWO 243
32. OVERSIGHT 252
33. D-DAY 260
34. GAME FACES 267
35. SICK OF IT 279
36. THE STING 287
37. THE CAT 297
38. JUDGEMENT DAY 305
END CREDITS 321
AUTHOR'S MESSAGE 323
I. THE DARKER TRUTH BEHIND THE SCENES 325
II. WHAT LIES AHEAD… 336

PROLOGUE

I could never have imagined that stripping naked at a dental Christmas do or collaborating with a retiring drunk would pave the way to becoming the fastest rising multimillionaire in one of the most corrupt industries in the NHS.

Forget dodgy doctors and nurses or anything else you may have seen in the news. What 'they' don't tell you is why dentistry, beyond all others, now has the highest suicide rate of any career in the UK.

Fresh out of Uni and stuck for a job I soon realised that if I were to get ahead in this game my ability to drill a tooth would count for absolutely nothing.

This account is based very closely on what happened. For the protection of certain individuals who wish not to be identified, all names and locations have been altered. For story form, the timeline of some events has been adjusted, narrative license used and characters fused for simplification, while other stories have been left out.

I will explain various discrepancies at the end. In the meantime, sit back, relax and enjoy… it's about to begin.

Michael Sydney

1

EXILED

The year was 2007. I was 25 years old and from a small town in Yorkshire. Having just graduated from the final training year known in the profession as Vocational Training (VT), I was less than six months in but, already, my career was spiralling – downwards.

Standing in a beauty salon on the outskirts of Leeds, I found myself faced with a 60-year-old, sun-beaten battle-axe who was ready to pay me 300 quid for the impossible dream. The dream being that I could make the huge bags under her eyes and grooved wrinkles on her face disappear to make her look 20 years younger.

To my right in the bay next to me, which was partitioned with only a stained blue mouldy curtain, was the dodgy salon owner I was working for, Sheila – another sunbed worshiper – who was pushing hard for the sale of a second colonic irrigation course to some poor punter she'd already been rogering for the last ten minutes with her pipe.

The room was dark. Everything in here smelled damp. Emanating from under the moth-eaten divide, which was a foot short of the floor, was a mild smell of poo which I was trying to ignore.

I was trying to ignore everything in this place.

As I picked up my needle and vial of Botox from my baby box, I saw to my left a fat woman gawping at me through the gap in the curtain.

She was being slowly spread-eagled on 'The Toner', another gimmick of the salon's, which was basically an ancient 60s stirrup machine that promised effort free abs and tight bums. All yours if you just pay the £20 fee to lie there and have your legs mechanically waved.

Mrrrrrrrrrrrrrrrrrrrrrrrrrrrrrrrrrrrrrrrrr.

Oh yeah – how could I forget – above me and coming out of every dust-ridden speaker the salon had, the inescapable sound of whale cries, cries that were the salon's guarantee to transport you to a tranquil place. A place where you're supposed to be able to relax to the sound of 70-foot killer whales swimming towards you.

"Are you sure this will make me look young again?" Barbara, my despairing client, asked me, her triple-bagged eyes clutching onto what I knew was an impossible hope of youth.

Holding up my needle, facing her at the end of the bed, I took a moment to reflect…

"Yeah," I inject.

How the fuck did it get to this…?

2

PRISON

To be fair, before I had sunk to this point and way before I'd got my career off the ground, I had been a prize dick.

Having qualified from Sheffield University* and completed all the necessary dental training, I expected my prospects to be good – I'd scored highly in my exams, I'd been awarded great grades for my clinical skills – I just couldn't get a job.

My classmates could. They were already working in cushy dental practices around town, whereas, for my first summer, following three months of painful rejections, I'd become well and truly stuck. The seeds of my problems were sewn just at the moment I was due to graduate and at the critical stage when everyone had to apply for jobs. Unfortunately, I'd made the wrong joke to the wrong nurse. Trudy was her name, a 38-year-old student hater and eternal gossiper. More importantly, she was also the only nurse on university clinic who just so happened to double up as the main drug rep serving nearly every dental practice in The North…

*Location changed

One afternoon during training, as she sauntered into clinic – late – the way she usually did,

"Well I must be doing something right," Trudy waded right into the middle of us ignoring the fact that, as students, all we really wanted was her assistance, "cos guess where they flew me last night?"

"Where?" One of my Uni mates had to ask her, getting used to the idea this would only be another brag about her drug repping job.

"Scotland!" Trudy lorded it once more like a queen.

This woman had zero qualms about taking the mick out of any of us and she had become quite the ringleader to the cohort of other dental nurses who were also being paid by the Uni to help. Annoyingly, when it came to actually assisting us, as they were supposed to do, taking Trudy's lead, none of them could be bothered to lift a finger.

Even our teachers were too afraid to ask them for anything! It had become routine for the dozen or so nurses to just stand around bitching and gossiping and leaving us struggling trying to treat patients by ourselves.

I assumed, like any other day, it would be OK to return the banter. After all, Trudy had taken the piss out of me several times about my being lanky, and even getting dumped by my ex. Surely then, any joke I made from here on in would be fair game, right????

Wrong – as I was about to find out!

"Yeah they flew me up last night," she repeated.

"Why?" I stupidly pitched in. "Are you that much of a high-class prostitute?"

"Gwaaah!" I was immediately met with gasps.

Fuck.

Even the other students were recoiling and I realised my intonation was way off. I'd only meant this in jest but standing between them and opposite me, Trudy started welling up. Clearly this remark wasn't going down well. Before I knew it,

"Sometimes Michael," her bottom lip quivered, "you go too far," she finished before stomping off.

Damn!

Chasing after her, I had to accept that I'd been an immature dick. Despite endless apologies though and doing everything I could to appease her, she was eternally scorned and the damage was done…

From this moment forth, as I was to discover, Trudy would have her revenge. Every single interview I subsequently attended, I failed. Trudy had made sure of this by going round every practice I was being considered for, warning them not to touch me with a barge pole.

I was finished!

I'd not even started when I was out and there was now nothing I could do…

About eight weeks later, a mate of mine handed me an industry circular he had been given which was advertising for a dentist to work in a maximum-security prison on the outskirts of Selby. Apparently, the prison was looking for someone to fix the backlog after they'd failed to employ a dentist there for six months.

I tried not to imagine the hordes of tooth-ached murderers and diseased psychopaths there, but I did wonder – what happened to their last guy??

Anyway, no time to be picky, grabbing the phone I called them straight up.

I spoke to the agency which was handling the position. It was clear that they knew very little about dentistry and without asking me too many questions they explained that they simply needed someone to fill the post. I expressed my willingness and without further ado, they offered me the job.

"Great!" I thought.

Two weeks later, after emailing my passport details and, ironically, having to complete their required CRB check to allow me to enter their prison, feeling nervous as hell, I stood for my very first day outside the huge steel gates of HMP Halsden* which was surrounded by nothing but farmland and appeared to be in the middle of nowhere.

I checked in with the guard at the gatehouse. With no idea what to expect, I signed in and was first locked into a bare room which had only three bolted chairs for company. Left alone and wondering what would come next, I heard the unlocking of a heavy steel door on the far side. It was the manager of the medical wing coming to collect me.

"Hello," the short woman greeted. "You must be the dentist they've sent. I'm Miss Hunt," she said holding on to a large ring of keys.

"Hi," I stood to shake her free hand. "I'm Michael."

In her 40s, short brown bob and glum face, Miss Hunt looked a bit like Angela Merkel but appeared to be friendly – to begin with.

"Come this way," she guided me along.

*Name transposed for identification protection

She escorted me through an empty courtyard with a series of 30-foot mesh gates. I still hadn't seen any prisoners yet. As we walked, she explained that the agency had yet to find them a dental nurse and having been so long without a dentist, they had quite a backlog. Furthermore, they were massively understaffed in nearly all other departments and it transpired that they wouldn't be able to provide me with a guard.

Marvellous!

Just the thought of how I'd soon be expected to trust my fingers between the teeth of whatever psychos they had waiting for me – only a latex glove for protection – I shuddered.

Finally we arrived outside the locked entrance of the medical wing. Essentially it was a 60-metre concrete block with no windows on the lower floor and only small barred windows on the top. Miss Hunt pressed the buzzer.

"I'm bringing him in," she said.

Bzzzzzzzzzzzzzzzz – a horrible electrifying sound unlocked the door.

Pulling on the huge heavy handle to open it, "Here we go," she gestured me inside.

Entering by the bottom of a stairwell, I could immediately hear the intimidating shouts of prisoners who were hanging around on the floor above – some of them loud…

"CUNT, OUT MI WAY," one shouted.

"MISS!" another bawled. "WHEN'S THAT DENTIST GETTIN' 'ERE?"

My God. It felt like I was walking into a wolf pit.

From where I was standing none of the prisoners could see me so I took a moment to peek up through the steel railing of the staircase. I spotted the gang of them waiting on the upper deck.

Gutted! Taking a deep breath I realised that my choice of clothes this morning had been a bad idea and I would stick out like a sore thumb. The prisoners were all uniformed in brown, and the permanent staff were all wearing grey. Not having known what to wear, I'd stupidly come in pleated white clinical trousers and a brand new bright white shirt I'd bought from Debenhams the previous week. In any other surgery, this would have looked normal. Suddenly, it dawned on me that, in a place like this I looked effectively like a gay sailor.

Eeee..

"Well come on," Hunt urged me to go on ahead.

Reluctantly having to ascend the first flight of concrete steps, I turned to the second flight to finally face the gang waiting above.

"ARRRR!" a burley Scouser shouted, pointing at me from the bannister. "Are you the dentist?!!"

"Ha!!" another sniggered making the rest of them stare. "He looks pasty as fuck!"

Hunt was still behind me leaving me no choice but to walk right into them as they blocked me at the top.

"Ooooop, move out of his way," the nearest teased.

"Lannnnky," another shouted from the back.

This felt intimidating.

We pushed past and Hunt continued to escort me to the end of the corridor leaving the convicts watching and waiting on the steps. She unlocked the last door.

"Right, here's your room," she revealed a surgery that looked like it had hardly been used. "Here's the list of cons you've got to see," she handed me a clipboard. "Oh, and if they try anything," she casually brushed, stepping back out, "just press this red button by the door. Ok?"

Huh? What?

Already she was walking off. What kind of induction was that?!

Hunt was obviously busy managing everything else.

As she left me to it in my barred surgery, I figured that the term 'maximum security' was a joke. I could only envisage trying to press the red button by the door while I was getting bummed in the opposite corner. This definitely wasn't my idea of maximum security.

"Come on dentist!" I heard a convict shout.

Anyway, pressured to get a move on and no time to adjust, I heard the impatient rabble had started shouting only twenty feet away. Switching the machines on and quickly grabbing a few tools, I rush read the list. There were 15 or so convicts I had to see. Mostly the names looked normal but the first one made me recoil:

"The Truck?"

Was this real?

Stepping into the corridor I called out the name,

"Hello is there a Mr Truck?" I said not knowing what to expect.

Soon, emerging from the back, a huge black guy stepped through the gang. Stomping towards me he looked so hard he could probably kill me with just his dick. I held the door for him. Wading past me he stepped inside.

The door was now closed behind leaving just the two of us but how was I supposed to be??

Should I act friendly?? Do I need to be cautious??

He sat in the dental chair which I then reclined. The silence was intense. I felt very uneasy. All of a sudden in the room next to me, a medical nurse shouted at another prisoner who was moaning…

"WELL IF IT'S HURTIN'," she laid into him with her no nonsense strong Yorkshire accent, "SHUT IT N' GET T' DICK DOCTOR!!"

Ha. Hearing this, I realised, nothing else for it, I simply needed to man up.

"How can I help?"

3

CII

To me, prison was crazy.

Though 'The Truck' turned out to be a nice guy, I knew that acclimatising to the rest of this place would take some time. Over the passing weeks I made friends with all the medical staff who worked alongside me on the wing. They were great, but some of the convicts we had to see were nuts.

This jail contained all kinds – lifers, repeat murders, robbers, even some charming crooks, and every couple of months or so, one or two of the more defiant ones would attempt a dirty protest. This involved prisoners covering themselves in their own shit knowing that the guards wouldn't want to handle them. Their protests appeared to make no sense, however, as the response by the guards was always the same.

No matter how often 'cons' repeated this performance, instead of stressing or letting the prisoner out, the security staff would simply push food through the prisoner's hatch and just leave them in their cell, now covered in turd but with all the time in the world to question whether this particular form of protest had been a good idea.

Imagine that! Imagine being the tough new convict having hoped to make a name for yourself or show everyone how 'dead 'ard' you are, only to find yourself abandoned, sitting alone on your bed, covered in your own gravel-juice and stinking. At some point, you'd have to think, "Shit (appropriately), maybe Billie's idea back in the canteen wasn't so cool."

It was insane. Out in the exercise yard, however, there were other strange habits and behaviours too. Sharing the same breaks as the rest of the medical staff, each day we would walk across to the cookhouse at lunchtime only to see the drone of convicts in the yard all walking defiantly anticlockwise in one huge unified circle.

Apparently this pattern still occurs across most UK prisons, and felons say it's to work time against the clock to shorten their sentence.

Good one – surely to make their theory correct though, wouldn't they be better to walk with the clock to speed time away?!

Maybe this is why we have prison.

Anyway, two months in now and I had seen all sorts, including a convict who was rushed into the medic bay after someone had thrown a pan of boiling sugar water in his face. Yes, prison could be a nightmare place for all concerned but I had no idea that I was about to face a nightmare of my very own...

Midweek and returning early from lunch I went into the medical building and climbed the stairs alone. All the wings were still on lockdown. When I opened up the surgery door, to my complete horror, I was confronted with a young skinhead convict loose inside my surgery and now ravaging, with his bare hands, through the sharps bin.

WTF?!

"Hey! Put 'em back!" I shouted.

God knows how he'd got here but aware that the nearest guard would still be on lunch three buildings away, I knew that the panic buttons were useless.

"Hey, put 'em back!" I repeated, trying to balance friendliness with authority.

His name was John. As a hardened convict serving for murder he was infamous for having CII on his arm. Apparently he tried to self-tattoo 'CITY', his beloved Manchester football team but, finding it too painful, he'd stopped half way through the 'T'.

"Come on man fucking drop 'em!!" I said, swearing this time for effect.

Ignoring me, John continued scraping like some rabid dog.

Shit.

Realising that he was hunting for the non-screw type needle which he could sell, one rarely used in dentistry but worth £300 on the black market, I froze just as he finally turned to face me.

"Drop what?!" John gritted.

Clenching fistfuls of live needles, his knuckles tattooed with the words "FUCK" and "OFF" – I didn't need his subtitles to figure that this was bad.

"The needles," I softened. "I can see them in your hand, put 'em back!"

My arse twitched. I knew these guys could switch in an instance and I was in full sight of the dots of blood which were now oozing from the pricks on his fingers.

"I aint got any!" John grunted, remaining ever-defiant by the bin.

"John. Fucking drop 'em!!" I tried firming with authority.

Watching his eyes dart, I was aware a quarter of the prisoners here had HIV, hepatitis or some other life-threatening disease so one wrong move meant I could wind up copping one.

"Come on man," I tried.

Eyes still scanning elsewhere, CII obviously intended to do something, but what?

Everyone knew that heroin and steroids were rife in here but that needles were about the only thing their friends couldn't get past the metal detector during visits despite security staffing shortages. Trapped in a standoff and freaking. Was this the prize he'd fight me for?

Suddenly we heard a door swing open fifty yards down the corridor.

"OK OK," John relented at the sound of footsteps marching up.

Still, he dumped only a few back in the box.

Clocking this sleight of hand, "Hey you've still got one!" I said when my position of power evaporated.

We could both hear that whoever had come into the corridor had now gone and my rescue was not about to happen. Without warning, "Do you FUCKIN WANNA GO?!!" John lunged at me.

"Hey-ey-ey," I backed up.

Shit.

I tried to keep a safe distance but CII was almost on top of me.

"COME ON FUCKIN PAD ME IF YOU WANOO!" he gritted right up in my face.

"OK open your shirt," I bluffed any command.

"See. Nothin'!" he flashed, boxing me by the door.

"Well empty your pockets!" I tried again, my authority vanishing.

"TOLD YOU – NOTHIN'!" he pushed even closer. "COME ON FUCKIN PAD ME!"

I was helpless.

Having me right up against the wall now, CII was raging for trouble. The chances were that he still had a live needle on him somewhere. Alone and with no one around, it would take a brave man to want to pat him for a bit of HIV.

With me being the only thing in his way, John barged for the exit. Scared, I quietly stepped aside.

Letting him slink off, I knew I should have been braver. I preferred to tell myself that he wasn't lying and had dropped all the needles back, but I guessed John had just left with exactly what he wanted.

Later that afternoon when the staff returned I didn't report anything. Perhaps this was wrong of me, perhaps I was ashamed but a lot of guards had become my friends and I figured that, if he'd lie to me, he'd lie to them and I didn't want them tasked with having to pat some ruthless bastard only to get pricked too.

In jail the evil underworld would never change and I knew that drawing other staff further into it wouldn't stop a thing…

4

FIRED UP

With everything seeming to settle down after this, the prison job was progressing well but it was only part-time.

Saddled with huge Uni debts and interest-rising overdrafts, I still needed to find more work and fill the rest of my week to make ends meet any way I could. My young dental nurse Natalie, who had eventually been supplied by the prison's elected agency, said she knew of a beauty salon where I could try offering tooth whitening.

"OK," I said. Fairly desperate by this point I decided to give it a go.

The address was on the outskirts of Leeds. On a cold early February morning, pulling up in my rust bucket Fiesta outside a run-down shopping parade, I spotted the salon shelved above a Chinese takeaway. Trying to block from my mind the number of dentists who would be frowning on me for doing this, I found the entrance and headed inside, thinking if this could help me pay off my debts, I'd be thankful.

Having arranged to see the owner already, I climbed the stairs before entering a small dark brown reception area to finally meet her. Sheila, a bleached-haired, leather-skinned 50-year-old. Surprisingly busy, Sheila was surrounded by six younger women all at little desks scrubbing their six customers' nails hard, while others awaited their turn. The way everyone appeared beholden to this woman, in this diverse little place, made her seem like some western brothel keeper. Sheila's blank stare also told me that she barely remembered my phone call.

"Are you the dentist?" she greeted.

"Hi yeah," I said realising I was the only guy there.

"OK I'll show you round."

She took me through a connecting room which was slightly larger than the reception. It was a mess and crammed with all sorts, but it was clear that if they thought they could make money out of any fad, they would try it, no matter how ridiculous. The level of bullshit they successfully marketed was unreal.

It was here, down one side, that I first saw the set of old beige coloured stirrup machines called 'Toning Tables' which could, supposedly, help your weight plummet without you having to do any exercise at all. Packed along the opposite side they had a row of treatment beds divided by dusty blue curtains which were moth-eaten and must have cost the salon about a quid. Regardless, it was busy, and over the whale music blasting out, Sheila explained the list of treatments they sold.

They offered everything from the infamous 'Flab-Jabs' (injections that could apparently dissolve fat) right through to £200 sessions of 'Cellugon' (a name they'd given to some magic vacuum cleaner which, if rubbed over a woman's legs, could, allegedly, banish cellulite). It certainly was an eye-opener.

I just couldn't believe people paid so much for this shite. As I took it all in, several overweight women on the toning tables stared at me curiously. We had one thing in common – we were all desperate. I felt a part of my soul die.

Standing there, I pitched to Sheila as to how I could provide tooth whitening for her clients. She, instead, insisted that I should take on the Botox clients. She wanted me to cover for a nurse who was on maternity leave and who normally visited the salon every week to inject Botox. Because of all the leafleting and banners they had pushed relating to this, it was in significantly more demand.

I didn't know a thing about Botox but Sheila explained how, for any dentist, doctor or nurse wanting to provide it, the training course took only three hours. With no other choice, I happily said, "Yes". I mean, it wasn't as if there was much else I could do was there?

The following month, having attended the three-hour training course over in Manchester, I returned to the salon ready to apply what I'd 'learned'. Unlike my prison job, however, which had been going relatively well, working here turned out to be a disaster right from the off.

Less than one week into injecting several rounds of their sun-beaten clients, I was called straight back to handle my first ever complaint:

"My face has stop working!"

"Huh?"

Fuck me. Seeing what I'd caused I almost jumped out of my skin.

Standing at the end of the bed, I was faced with Jean, the 40-year-old biker chick who had been my very first client. As she told me what was wrong I was freaking…

"My face doesn't work."

"What do you mean?"

I really didn't need to ask.

"It dun't work," Jean barked. "And when I smile, I smile to one side and I've now got more wrinkles than when I started!"

This was not good.

Unfortunately, in the three-hour training lesson they'd failed to teach what to do when it all went wrong.

"OK, no worries, no worries," I said, panicking about what the hell to do. "Give us a smile," I first prompted, trying to act like everything was still cool.

Shit.

As I stared at Jean's face now, which was twisting up with some weird rotation, I felt an overwhelming urge to quit right there and then. As a result of the Botox (or Botulinum toxin – its correct term) Jean was grimacing at me like she was mental. The toxin had, somehow, spread sideways, stopping one half of her face from lifting.

"Hmmmm," I paused with a questioning expression.

On the inside I was freaking, realising I'd effectively just given Jean 'Bell's Palsy'.

"It appears…" how the fuck could I get out of this, "that the Botox, unfortunately…" I delicately started to explain myself as professionally as possible despite the sound of whale cries overhead, "has propagated to the lateral facial muscles," I used as many big words as I could, "and it has temporarily paralysed the ones used for expression."

"Well how you gonna fix it?!!!" Jean half scowled. (A full scowl being impossible)

This was the million-dollar question.

Having already been injected, the toxin couldn't exactly be sucked back out. Equally there was no way I could leave her lopsided for two months until the Botox wore off.

Trying to think.

Mrrrrrrrrrrrrrrrrrrrrrrrrrrrrrrrrrrrrrrrrrrrrrrrrrrrrrrrrrrrrrrrrrrrrrrrr.

Another track kicked in.

Stupid whale…

"Don't worry," I exclaimed.

Suddenly I had an idea. "I can sort this!"

Pulling the privacy curtain round and grabbing another vial of Botox from the baby box I used to store it in, I got to work. Ignoring reception staff, who were peering at me anxiously through the curtain gap, I proceeded to inject the working side of Jean's face.

Five minutes later…

"There!" I stated, quickly wiping her pricked skin which was still bleeding like Hellraiser.

"Is it fixed?"

"Wellll… kind of," I skirted, having just paralysed both sides of her face. "You might not be able to smile for a bit but at least you'll be symmetrical!"

Phew. Amazingly she accepted it; an emotionless face but less creases… the silver-lining that Jean, for now, was willing to accommodate. I knew that this was a lucky escape, however, plying a drug that sounded not far off 'Botch-your-line-erm' toxin, what the hell I was doing??

Throughout the rest of the week, regretfully, more complaints came in. I found that when it came to providing injectable cosmetics, apart from Jean, who'd been more than reasonable, roughly one in three women would complain no matter what. After a lifetime of being frazzled by sunbeds, they expected Botox to perform absolute miracles but their demands for eternal youth were insanely unrealistic!

One ferocious woman I had to see repeatedly complained,

"Av measured mi face and when a lie on mi back mi eyebrow's move two millimetres higher."

"WELL WHY DON'T YOU STOP MEASURING YOUR FACE YOU CRAZED MENTALIST?!!!"

Obviously I couldn't say this.

Almost every day now as I came out of the prison, I would find four or five answerphone messages waiting for me from angry salon clients. It was becoming horrendous. Suffering endless moans about exaggerated lines, temporarily bruised skin or some other normal healing stage they'd all been warned about, I'd have to rush over to the salon each evening just to calm them down. It was a nightmare and I could no longer sleep!

Working in beauty salons was clearly not for me. I was good at dentistry, and patients liked what I did. Selling the salon's bullshit though was nothing to do with what I had spent six years training for. Even though quitting would make me somewhat short on cash, it was a course I would have to take – quickly – to keep my sanity. I decided I'd just have to stick with the proper dental job I had in prison. Unfortunately, even this was about to come rapidly to a close...

Having worked well together, my nurse Natalie and I had managed to reduce the prison's historical backlog to the lowest level it had ever been. We were flying, the prisoners loved our work and on top of that, the other medical staff were impressed with what we'd achieved. Things were going well. Despite this, conscientious Natalie, who'd been brought in by the same outside agency that the prison had used to find me, was about to make one innocent mistake that would end us.

Unlike the regular staff, the two of us were being paid by the prison's elected agency. We would invoice them at the end of the month.

So far, I'd been paid well. Natalie joined me later and it was her first ever invoice. Wanting to do everything properly, she had made herself a chart which marked up her hours along with her hourly rate. None of this was necessary but, wanting to be diligent before sending it to the agency, Natalie asked Miss Hunt, the medical wing's manager, if she could counter sign her invoice as confirmation.

I'd never done any of this for my invoices and knew that Miss Hunt had nothing to do with staff wages. Sharing this kind of information made me uncomfortable. Hunt was employed directly by the prison not by the agency and her role was only to ensure the smooth running of day-to-day services.

Natalie, nevertheless, wanted to be fastidious, so showed Miss Hunt her chart in the surgery asking her to sign it. Right there and then I saw that this was a huge mistake.

Natalie was being paid £170 per day which for any dental nurse was great. She must have been on way more than Hunt and I was being paid even more. Hunt's green eyes of jealousy were impossible to hide.

Staring at Natalie's form, Hunt remained fixated on her wage in addition to the travel expenses which, besides me, I quietly knew none of the permanent staff got. After a few long hard seconds,

"Have you got one of these too?" Hunt turned to me, pincer gripping Natalie's form with a patent loathing.

"No no," I backed, "I just email the agency directly."

Gutted.

Watching the Merkel lookalike almost scribe her fountain pen right through Natalie's neat invoice, I tried to tell myself that her cold attiude was related to something else...

Two weeks passed.

On what should have been a normal Monday morning, Natalie and I arrived at work and were let into the surgery to start our session like any other day. Carrying out our routine tool check we saw, however, that Drill 2 was now missing.

"What do we do?" asked Natalie, freaking as she banged through each cupboard.

"I dunno." I quickly joined her rushing to recheck every draw. "No one had access to the room at weekend, did they? And Friday's tool count was proper, right?"

"I think so."

Shit.

This had never happened to us before, but a strong feeling of foreboding came over me.

Each day we'd fastidiously check the tools at the beginning and end of every clinic to ensure nothing was stolen. Obviously a murderer running around prison with a scalpel wouldn't be cool. Up to now though, we'd kept everything in check.

"It's gone!" Natalie finished.

Fucking hell. Maybe I was being paranoid here but was this Hunt's way of testing us to see if we performed tool counts properly?

It could be. After all who would steal a drill? Not a prisoner... they'd have stolen the needles just like CII tried and to make a dental drill work, they'd also need the huge compressor but for what? To mildly groove a hole in the wall?

The drills were tiny and this was Yorkshire not Shawshank!!

"We gotta report it!" Natalie freaked.

"No, wait!"

From other staff I'd heard rumours that stumpy Hunt, apart from being the most widely hated Manager of Health, was a ruthless jealous type who had done things like planting a loose blade in a physiotherapist's cupboard as an excuse to get rid of her. Apparently, this was because the woman was so well loved.

What if, because of discovering our wages, Hunt had set us a similar trap?

Then again, what if like most Chinese whispers, the rumours about 'The Merkinator' were bollocks and this really was just a spot test?

I couldn't be sure.

"Lets tell her!" Natalie begged.

"Fine."

Against my better judgment, trudging to the grimy office at the opposite end of the wing, we knocked on the door.

"Enter," Hunt summoned.

"Hi, hello," I opened it. "Mornin'," I nervously stepped inside. "Err. We are just letting you know that one of our dental drills appears to have gone missing."

"What!?" Hunt immediately spun from her desk while Natalie and me stayed hovering by the filing cabinets. "This is disgraceful!"

"I know but it's not our fault," Natalie rushed.

"Well it must be your fault!" snapped Hunt.

"But we've only just accessed the room," Natalie begged, "and without having a surgery key we don't have any control."

"Pff," Hunt cut her off like she was more than ready to lay it on. "This had to have happened Friday then and your tool count was wrong!!"

"No, we did everything right!" I joined.

"You can't have!" the Hunt-Merkinator barked. "Which makes this an unforgivable breach of security as that drill could be with anyone!!"

This was all feeling far too rehearsed.

"But someone else must have accessed the room!" Natalie tried.

"Impossible!" Merkel stood now. "This had to have happened under YOUR watch," she pointed at us both, "and as manager of the ward, I simply cannot afford to have this kind of mistake from either of you."

"But please," Natalie again. "It's not us."

"Yeah it can't be!" I added

"Well I'm very sorry!" Merky was having none of it. "It's both your fault and as a major breach of protocol,

I will now have to inform the agency that your service will cease today!!"

"Oh come on," Natalie tried, "we haven't don-"

"My decision's final!!" Merky cut "YOU'RE BOTH FIRED!!"

Fuck!

So there it was – there was the end of my career before it had even started. I knew I should have listened to my instincts.

Escorted out of the building, Natalie and I swapped our sorry goodbyes with security at the gate. Hired by their agency, we didn't have any right to resist and Hunt knew this. Eventually it was down to just the two of us in the car park.

"We shouldn't have told her anything should we?" Natalie whimpered, teary-eyed.

"Ahh," I hugged her, "I'm sure she would have still got rid of us."

"Really?" she sniffled. "I've never been fired before."

Eventually saying goodbye to her too, I knew Natalie would be all right. She already had another part-time job where they wanted her to become full-time.

Me though, watching her drive away and feeling that cold sense of failure wash over my skin, I was screwed. This was The North. Dentistry was a small world and because of the drug rep Trudy, I'd effectively been exiled. All other options now exhausted, it appeared that there was only one place left that I could try.

Being from a small town, just the thought of the place I had in mind intimidated me. I knew, however, that from this point forth, if I wanted to win, I'd have to seriously wise up and somehow learn to outsmart, out think and outmanoeuvre all the cut-throat bastards that filled it.

I was scared, alone, away from my friends but it was now time to execute bold moves on my own.

It was time to hit London…

5

BLAGGING THE JOB

"The streets are paved with gold."

Whoever said this about London must have been tripping, because for me so far, the streets – and my career – seemed to be paved with nothing but rejection after rejection after rejection.

Following two miserable months of being here, I'd hunted like a maniac trawling through dental web-boards, registering with agencies as well as cold-calling every ad there was. Unfortunately, this didn't get me even a single interview. Absolute zip!

While more and more of my days began drifting into watching endless reruns of Jeremy Kyle, I was dismayed to discover that against a constant influx of experienced dentists flocking to our nation's capital, all fighting for the same few jobs, my CV didn't stand a chance.

Worse still, I was bouncing from one credit card to the next and had contracted to a lower ground squat in east London. I was living in a broom cupboard so dark that a solar-powered calculator would struggle. For the rates they were charging, the streets ought to have been paved with diamonds, let alone gold! It was ridiculous.

Anyway, my only comfort and contact with the outside world was Justin, my friendly, Italian 35-year-old actor flatmate. Most nights I'd wait up for him hoping to hear his stories – anything basically that could help keep my mind off seeing my debts spiral faster than those of a smack-head borrowing from Wonga.

Weeks dragging on, I was truly lost for what to do next.

I knew that watching Cash in the Attic wouldn't help and if I didn't come up with something fast, I'd likely end up on one of those CCJ adverts myself…

Yet another mindless week melting into the next, I rechecked online for the thousandth time when suddenly I saw a job opportunity that might just be the one!

Posted on the British Dental Journal website was a new position which was full-time, required an immediate start and didn't even need many years' experience.

This had to be me!

Staring at the screen though, before I could get excited, I just knew that with my CV and 'The Merkinator's' decision to fire me from prison, applying in the normal way would not go well. I needed some magic – but what?

Hammering down my third bowl of Alpen, temporarily borrowed from Justin's cupboard, and finishing the milk from the bowl, I had a cheeky idea.

The first thing I needed was to tap into all the confidential information of those applying for the job and to see how many people I'd be up against…

Grabbing my waning credit card, I called the same job website and immediately paid their £250 advertisement fee to post an almost identical job right next to the original one to lay my trap.

My theory was this. All the people applying for the real job would almost certainly also apply to my fake ad. This would let me know how many I was up against but, more importantly, it would provide a private copy of each of their cover letters and CVs.

Yes!

Within a few hours of posting, five people had applied and sizing up the competition I saw that things were better than I thought.

Apart from one weirdo in India declaring he'd "never done dentistry but could surely pick it up" it seemed I might actually be in with a chance. Up to now, two dentists applying were requesting part-time and in the end there were really only two full-time contenders I needed to worry about. I could see each had more experience than me but both said they were free to attend interviews only in the week following…

Ha. Quickly adjusting my CV, and deciding to bend the truth on all areas I dared, I finished off by rewriting my cover letter, stealing the best bits from theirs while making sure to highlight that I was available for interview THIS week.

Just before I could send everything, however, there was still one last thing I needed to fix: the reference!

If 'Witch Merkinator' back in the prison was contacted, she'd no doubt gloat about sacking me and this was a risk I could not take. Putting my trainers on I sprinted straight out to buy a new pay-as-you-go sim card.

Telling the girl in the phone shop it was a surprise gift for a friend, I eventually convinced her to record an answerphone message which in her best voice greeted:

"Hello, I'm currently at meetings in the prison. Please use my preferred contact which is my email address... hunt9666@hotmail.com."

Switching off the phone and having already set up the fake email, I swapped her old contact details for a good friend's home address before sending off the polished CV and cover letter to wait for a reply.

My bait was cast – but would it work?

6

I JUST LOVE TEETH

Boom!

That afternoon, feeling rough from having nailed three further bowls of Justin's cereal along with an old tin of pineapple I'd found, I refreshed my inbox to see an email had arrived from an Evette Robertson:

Dear Mr Sydney,

Thank you for your application and CV. As part of a formal assessment, we would like to invite you to attend an interview with the principal, Dr Clive Hallam, and myself, on Wednesday June 20th 9.15am.
Please confirm that you are available to attend.

Evette Robertson
Practice Manager
Clive Hallam Dental Practice
Carrington St
Bethnal Green
*London**

*Location changed for identification protection

Get in!

I replied straight back. Stage one was complete but next would be their interview in which I would need to blag my heart out. I had no clue how it would go...

The next morning having barely slept I awoke just as both my annoying alarms blasted from the opposite side of the room. It was 7.20am. For my evolved body clock this felt a real struggle. Clambering out of bed and zombie-ing into the shower I dressed and quickly headed out, managing to check through the overground ticket barrier just before 8.

Waiting amongst the intimidating city slickers, I realised just what London commuter life was all about.

Squashed between suit after suit and forced to listen to the loudest and most public business calls ever – *"yes Jeremy tell Polly to email me the power point..."* – provided a sobering reminder that entering the capital's inauspicious rat race along with the rest of these money whores, I'd somehow have to fit in.

According to the address the practice wasn't far. Jumping onto the outbound train and perching on the edge of my seat, I began using licked thumbs to try to iron the last of the wardrobe-hardened creases out of my one and only interview suit. A suit that I clearly wasn't used to wearing.

Receiving disgusted looks from other passengers, I accepted that, along with the ill-fitting fake leather shoes I'd bought from ASDA only the night before, I already did not look the part. Not only did the discounted clodhoppers look so shiny they passed me off as some double-glazing salesman, their sharp plastic rims were cutting so deep into my ankles that they were forcing me to tiptoe lighter on each step. If this got any worse, I might end up having to river dance to this thing.

Anyway, with the train journey over and having staggered a painful kilometre, I finally arrived outside the large mirrored glass healthcare building with 20 minutes to spare. As per instruction, taking the communal lift, I pressed for the top floor where I was told the practice would be.

Nervously climbing each level and peering through the lift's window, I could see that just like the GP Surgery on the ground floor and the Sexual Health Clinic on the second, this place was typical of most public establishments – endless combinations of soulless fixed wooden benches, cold industrial carpet tiles and those blue disabled safety bars they manage to wrap around just about everything.

Shish – each service as thorough as they come, I realised that minutes from now whoever ran the dental practice would be scrutinising my CV with a fine-tooth comb. I'd better be careful – I hadn't exactly told the truth.

Arriving on the top floor (an irrational pang – could my finger catch an STD by pressing the lift buttons?) I saw up ahead two receptionists bobbing their heads behind the huge rosewood desk while they dealt with the queue. Shuffling patiently (it was taking forever) I spotted what must have been the manager.

As a blonde curly haired woman in her 40s, she had a charmless face which was caked in so much white-powder makeup she could have been Elizabethan. Frowning at both receptionists, it looked as if she was already having a bad day. Soon it was my turn.

"Hello," I approached as my hopes for someone friendly faded, "I'm here for the interview," I directed my smile at her.

"Name?" the manager responded, pausing to look down at my scruffy rucksack.

"It's Michael Sydney," I suddenly wished I could magic my bag into a briefcase.

"Hmm," she started coldly fingering through a wallet full of CVs. "I'm Evette," she finally found mine. "Take a seat," she pointed to the waiting room.

Before long Evette returned. It was time to do my thing.

"Dr Hallam is ready to see you now."

Trying to keep my bag out of sight, I followed her behind the reception. Marching me into a tight corridor, she knocked at the door.

"Come," a posh voice summoned.

Stepping aside she opened it to finally reveal a huge fat grey-haired man in his early 50s, squashed on the other side between two desks.

"Hello," he swivelled, nibbling the arm of his glasses like a pipe, "I'm Dr Clive Hallam. Do take a seat."

Quietly lowering myself into the chair behind him, I waited as he took a moment to peruse my CV. Keeping silent while he had his back to me, I gazed at the walls to see numerous pictures of him standing by what was, presumably, his grey Porsche.

Eventually having read what I'd typed, Dr Hallam spun around.

"It says here," he stated, "you're from The North?"

"Yes," I smiled, "I've just moved down."

"Ha, quite," he snooted glancing a second at his Rolex. "I've never worked with anyone from The North. In fact, I'm surprised they even qualify people there.

Huhuh," he suddenly tittered before turning back to Evette who had parked herself neatly by the filing cabinet behind.

"Huh huh, yes," she tittered straight back.

"Huh huh," I decided I'd better copy.

This was weird.

"It also says," Clive read further, "you worked in a prison. Tell me, why did you decide to leave and move to London?"

With the two of them now focusing on me, I breathed in.

"Well..." I said, my mind screaming not to leak the truth, "after being sacked by their manager and escaping a load of Botox nightmares in a beauty salon, not forgetting having my reputation destroyed by a drug rep Trudy, I had no choice really."

As if... my CV didn't even mention Botox!

"Well..." I started, careful to deliver the line I'd rehearsed with Justin late the previous night, "although prison was a great experience for me, I felt that after helping a wide range of challenging patients, moving forward to a city like London would be the next natural step."

"Evolution you mean – you northern monkey. Huh huh," Clive chimed in once more.

"Huh huh, yes," I rushed, making sure to beat Evette to it this time.

"Huh huh," she caught right up.

Jesus.

As I precariously handled what looked like Clive's first ever interaction with someone from The North, the door swung open to my side. A well-kempt, moisturised-skinned Asian guy in his early 30s stepped in.

"Oh hello Kam," Clive smiled at him.

"Hiiii," he drawled in what seemed to be a long drawn out American accent, his tight dental top tucked perfectly into his narrow leather belt.

"Kam is my senior associate," Clive introduced us while Kam, still ignoring me, searched through a drawer. "Kam is from New Zealand," Clive continued. "And this here," he caught Kam's eye, "this here is Michael. Michael is from The North."

Stopping a second, Kam took a look at me with disdain.

"Huh gawwd," he mocked. "I think the last person I met from up there tried joining our golf club and didn't even have the appropriate attire."

"Hoh yes," Clive immediately waved "I do remember... God he was wearing some awful stuff wasn't he, huh huh." They scoffed in unison.

I hid my George shoes under the chair.

With Kam disappearing, Clive wiggled himself a little deeper onto his tiny saddle stool, the single steel spike almost disappearing under his chunky thighs like it was his giant anal love bead.

"Tell me," he leaned forward now, eager for a more serious tone. "Do you enjoy root canals?"

Shit.

Besides spying the car pictures, I'd clocked his multiple root canal certificates on the walls. I hated root canals – nearly every dentist did. But I needed this job at all costs and was ready to say anything to get it.

"Yes," I nodded, "I love root canals they're my fave..."

My lord – I felt the devil now owned my soul as I watched Clive scratch one of the curling grey hairs on the underbelly of his chin.

"Splendid," he smiled. "I specialise in them."

I'd answered correctly – phew.

Throughout the next 20 minutes I did my absolute best to scrabble for descriptions that were sliding further and further from the truth. I lied, agreeing with him about the specialist root files I preferred, something I barely had a clue about. What I was saying seemed to be working but I could feel myself cracking under the pressure. I just had to make sure I didn't blurt out anything too ridiculous as I'd made that mistake before.

Back in dental school when I was trying to get in, I'd been asked the big question,

"Why do you want to be a dentist?"

Having been denied by two universities already and desperate to get accepted by the third, I gave the admissions board all the plausible reasons I could think of. I said I liked to help people. I said I liked the art of it. I said I liked using my hands. Met with nothing more than silent stares, however, I realised that this was clearly not going to be enough. Simply put, I was stuck for what else I could say when I begged,

"Please… I just love teeth!"

How bad is that?!

Mmm teethy teethy.

Anyway, back with Clive and cringing now at the falsehoods that I could hear myself bumbling while beads of sweat trickled down my sides, I finally started clawing back some dignity right before that classic, "My only weakness is I work too hard" poured out…

With experience, one thing I've learnt when it comes to interviews, is that the tip of your tongue is never the tip of your career.

What I mean is, being nice is expected, but if you kiss arse too much you just look desperate and it will never serve you for anything big. Most interviewers aren't actually trained to ask the right questions so being in a higher position of authority, they will prefer to spend the time bragging and embellishing their own success, especially if another colleague of theirs is present in the room. Also, despite what they teach in school, bosses rarely recruit the best person for the job. Instead, to protect their own interests, they aim to hire a barrier ring of weaker subordinates who they feel they can most control, ideally carrying a flaw they can burn at any time, be someone who will not pose a threat to their own career and who can leave them feeling good about themselves.

Knowing this and appreciating that it's easier said than done, I began redirecting as many encouraging questions as I could towards Clive and Evette, making sure to ham up my best impressed face as he lorded it about accolades of God knows what.

Following another five minutes, he finally unwiggled himself off his stool.

"Well," he concluded, "I think we may be interested but we do have more interviews and obviously we must speak to all references."

"Certainly," I smiled, standing to shake his hand. "Oh, and if you want to speak to my old manager Miss Hunt or anything, I know she's often busy in and out of meetings but I'm sure if you call her it will be fine."

"Very well."

Jesus.

Hot-toeing out of his room before my serrated ankles gave way, I made my way home and waited.

A day later 'The Merkinator's' fake hunt9666@hotmail.com received a magic enquiry. It was from Evette. She was requesting a reference. Nervously I wrote what could only be described as a glowing report back.

Three days later I got the call.

"Clive here..."

"Oh hi," my voice shot into the high octaves of angels.

"Yes hello, I think we may be interested," he continued. "As it stands we've booked a meal for the departing dentist and Evette says that, as one of the associates has just dropped out you may as well attend."

"Thank you," I said, still confused as to whether this was an offer or not, "that's great."

"Hmm," Clive finished, "We'll see..."

7

HIGH HATS

Ending the call I knew this dinner would be the be-all and end-all. Pull this off and I'd got a job, income, security and perhaps a future in one of the most expensive and grinding cities going.

Fuck the dinner up, however, and I'd soon be on the next train back north to a life of couch surfing at friends' flats until all the debts I'd accrued could be paid off – somehow.

I'd lied and lied again to get this far. My CV was about as accurate as the Bible. The interview answers I'd given were a mile from the truth. There was no room to fuck up now!

The dinner was booked for the Friday night. I struggled back into my £15 ankle slicers again. The plan was to join the rest of the dentists and Evette as they celebrated the outward emigrating colleague I was hopefully due to replace.

The meal was at Galvin at Windows, Park Lane.

Being fairly new to London and still basing what I knew to be posh or not on the Monopoly board, I nodded to the top-hatted commissionaire outside before heading into the lobby of the Hilton Hotel…

Wow – emerging through their huge revolving doors I realised this was a whole other league of fancy. The décor was stunning. Wandering over to the bay of lifts at the back, I took one to the very top floor. After I stepped out into the reception I saw, for the first time, what had to be one of the flashiest and poshest places I'd ever been to. It was amazing. Michelin starred and on the 28th floor of the hotel, the restaurant looked spectacular and with its far reaching views that spanned the entire city, you could see everything… like everything… the BT tower, Hyde Park, Mayfair, some hills!

(The Shard hadn't been built yet)

Spotting the rest of the dentists along with Evette over by the bar area, I started worming my way across and waited for Clive to finish his joke. Unintentionally dimming spirits a little, I waved my hand in to break their circle of five.

"Hello everyone," I smiled, lingering from the side.

"Oh hello," Clive turned, Kam never breaking once from sipping through the tiny black straws of his cocktail.

"This is Penny," Clive gestured to a plump girl in her early 30s, her short black hair rounding her face. "And Alex," he continued, "the leaving dentist you haven't met."

"Hi.. Hello.. Hi," I nodded around, a bit self-conscious that Evette wouldn't stop staring at my faded jacket.

Left standing a moment, I was not sure what else to say when Penny leaned in.

"So you must be the other candidate?"

"Other? Err.. I guess."

Shit – suddenly I realised this was why Clive had acted a bit off with me when he invited me here – I was probably his second choice. Under more pressure then to do everything I could to fit in.

"Would anyone like a drink?" I half retreated, praying that at these prices nobody would actually say "Yes" or worse, "Sure just a triple JD and Red Bull."

Thankfully, everyone was stocked.

Conscious that I had only £38 left in my overdraft, I stepped away to quickly order the cheapest beer at the bar.

The barman took an excruciating minute to wait for my card to clear payment and when I turned back I saw the rest of the group were already being led to the table.

Grabbing the bottle and flurrying behind I managed to catch up just as Clive took his seat.

"Oh, the food here is exquisitely divine," he announced picking up the menu.

"Hmm yes," Penny agreed, taking one of the cloth-covered chairs by his side. "I've been here many times."

"Who hasn't?" Kam scoffed as he sat to my right. "The tartare and seared polenta is the best."

Settling to join them, "Hmm," I nodded. I felt like I'd stepped into a vicar's tea party which was only making me drown.

While Kam and Penny continued excessively commenting on anything that could pass them off as esteemed intellectuals, I ducked behind my menu. Having lived like a student for most of my life, I hardly recognised the stuff I was reading. Scanning each food description, I tried to decipher the few at the top – right 'pea purée' that's just mushy peas, so I've got that one –

"Hey excuse me!" Clive suddenly interrupted just as I was half way down. "Excuse me! Everyone... Everyone," he started sine waving his big sausage finger around the table to the waiter standing by. "The man here is asking which wine we wish to choose?"

"Oh do go with the Ornellaia '89," Evette lit up.

"Yes," Penny joined, "the '89 would be great."

Shit, praying Clive would be paying for this as I freaked at the prices (so big they hadn't even bothered with the £ signs) I hoped surely we would go with the one just after the cheapest right??

"Two '89s," Clive nodded.

Oh fuck, he'd actually ordered it. I strained my worried smile as I swear facial muscles I'd never used before started cramping at my cheeks. It seemed like my beloved pound-a-pint nights back at Uni were long gone.

Ordering the food was next. Normally this wouldn't bother me but here I suddenly felt uncomfortable that certain words spoken in my parochial accent would stick out like a sore thumb to these people. The waiter started going round the table and everyone began ordering duck or "dak" as they were pronouncing it.

"Dak."

"Dak."

"Dak," they all chimed.

Soon coming to my turn, to be part of the group I knew I'd better copy but I could see Kam and Penny were already smirking waiting to see how I'd say it. Hmm – I didn't want to come across a fake. Equally, as most of my friends up north would do, there was no way I could say phonetically, "Aye duck luv" either.

I know…

"Um I'll just have the same please," I rushed in with an almost schoolboy-like voice.

Phew – shamefully disowning my heritage I was still blending in. More wine was served and the night flowed on.

By the time the meal ended having finished on desserts, I had listened to about ten different golfing stories, each one of them increasingly lame. Finding it harder and harder to keep my titters going – as they mixed their stories with scoffs of how clever they were compared with the rest of society – I started to feel empty inside. I know everyone can act snobbishly at times but listening to the endless pomposity I thought of a lot of decent people I cared about back home. People these guys would probably look down on just because of their roots. It felt horrible

Nevertheless, as I did my best to keep fitting in and nodding back like some Churchill dog, the progressively drunker me found it tougher to keep agreeing. Ending the meal, Clive invited us to his house. It would be here that, for all the yarns I'd spun in the interview, I was about to get busted.

Riding along in the taxi I had to half mime to their tralala songs in an attempt to sing along. I knew instinctively I shouldn't have allowed myself to relax but I was plastered and as we arrived at his house the party was set to continue. Clive sorted out his front door key a moment and we bumbled through darkness into his living room. Finally, he switched on the lights. To my horror, placed there in all its glory waited a full set of drums.

Oh fuck.

Back in the interview, Clive had asked what I got up to on my days off. (I could hardly tell him I was giving

Botox in beauty salons. Any dentist worth his salt knows that this form of work would be judged like hell and for me, struggling to get a proper dental job, it would mean the difference between success and failure.) Already on a back foot having to fumble my way through how much I loved root canals – the tedious area of dentistry I knew relatively little about – I don't know why but, desperate to divert the pressure, I'd stupidly blurted a whole convoluted story about how I was a drummer in a band.

Why on earth had I chosen this?

He'd only mentioned he liked music and I didn't have the first clue about instruments!

With everyone moving around the drum-kit I stayed hovering by the wall. Drinks were being passed around but almost on cue,

"Hey rock star," Penny turned to me. "You're in a band, let's hear you play."

"Huh?" I looked up thinking I could remain hidden behind my glass.

"Yeah," Clive lit up, "let's see you!"

"Yeah come on!" Kam joined, now finding me interesting.

Shit.

Struggling for a good excuse as my drunken mind drew a blank, "Ah I'm OK," I grimaced, "I'll just chill."

Clive insisting, however, had already taken to patting on the stool.

"Come on!" the others chanted. "Let's hear you!"

"Yeah," Penny began frog-marching me to it, handing me the sticks. "PLAY. PLAY. PLAY!"

Having to sit at the drum stool now, I noticed that Evette had even turned the music off to ensure everyone's attention. They were waiting for something epic.

"Come on!" Kam prompted.

"Just a second!!" I stressed.

Not sure if I could blag this one, I prayed that some sort of black rhythm God would pass through my soul.

Fuck it!

I hit the cymbal. Tap

Bash Clash. I hit two more, trying to fake it with a face of intensity.

Tap Dunk. I pressed the pedal…

Tap Dunk Tap.. I hit some more.

Clunk, Dunk.

Zero beat emanated while excitable Penny, right in front of me, did her best to dance.

Clunk Clunk.

As I watched their faces of awkwardness begin to match my receding hype, Dunk Tap, I paused a second to sip my wine.

"You know what?" I finally lifted my head from out of the huge glass, "I'm too drunk, Clive should play."

"Yeahhh," the mob switched, "Clive! Clive! Clive!"

"Yeah come on Clive," I clapped.

Thankfully Clive beamed like he'd been waiting for this moment his entire life.

"Pass the sticks!" he gleamed.

Thank God.

Handing them over I moved out of his way. Clive started drumming to his disciples while everyone finally danced. I was relieved. They all seemed too inebriated to have registered. Clive, however, started again.

"Hey," he looked over at me while playing. "You know what a Hi-hat 8 is don't you?!"

"Err.. huh," I pretended I couldn't hear him.

"You know?" he pressed. "A Hi-hat 8?"

I guessed this was a drum term but nodding and quickly sidestepping away, “Mmhmm,” I dipped my head pretending I was suddenly well into my dancing.

As the night fizzled out and taxis arrived, Clive saw me to the door when, finally, he handed me the contract.

“We must talk more about your band,” he said, shocked that I was already flicking for the signature page. “I’d like to see them sometime.”

“Certainly,” I grabbed the pen by his telephone, “I mean I don’t really play much with them now but yeah, we must organise it.” I handed the contract straight back. “Anyway I’d best go but thank you for tonight.” I started escaping down his driveway, “Oh and tatar,” I waved back one last time.

“Yes tatar,” Clive waved, slightly perplexed.

Climbing into my cab I realised that I’d just said “tatar”, a word I never thought I’d use; who was I?

All signed though I’d done it. And although I had to celebrate by asking the confused taxi driver to pull immediately around the corner to let me switch to the night bus, finally I was in!

As I waited by the bus stop my thoughts drifted ahead to day one. These dentists may have their nice sides but undoubtedly they were cliquey. I knew that when it came to working with them, I’d just have to make sure I didn’t slip up with anything else that might expose me and make me the unwanted outsider.

Fucking rock band....

8

A BAD FIT

It turned out that faking being a drummer would be the least of my worries as five months from today I'd be seeing myself sacked for stripping naked in front of Clive and his staff. Right now though I wasn't to know this and Monday, 8.45 am, having had to wait a further SIX weeks just so that the Primary Care Trust (the NHS's regional body that, until recently, regulated all NHS practices) could process all the paperwork needed for a new dentist to work in their borough, I was desperate to get stuck in.

I'll never forget the first morning when, excited to finally start and be part of society once more, I re-entered Clive's practice double doors only to be met with maudlin nods from his two receptionists.

"Hi, I'm Michael," I properly introduced myself to the girl nearest to me at the desk, "I'm the new dentist."

"Yeah, go see Evette," was all I got back.

God.

Brief greeting over with each of them, neither of whom Clive had invited to the dinner, I soon noticed that something wasn't right...

Moving out of their way and unzipping my coat I saw Evette coming out of her office.

"Oh you're here!" she looked flustered.

"Hi yes, I came early," I smiled.

"OK, well I'll show you to your room."

I followed behind her. It would soon become apparent to me that, despite all those rara jokes Clive and his dentists had enjoyed sharing with such familiarity back in the restaurant, when it came to actually working here, his staff were fucking miserable!

Finally standing outside my soulless surgery, Evette hovered by the door and just pointed to the computer. As practice manager, she seemed nervous to introduce me to the dental equipment or to delve into any detail. I gathered that, having come from accounts and being given the job because she was the sister to Clive's long-term girlfriend, she didn't know much about dentistry. Kindly handing me a spare cup of tea, she quickly added that my nurse was still in the sterilisation room but should be through any minute. Brisking off, she left me to it.

Alone in the room for a while I was not sure what I should do. Sitting by the computer I drank the tea and began reading through my day list. Having checked it thoroughly, I heard the door handle rattle. Turning, I finally faced my nurse.

"Alex doesn't put his cup there!" was the first thing the 40-something barked, a veiled Asian with beady eyes poking up against thick-rimmed glasses.

"Hi, oh sorry," I shuffled as she stepped towards me. "I'm Michael."

"I'm Bilge," she gritted back.

Jesus.

I immediately reached for my offending mug while Bilge forced me to watch painfully as she slid it at an excruciatingly slow pace to an area along the worktop which, to me, looked no different. Finally satisfied with her mini victory, "Right," she left it parked, "your first patient's waiting. You'd better get him in!… Come on, hurry!"

She was a witch!

Collecting my patient, I wondered whether it was just a coincidence that Bilge had been named after a water-sucking boat pump. She certainly offered about as much charm. Brushing this off, I returned before parking my guy in the chair. It was time to start performing my best.

"OK, open wide," I smiled to the nice fella in his 50s.

As the patient opened his mouth, Bilge leaned over us both from her side.

I figured I'd better carry out the examination in silence. Finishing this, I told the patient that his teeth were good apart from a chip that we could sort out there and then.

"Great!" he exclaimed.

This made him happy and would save him from having to come back. It wouldn't take long either. Bilge, however, glaring at me now like some angry hawk, was clearly having none of it.

"This patient is only booked for an exam!" she barked.

"Yeah but our next one's cancelled," I smiled, "so couldn't we just fix it?"

"It's supposed to be just an exam!"

What a miser. The dentist is the one who calls the shots but, not wanting to get into an argument here, especially in front of the patient, I'd have to be delicate.

"If it saves him coming back," I softened, "couldn't 'we' just do it now??"

Bilge must have known I was talking sense but slamming her cupboard doors to make a point she thrust me the tray of tools I'd need.

"Thanks," I nodded. "Oh and can you just aspirate for me too."

Fuming as she stood over me, Bilge (or 'Bilgie' as I'd mentally nicknamed her) fired up her suction machine, tipped the aspirator pipe into the patient's mouth and gripped it like it was my throat.

What could make someone so unhappy?

Speaking to the cleaner later I would discover that Bilgie was fifteen years into an arranged marriage and hated life. It seemed that for some time now, her only pleasure had been to fantasise about escaping with this Alex rugby-playing dentist I'd just replaced. Evidently, his eloping back to Oz without her meant that I was now the enemy.

Great!

"And can you just pass me the cotton rolls," I teetered. "Thanks."

While the patient and I continued doing our best not to piss off Queen Miseryguts any further, she twisted for the hand mirror when suddenly I noticed how her body had been completely shaped by the way she resisted her job. This shocked me.

I know this sounds judgemental and I'm certainly no pinup myself but, just to give you an idea, through years of hating the world and doing workwise what must have been the absolute minimum, Bilgie had developed an actual right-angled parcel shelf around her hips. To get by in nursing she was only bothering to use one arm despite both of them working perfectly. I could see that her poor left, which rarely got a look in, was now significantly fatter than the lucky right she occasionally stirred!

It was alarming!!

I've only ever seen this same arm disparity in professional tennis.

I doubted she played tennis.

Anyway, completing the filling on the patient, who by this point looked sorry that he even owned teeth, I let him dart off. With minutes to spare before the next one was due, I decided I'd escape for a breather myself. I headed off to the break room next door to make another cup of tea. Kam was already there.

"Hey man," I greeted him as he stood by the sink.

"Hey," he replied, sipping on some drink.

We hadn't really spoken at the restaurant and I hoped he'd at least be easier to talk to than the other miseries I'd met. Starting friendly then, "It was a good meal last month eh?" I smiled desperate to build up a relationship.

Merely raising his perfectly plucked eyebrows back though Kam forced me to fill his silence.

"Ah, you go to the gym?" I noticed he'd been mixing some protein shake.

"Yeah," he eventually spoke.

My God – not exactly the warmest of guys just giving me one-word answers – I remembered he was single so defaulting to the conversation most lads have when they first try to bond…

"Hey, Penny's pretty fit isn't she?" I smiled.

"What do you mean?" This stopped him stirring his powder.

"Well, with those fuck-me eyes she looks a great shag doesn't she!" I bowled on, stupidly following this up with an air-arse spank, certain this would break the ice...

"Penny's my girlfriend!!!" he exclaimed.

"Is she??" Fuck – my voice suddenly lifted to that of a choirboy's. "Ahh I didn't realise – haarr."

God this was awkward.

Pretending to focus on the kettle waiting for it to boil, I had to stand there for ages while Kam stayed washing his shaker out in silence. Finally rush-making my two cups of tea, hands full, I quickly reversed from the tiny room and carried them back to Nurse Motivator. I hoped my peace offering there might do better.

"Hey," I tapped on the surgery door, "I've made you this drink." I smiled as she opened it.

Bilgie took one look down, "That's not my cup!!"

Oh fuck off.

"Isn't it?" I gritted.

Someone shoot me please!

Grinding my way through the rest of the morning I fantasised about gouging my eyes out with the drill and was thankful when it was eventually lunch. With the patients gone, we were called into the waiting room to have our monthly staff meeting.

Cool, I thought. This being a great chance to meet the rest of the team, I became re-energised again. Sitting as everyone gathered, I smiled to the others including three nurses I hadn't met before. All just nodded back mutely. It soon became clear it wasn't just Bilgie who appeared depressed.

Facing Clive (Kam and Penny had made sure to position themselves by his side), Evette kicked it off.

"Right," she took out a typed list, her voice firming as though she had some super grave issues to announce. "Someone has spilt coffee in the break room again and it needs to stop!"

What – this was top of their agenda!!

They should try dealing with a needle-pricked prisoner with anger issues.

Anyway, we listened to her roll on blaming the receptionists and nurses with one petty thing after another until she finally ended on the complaint that paper towels were wrongly being flushed down the patients' toilet (I couldn't fathom how that was possibly the fault of the staff). It was no wonder everyone wanted to jump off a cliff – the staff here were broken!

Clive was next and wading in with an even bigger wave of negativity,

"I'm also very disappointed!" he scowled waving his big sausage finger around the room. "The PCT (Primary Care Trust) report shows we're still behind target and the deadline is March!"

Wow – I was surprised that he was solely glaring at the nurses and receptionists.

Although Clive had a valid issue, choosing to blame the non-dentists for practice underperformance, his scowling needlessly mirrored by his henchmen Kam and Penny, was bizarre. This was nothing like the Clive I'd seen back at the restaurant.

His point was relating to the fact that, in dentistry, an NHS practice must achieve an agreed quota of treatments for the Government each year. If they fail to meet this by March 31st, their annual contract – which dictates how much treatment a practice may offer and, therefore how much income they can receive from it – is either permanently reduced or, in some cases, irreversibly revoked.

In the 80s and 90s when this restriction didn't exist, catching up on patients and treatment totals wouldn't have been a problem.

Since 2006, however, the Government literally doubled the number of dentists either qualifying in this country or being allowed in from abroad. This meant that finding enough patients and achieving treatment totals on time was now as competitive as hell.

In a dentist-flooded London, with everyone finding it harder to meet targets, it was clear that Clive needed his team to work well.

Looking around at these morale-sapped faces, however, I just couldn't believe that Clive and the other dentists were still upholding such an ignorant stance.

To perform good dentistry, a motivated team is essential. Even if you like to think you're the best dentist in the world, spending every minute criticising the nurses and receptionists – vital support staff – with endless petty irrelevances, while simultaneously making sure to lord it over them as some infallible God (a common trait of many snobbish dentists) is just asking for disaster and will, at best, produce only minimal results.

The meeting was soon over and, as everyone left in silence on what had to mark the least motivational pep talk of my life, I realised I had a long and lonely slog ahead of me. For now, getting on with the job and just keeping my head down was all I could do.

Nothing much happened to begin with. The days slowly inched into weeks – the weeks into a month – while me and Bilgie were just not working out. She knew it and I knew it. There was nothing I could do to cheer her up and she simply hated life. Finally, having adopted the same miserable rhythm, I got some good news.

Evette walked in to let me now that Bilge was transferring to reception and that I was about to get a new nurse.

Boom.

Enter a legend.

Enter somebody who would help save my mind.

Enter Tiesha.

9

TIESHA

There was no doubt about it. I needed a partner in crime, somebody human, normal, funny and on my wavelength if I wasn't going to lose my mind.

After all, in between suffering the miserable Bilgie and Clive along with this relentless PCT quota, somebody had to brighten my day. Finally, that somebody had arrived.

Tiesha (or Tiesh as I came to call her).

A slim 33-year-old single mum from Jamaica, Tiesha had come over illegally with her child and 'baby father' as she called him, to start a new life in England. She was abandoned by her fella soon after, however, and he'd dumped her in London without any support. Having worked a few dodgy factory jobs that paid cash in hand and doing everything she could to survive, Tiesha had somehow managed to get hold of an £800 black market fake National Insurance number which would let her work legally (or thereabouts). No one in the practice knew this of course and it would be months before she'd reveal this predicament to me. It was at this crossroads in her life that we were both about to meet.

"Hey yo!" was the first thing Tiesha greeted me with as soon as Evette, who had been interviewing her and a string of competing nurses all day, left her in my room. "You'rrralankyboywahgwan."

"Uh?" I turned, not having a clue what she'd just said.

"Yougonnahelpmegetpickedforthisjobmanorwhat?!"

Ha, I liked this girl straight away but since I had no choice in the hiring I'd have to find ways to persuade them that Tiesha was the one.

Right from the off, Evette, unfortunately, didn't like her. Perhaps it was the accent. Or to be more precise, perhaps it was the fact that Tiesh spoke a million miles an hour and had a strong Jamaican patois that most chavs could only dream of. To the middle-aged white Evette – the anxious protestant who couldn't understand a word – Tiesha probably sounded intimidating. I knew she would be perfect though. I pleaded with every reason I could think of as to why Tiesha would be great and after lengthy deliberations (along with, I suspect, a healthy fear of being deemed racist), Evette and Clive finally relented and gave her a chance.

Yes – she was in and just as I'd predicted, she was amazing!!

Working alongside Tiesh every day, my painful, mortifying environment changed immediately to pure joy. As a girl who'd suffered way tougher hardships than any of the other staff and, having a top sense of humour with a tireless work ethic as well as being able to bat off any problems, she was a tremendous relief for me. She was brilliant and at nursing she operated like a whippet! I mean, don't get me wrong, Tiesh was cheeky as fuck too as every so often she would just come to me and say,

"Hey yo bredren."

"What?"

"Gimmi twenty pounds!"

"Why?"

No rhyme, no reason, she just wanted it! But always with a smile and since she helped me to start meeting targets like never before, I gave it to her every time.

As the weeks rolled on we grew into a well-oiled unit. We even started outdoing the other dentists in the practice but frustratingly it wasn't long before jealousy crept in.

At the next thrill-a-minute staff meeting, Penny started first.

"Well, you must be cutting corners," she sniped.

"Or doing something chop shop," Kam added, with Clive nodding in agreement.

My God, no matter how hard we worked for these people to tackle what was actually important, it seemed that nothing we did could ever be good enough. Neither of us cut corners nor did we do anything 'chop shop'.

What Clive and his posse wouldn't accept was that, instead of sitting idle between check-ups like they did while making their nurse do everything for them, Tiesh and I shared the workload evenly and were breaking our backs to finish off patients' treatments right there and then.

There was no magic to it, just hard efficient graft!

As the next month rolled on and we smashed everyone's targets, yet again the sniping evolved.

"Well Tiesha's nails are too long to be safe on clinic," Evette added, and, "Her socks are too bright for surgery," said Clive.

I couldn't believe these dicks?! You'd have thought they would be happy with how we were saving things!

Nevertheless, arriving at the third month, December now, it seemed that staff morale couldn't sink any lower. Despite this, the Christmas had been booked – a night when everyone should relax so Tiesh and I figured we'd earned it and would therefore do what we could to have fun…

The restaurant booked was tapas. Pulling up outside just before 8pm and hoping to kick the night off with a little light-heartedness, Tiesh and I had decided we'd come dressed in half-Santa-half-drag outfits she'd borrowed from a mate.

We looked ridiculous in matching tights, hot pants and ill-fitting furry red coats as we stepped out of the taxi. Tiesha may have appeared confident but I still wasn't sure what we were supposed to be.

Anyhow, making our way into the restaurant as randoms laughed at us on the street (which I suppose was the desired effect) we searched for our clan. I didn't notice them at first but I was glad to see that the place was full of other work parties also having fun. I was relieved to discover that I wasn't the only one in stupid fancy dress. Pushing past a man dressed as a giant Brussels sprout, Tiesh and I managed to work our way to the back where we found our waiting table of miseries.

Oh dear. In complete contrast to everyone else – their sorry faces said it all. Sitting down, I took a seat opposite the nurses but my daft costume didn't even raise a smile. This was going to be a long night…

I just couldn't believe that none of them would allow themselves to have any fun. Looking over at Clive and Evette, I could understand their predicament. They had been the main culprits for enforcing this icy atmosphere. After all the berating they'd dished out right up to this event, it would be impossible for them to now relax even if they wanted to.

As a duty to their staff at Christmas, they were expected to show their fun side while at the same time, as boss and manager, somehow enforce their usual cloak of authority the only way they knew how. Impossible to do both and clearly anxious at having to socialise outside their dental only clique, they obviously felt awkward as hell.

In a weird way, I guess I felt sorry for them but for the rest, thinking they ought to let themselves go, it was time to get some shots in…

Hoping that a few drinking games might lighten the mood, I soon returned from the bar with a tray of tequilas which I offered to the table.

"No thanks", "No thanks", "No thank you" was all I got.

My God – these guys wouldn't budge for anything! We were surrounded by other staff parties who were downing booze and having loads of fun, which made our situation even more painful.

The first long awkward hour rolled on and as I sipped through my quietest tequila ever, we were thankfully interrupted by the raffle.

"Ladies and Gentlemen…"

I suddenly had an idea…

I know this sounds like I was on a mission here but, having tolerated five months of pure misery without any sense of teamwork or even just a reason to celebrate, tonight was the night I was determined to change things. After all, some of these staff were decent people and had suffered long enough.

Sinking the leftover shots that no one seemed to want, I turned to watch with everyone the little pot-bellied restaurant boss stand proudly on the stage. Kicking off his raffle,

"Prize number one," he called into his mic. "A free meal for two."

"Wooooo woo!" some of the tables cheered.

OK, so his entry prizes were small but the crowd got into it as they clapped the first winner onto the stage.

Soon rolling to the next one,

"Prize number two," the pot-bellied man continued.

What everyone really wanted was the biggest prize which was waiting at the end – prize number five.

As the first guy left with his gift,

"Prize number 2 – a £20 voucher for Boots."

"Woo woo!" – some more people cheered.

The next punter already getting up to collect his win. This was moving fast. I had to be quick.

With the others sitting quietly watching the stage, I leaned over to Tiesha,

"PSSSSST Tiesh!" I hissed.

"Wat?"

"Pass me your tickets."

"Why man, wat-yah-goan'du?" she whispered reluctant to hand them over (even though I was the one who had bought them for her).

"Nothing just pass them quick."

"Prize number three," the boss continued before shouting out the corresponding ticket.

Sitting at our table while other staff parties cheered and celebrated their win, the pressure was mounting for me. Everyone in the room was still gunning for the big prize. With hardly any tickets from our table and up against other groups who had literally bought reams,

I realised the odds of us winning this were not good. Carefully then, I started laying out on the table a ticket of each colour to get my blag underway.

"Prize number 4," the announcer called.

Ohh he was getting close!

"Pink 215."

Not even sure if this would work, perching on the end of my seat I waited for the penultimate punter to collect his prize while everyone started gearing up for the finale. After he exited the stage, the boss called again.

"AND NOWWWW," his voice began bellowing like a voice over. "We commme to the last and final priiiiizzzzeee.... Pleeeeeeeease give it up for the GIANT CHRISTMAS HAMPER!!!!"

"Yeahhhhh!!" everybody cheered.

This was it! This was the one.

The crowd was excited now as I hovered by the edge of our table knowing that this was the one we needed to win. All eyes on stage – the boss reached into his tombola.

Come on fucker...

Pulling out the ticket,

"And the winner isssss...." he kept everyone hanging "BLUE........256"

"BOOM!" I shouted. "I WIN. I WIN!"

Before anyone even had chance to breathe, I waved and yelled making the lights turn on me. With this the audience let out a massive cheer as I started bounding up to the stage. In my hand I had nothing like the winning ticket but that didn't matter now.

To the audience still cheering I headed to the stage steps where their dweeby assistant was waiting to check my ticket to verify my win. Stomping straight towards him and smiling all the way, I purposefully ignored his reached-out hand. Instead, I cheekily flashed my same-coloured Blue 324 ticket right past his eyes, too close for him to focus, before lunging straight on up to the stage, leaving him no time to react.

Almost immediately shaking hands with the waiting boss, we posed together for the cameraman as I was neatly handed the hamper.

Ha – crowd clapping, I couldn't believe it!

Thankfully the poor assistant, hanging back, looked too embarrassed to interrupt. Also since no one else challenged my win, I guessed that the real winner must have thought he'd misheard. Smiling for the picture and clutching the hamper, I made sure to exit by the opposite side of the stage before returning to our table victorious!

Popping the champagne and filling everyone's glass, I knew that no one on our table had a clue what I'd just done. I handed posh crisps and tins of salmon to everyone like some small-time Robin Hood when finally – FINALLY – after months and months of nothing but broken spirits, finally, finally, finally our table was happy!!!

I was buzzing.

Even Bilge was enjoying herself. I could see this by the way she was using both her arms to help herself to the biscuits. Clive and Evette were smiling too. For me this was the icing on the cake!

We were on a roll!

But this wouldn't last long…

10

THE SACK RACE

Sometimes in life, you should quit while you're ahead.

I stupidly thought I could take this team further so when Mariah Carey's Christmas tune started blasting I grabbed the two receptionists telling the others to come and join us on the dance floor… in hindsight this is where it all started to go wrong.

In the same way Clive and Evette must have lost sight of why they used misery to control people, I too had lost sight of myself. Being on too much of a counter mission to cheer everybody up, as well as nailing shots and chugging more table wine, I have to accept that the festive season had definitely got the better of me.

I never intended any of this…

With Tiesha and Amanda, the receptionist, accompanying me to the empty dancefloor, I began taking it in turns to break out into daft dance moves. This surely looked like fun as soon more of our crew wanted to join. People from other tables also gathering created a single circle which started to grow bigger. Everyone took turns to dance in the middle and play out more and more stupid moves. It wasn't long before this turned into the entertainment of the night...

'Ice Ice Baby' was playing now and I got carried away as even more people joined embracing the Christmas spirit. I was loving it and was taken right back to my student years of sharing nothing but innocent fun.

With our daftness progressing it was back to my turn to be clapped into the middle of the floor. Elected as some sort of ringleader, I felt I had to bust out more extreme moves so I started throwing my gangly body around like an idiot. Everyone was laughing.

Being well-inebriated and egged-on to keep going by smiling faces and people clapping, I decided to kick it up a notch so stepped onto the empty raised stage. People cheered me all the way. Me, the six-foot-six-inch lanky idiot gyrating now in my half-drag-half-Santa outfit – the ridiculousness only encouraging everyone else to let themselves go. Before long a few horny cougars joined and coming right up to me, one of them started pulling at my leg.

"Off Off Off," the big boobed woman demanded as her friend began yanking at my belt.

"OFF! OFF! OFF!" the rest of the mob joined, chanting along with them.

By this point I couldn't see Evette or Clive or our table anymore. However, right in the thick of it with these people and a couple of nurses, I didn't want to disappoint.

Swept up by the energy of Queen's 'One Vision' now blasting through the speakers and with the night having built to its maddest point, blinded by the lights, fun, booze and everyone finally enjoying themselves, I became way too caught in the moment when,

"OFF!! OFF!! OFF!!" the crescendo hit.

Spinning around to shouting, I dropped my pants to reveal my nob and balls to the entire 100 partygoers.

"Ahahahahaha," they all fell about laughing.

Amazing.

Given the seriousness of the last five months, it was such an elation to see everyone rolling about in hysterics. For this instant at least and with our crew even laughing, the daily grind was gone for us all.

What a result.

With the clapping soon over I picked up my strewn clothes from the floor. As I put them on, people were still congratulating me. I returned to our table where I naively expected to reap more glory. It was safe to say, however, that glory was the last thing I got.

Sitting opposite Clive with a huge grin on my face, and oblivious to the atmosphere at the table,

"Good eh?" I nodded.

But glaring straight back,

"YOU FUCKING CUNT!" Clive screamed against the music.

"Huh?" I stopped, half smiling still naively believing that with the dance-floor now filled, he'd be buzzing the same as everyone else.

"You fucking cunt," he repeated.

"What?" it started to sink in, "But it was funny right?" I said, just as the sickening feeling that he might actually be serious waved over me.

"NO YOU FUCKING CUNT!!" he shouted again, pointing his finger in my face. "YOU FUCKING CUNT! YOU FUCKING CUNT!" he couldn't stop himself.

With his angry strobe-lit face looking like it was about to explode, I struggled to hear over the loud music the rest of what he was saying. At the worst possible moment, an unaware stranger from another table waded right in between us and blocking Clive he grabbed my hand.

"Mate, mate," he clasped it congratulating me. "That was fucking brilliant mate!"

"Ha thanks," I rushed. "But now's not the time."

As I quickly pulled my hand back, he danced off only to reveal Clive's fuming face again and his resumed finger pointing,

"YOU'RE SACKED YOU CUNT," Clive continued. "I'M GOING TO GET YOU STRUCK OFF FOR THIS YOU FUCKING CUNT. YOU FUCKING CUNT!"

Shit.

Turning to Kam and Penny a second, I saw they were smirking by his side while Evette gritted opposite.

"You don't shit on your own doorstep," she glared.

This was bad.

In fact, this was horrendous.

In a horrible moment of loneliness, as I was surrounded by these four humourless bastards, I saw that the nurses and receptionists I'd done it for were all still on the dance floor. With glaring eyes before me, I sat wishing I could just vanish. Instead, I had to struggle to pull up my ripped fishnet tights while I couldn't believe what I'd done.

I'd only wanted to cheer everyone up.

Feeling that cold flush of failure, tears started building in my eyes and I excused myself to the toilet. I was totally gutted.

For some reason, society seems to think that dentists are all 100 years old, grey-haired and have to be serious 24 hours of the day – whether we're treating patients or not. I don't know why this is. Unlike other professions, it's appears we're not allowed to be human or ever have any sort of fun side. Obviously, I'm not trying to justify getting naked in front of the boss but on a night out why should it matter what I do – I'm not going to be required to drill anyone's teeth am I?

Anyhow, hiding in the toilet downstairs now and washing my blotchy face in the sink, I heard a knock at the door. Tiesha was shouting me from the other side…

"Open up man!"

Unlocking the door -

"Rass, dat was off de chaart!!" she said smiling. "Bare people loved it."

"Ha thanks," I sniffled, still wiping my face, "but did you hear what Clive said?"

"No," she laughed, texting away on her phone. (This was before iPhones had video and the habit of filming everything was not yet commonplace.) "Dey av' all gon' home why?"

"Who's still here then?" I asked, my mind already a world away.

"De oda girls. Amanda's wid som fella and Kam and Penny went wid Clive and Evette, why?"

"Fuck Tiesh, Clive just fired me."

"Waaaaat??" she backed, obviously not having a clue. "Fah real?? Nooo. He cann' ave! Dat was propa funny!!"

"Yeah that's what I thought but I'm fucked man."

"Pffhhh…." she waved, blasé. "Yuh wont be. You'll be fine."

But teary-eyed I knew she was wrong.

While everyone else was still dancing and having a good time, I realised what I'd just sacrificed. I'd lost my job. Slipping out by the fire exit and leaving them to it so I could walk home alone in the quiet cold air, I began mulling over what I'd just done.

It's strange because, to this day, I'm not ashamed of what I did but at the time I was devastated to the core. After making everyone laugh, I'd come to learn that in this world there's always some bastard who has the power to stop the fun and hold everyone back. This pisses me off. Like many others, Clive and Evette typify the kind of people who always place a misguided importance on permanently keeping up appearances over and above embracing the rare opportunities in which everyone is able to truly connect through laughter and fun. There are enough real problems in life and it's for this reason that genuine laughter can let us rest our burdened minds and relieve us when we need it most. I'm not saying that stripping naked in front of your boss is the best way to go about things, clearly it's not, but, if it's causing no harm, no one should have the right to destroy the good times, especially not a pompous dentist.

Anyway, now rambling home drunk as I munched on a kebab, I continued spouting a one-sided torrent of how much of a nob Clive and his posse were, while replaying what I should have said instead. God, I really wish it had been a FUCK YOU moment. Unlike in the movies, however, just left to pull up a pair of ripped fishnet tights in front of four humourless dentists, I realised it was nothing of the sort.

Still, bumbling along, even if a small part of me did accept I may have gone too far… for now, fuck 'em; it was CHRISTMAS and on these empty streets, kicking over a wheelie bin for standing in my way – I felt that no one could tell me I was wrong.

No – that could wait 'til tomorrow…

Stupid wheelie bin.

11

BACK IN – FOR A BIT

Waking up the next morning, what the fuck had I done?!!!!!

In my own sanctimonious bid to liven up and motivate a team of people who didn't seem to care anyway, I'd now lost my job while Clive had declared that he was going to get me struck off!

Realisation was dawning.

Rolling out of bed with my Santa drag suit still half on and dying for a massive wee I scratched around under my sheets and a heap of clothes to find my phone.

It was flat. Plugging it in and leaving it to power up I rushed to the toilet and had to pee through a ripped hole in my fishnet tights. Still feeling foggy I waded back to my bedroom just as missed calls, texts and four answerphone messages lit up on the screen.

Shit – I hoped one of them was from Clive....

Scanning the texts to see both were just jargon ads from O2, I dialled the answerphone and listened with trepidation.

The first message was from Amanda, the receptionist, left at 1.07am. She was inviting me to the club.

Hearing Tiesha on the second, then the third, all similar, shouting over loud music, I prayed the fourth would be from Clive saying everything was OK.

Left at 3.05am…

Damn – all I got was Tiesha again, this time in a taxi, laughing, saying I should trim my pubes.

Not a peep from Clive. He must have meant every word.

I needed to call him.

Searching in my interview suit I managed to find an old business card that I remember he'd handed to me on my very first day. I wasn't sure what the protocol was for Sundays but knowing he'd changed his mobile I had to dial his house.

Ring-ring. Ring-ring….

Man, I really should have prepared something but Clive picked up before I could change my mind.

"Clive's residence," he hailed.

"Oh hi is Clive available please?" I asked even though I knew it was him.

"Speaking," he returned a long drawn-out sigh.

"Oh hello Clive hi, it's Michael," I bumbled. "I'm just calling about last night. I'm so sorry. I really want to apologise."

Sighing once more, "What you did last night was disgraceful."

"Yes yes I know I know," I couldn't help but jump over his words, "and I'm so sorry I was just really drunk and had far too much wine."

"Well you're not at university anymore and those actions were inexcusable."

Rushing again, "I know I know," I was unable to stop talking over him, "I'm so sorry. I just got far too carried away with all the table wine and everything and I'm really sorry... Please Clive, please I need this job and I really love it at yours and I can assure you it won't happen again... please."

Fucking hell... by this point, literally ready to suck the man's dick, I was doing all the grovelling and pleading I could, until finally,

"Very well," he relented, "I will allow you to return."

"Ohhh thank you Clive, thank you so much," I jumped.

As he finished, however, Clive's tone was not half as excited as mine.

"Let's just consider this water under the bridge shall we and we can start afresh in the New Year."

"Yes. Thank you Clive, thank you again," I said.

Putting the phone down, I gave a little dance around the room – that seemed to go a lot easier than expected. Though I didn't read too much into it at the time, I would soon discover why....

Following ten days of annual leave and excited to start the New Year, I returned to work where I realised Clive's decision to let me come back had been nothing more than a short-term chess move. With his other dentists still behind their annual target due in March, Clive needed the immediate over performance of me and Tiesh to help the practice average out on top.

If he'd sacked me at Christmas, he wouldn't have had the time to advertise, interview and get a new dentist in, and what's to guarantee they'd be just as quick?

Nah – this would be too risky.

After March, however, his practice would meet all targets, clearing him for an automatic NHS contract renewal which would give him all the time in the world to push me out.

Sitting in the January staff meeting I could already see his antipathy towards me was bubbling under the surface. Evette kicked it off. We listened to her usual drone about coffee stains around the sink, then Clive got going on his imminent practice targets again. This time he wanted suggestions on how we could entice more patients in…

"….so how could we do it?"

"Well I have an idea," I said, eager to answer him, given no one else had. "To get more patients in we could advertise on the outside of the building and put up a huge banner."

I'd seen this work well for the beauty salon and although we were on a main road, we were hidden at the top of a glass-mirrored building. None of the passing traffic even knew we were there so, to me, a banner made every sense.

Clive, however, couldn't wait to shoot me down.

"A banner???" he scoffed. "Pffff. Don't be ridiculous. I said intelligent suggestions!"

Scorning, his face of disgust was copied by Kam and Penny.

OK – maybe I should just keep quiet.

About a week later a good-looking Asian woman in her 40s came from the Primary Care Trust to visit Clive in his office. I just so happened to be passing by. Clive, seeing me through his part open door, summoned me in.

"This is one of my associates." He introduced me to Mrs Shah, a PCT manager who I vaguely knew helped handle NHS contracts for the borough.

"Hello," I nodded to her, not quite sure why I'd been called.

"Hello," she smiled back.

She seemed nice. Standing in the confines of the small room though, I stood as Clive refused to say any more. Making it awkward for us both while leaving me stood waiting like a lemon, neither of us were sure what he wanted next…

"WELL GO THEN!" Clive suddenly snapped, breaking the awkward silence. "She's not here to speak to you! GO!"

What the fuck was that all about?

Confused I left, tail between my legs, just as the attractive Mrs Shah tipped her head looking as embarrassed as I was. It seemed Clive had just wanted to indulge himself with yet another form of belittlement and make me look like an absolute fool.

As the weeks passed his disdain towards me became more and more blatant. I tried everything I could to appease him but nothing would work.

He would barely even acknowledge me in the corridor. I offered him cups of tea. I tried complimenting him and even surpassed all my targets.

There was simply nothing I could do.

He hated me.

With the March deadline steaming into view the panic for my future wrenched at my guts. My options at this point were grim. Searching online I saw that there were next to no jobs at this time of year. On top of this, Clive was well known in the industry. He'd addressed conventions and audiences at the highest level. I knew that he would slag me off to any employer I applied to. Also, being registered with the PCT and with the new NHS.gov.uk issued emails we all now had to use, I knew that faking my reference, like I could before, was impossible.

I was screwed and starting to feel worthless. As each day ran down, Clive was just waiting to close on me.

Before long we were down to the last month when I picked up March 1st's edition of the *British Dental Journal* magazine. There were no new jobs again but, reading the miscellaneous section, suddenly I spotted what might be the answer to all my prayers.

WTF!! I couldn't believe it!

In bold letters it read:

"Invitation for tender."

Wow!

As a once in a lifetime opportunity, the PCT was offering up a brand new NHS contract worth half a million pounds!

Reading on and researching further details online, I discovered that a tired practice had apparently been hit by the credit crunch. It had failed to meet its target so the PCT had revoked its NHS contract. As a result the PCT was now inviting bids to start a new contract from scratch.

This was amazing. In order to acquire the contract, applicants had to demonstrate how they would provide brand-new dental services that could meet all NHS requirements, be located in a suitable ground floor premises within 100m of Mile End High Street* and set it all up within two to three months, (a very short space of time!!)

Surely I could do this!

*Location changed

Downloading the application form, I worked like crazy. In the space of eight frantic days I filled out pages and pages of how I could provide the best service ever and, following a business mate's top tip, made sure to spell out line by line at the end how choosing me would directly benefit the person making the decision... a crucial finisher he'd taught me which was something that most bidders rarely knew to add.

My application was strong and by pure chance I had also managed to find a suitable location that was just within the NHS criteria. This was so lucky.

Right up to the very last day of submission there hadn't been any suitable premises to be found but, hanging on and cycling all over, I, fortunately, found a place in the nick of time. It was off a side road and was just about to go on the market.

The landlord there wanted an extortionate rent so I verbally accepted this on the proviso that he'd write a letter confirming that I had first refusal. I attached this to the application and worked right through the night to make my application look perfect. I finally submitted the completed tender to the PCT just before 8am.

Now all I had to do was wait...

Get in!

Arriving in the post one week later was a letter from the PCT that said I'd been shortlisted for an interview where I'd have to present my proposal to their board for the final decision.

Apparently, I'd been shortlisted along with two others from twenty-two (this I was told later).

Walking into work the following morning with the exhilarated feeling that I might actually escape Clive's clutches and finally have a chance to better myself, I was summoned into his office 'for a chat'.

"Morning," he shut the door, clearly something pressing on his mind. "I understand you've been in contact with the PCT?"

What the fuck! How could he have known about my application – I hadn't told anyone!

Purposely holding out a prolonged unnatural silence – my only negotiation tactic – I forced him to spill what he knew. He spoke,

"A little birdie tells me you've applied for a contract."

What!! So he did know!!!

Keeping silent again I just shrugged…

"Well have you?" he had to ask.

Shit. This really wasn't good but I figured that I'd better play him at his own game if he already knew,

"Well Clive, all it is is, you told me I needed to know more about NHS protocols," I acted dumb. "So I just thought this would be a good learning exercise like you suggested."

"Hmm," he didn't quite know what to say.

Deciding I'd better get out of there before he asked any more,

"Listen Clive, I must dash," I nodded, "I have a patient."

I scurried out but fuck, that was tense.

Over the next few days I did all I could to keep out of his way while still hitting my targets with Tiesha. With only a day to go before my big presentation, I made a quick call to the PCT for some last minute checks.

Mrs Shah, the good-looking Asian I'd met, answered – "Oh, hi," she said, being nice to me again…

After formally confirming the order of presentations and the board's compatibility for computers and PowerPoint, she finished our chat with a tip I never expected.

"You know you may want to consider asking Clive for some assistance on this."

"What?" I replied, completely thrown. "Do you think I need it?"

"Well Clive is well known round here and perhaps the approval of a principal like him could help make your proposal even stronger."

Fucking hell – did she not remember him shouting me out of his office??

"Anyway," she finished, "I'm only in and out assisting tomorrow but hopefully I'll catch your presentation in the morning."

"Ok thanks."

Ending the call I was now left with a horrible dilemma.

Even though my written tender was apparently coming out on top and the tender advert itself described how they wanted a fresh new dentist to provide their services, I couldn't be sure whether Mrs Shah was subtly warning me that I might be considered as too much of an unknown.

If I asked for Clive's approval, however, how bad would this sound?

"Oh hey Clive, I know you hate me 'n' everything, but do you fancy helping me become a boss?"

Cos that wouldn't be awkward would it!?!!!

All night I lay awake debating what she'd said.

Fuck it – waking the next morning I figured Clive's approval might just be the advantage I'd need to persuade the board I was bulletproof.

Having booked the day off work and now with only three hours to spare before the interview, I told myself I was just being paranoid so on the way I popped into Clive's surgery to proposition him... after all, what could I lose?

Right off the bat, "Well this is preposterous," was the first thing Clive barked when I asked him.

"I know but it's just as a mentoring thing," I tried. "And if they ever gave it to me I'd still work here of course. I just wondered if this was something you would approve?"

I watched as Clive's face turned to disgust followed by his series of reasons as to why the PCT's proposal was no good. Eventually, however, Clive agreed he would advise me if needed suggesting all the while that he had my interests at heart.

Boom! Backup was sorted.

I rushed off to give my presentation to the board. This involved a slick PowerPoint after which I was able to impress them with thorough answers to their questions. Mrs Shah, who had luckily managed to catch it, escorted me to the lift...

"Just between the two of us," she whispered, "out of the three presentations, yours was the best and you've been the only dentist who's managed to secure a suitable premises in the timeframe."

Things were looking up!

Later that evening, trying to kill time by walking along a quiet path near the River Thames, I nervously waited for the panel's decision. Finally my mobile rang.

"Good evening," a tinny voice said. "This is Mr Darlington, from the PCT."

"Oh hello," I crossed my fingers, coolly trying to pretend I took calls like this every day.

"First of all," he said, "we wish to thank you for your application and we have to say your presentation was excellent."

"Thank you," I started grinning, excited to hear what this meant.

"Yes, however," his tone was already starting to dive, "the competition, unfortunately, was fierce and as a result the board has decided to hand it to someone else."

"What!!" I was shocked. "But did they have a location?" I demanded, knowing full well they didn't.

Coughing his answer,

"Er well erm," he struggled. "They already operate a practice elsewhere and could offer more experience."

"Yes but I thought you wanted fresh talent," I countered, "and like your advert says, you specifically wanted dentists who didn't already run a practice!"

"Well, erm, I'm sorry," he squirmed now, "I'm not at liberty to discuss such matters."

"So who is then?"

"Listen, I'm not calling to argue!" he closed. "The board's decision is final so thank you and goodbye."

The phone went down.

Motherfucker.

I would discover later that asking Clive for help before my presentation revealed to him how far I had actually come.

Shocked that I had made it this far, he had, apparently, jumped on the phone to the PCT and told them categorically not to let me win the contract. Thus, despite the fact that my tender and presentation had been the best, I lost.

Clive – now it's time for me to say to you, FUCK YOU YOU FUCKING CUNT!

Bumbling along the riverbank, as the winter's night air washed a horrible chill over my skin, I felt my phone buzz again.

It was a text from Tiesha.

She'd just seen an advert go online for a new dentist at Clive's.

I was broken.

12

UNFINISHED BUSINESS

Back in work on Monday I watched as Clive wasted no time arranging interviews.

Catching me in the corridor,

"How was the presentation?" he smiled.

"Yeah good thanks," I returned, trying to keep as nonchalant as possible.

Fucker.

He knew I'd lost but I was not about to let him schadenfreude my arse.

"So where does this leave us?" he trifled further, still gunning for his pound of flesh.

"Well, like I said," I shrugged, "I'll just carry on here as normal which was always my intention."

"Oh?" Clive stroked the underbelly of his chin. "Really?"

Ok, so I knew what he was getting at but being the final week of March and not ready to roll over dead just yet, "Yeah you see for me Clive," I stood tall, "the presentation was just a learning exercise because like you told me many times, I need to know more about protocols, so I figured this was the best way."

Ha – Eat that twat face!

"Hey I see you're interviewing people," I was still on a roll. "What's that for?" I was determined to turn this charade back on him.

"Oh nothing," he waved, "just spare surgery sessions that aren't being used – that's all."

Yeah right. Having seen his advert online – full-time and five days a week with no spare surgeries – it was clear how he intended to create one.

"Cool. Well Clive, must dash," I nodded. "I don't want to keep my patients waiting."

"No," he smiled.

Leaving me to it – we both knew the plan.

To ensure there'd be no gap in service, Clive was going to string me out for as long as it took to set up a new dentist. Once all the paperwork was complete and he had his replacement ready, he would be in just the perfect position to sack me.

I headed back to my surgery. Tiesha was waiting for me. She was trying everything she could to calm me but it was useless. I was screwed. With the countdown closing and regardless of the fact that I was hitting all Clive's targets, I knew he would act. I needed something fast.

A week on we'd cleared the March deadline. Clive was now holding interviews which was making it torture as any day now I'd be getting it. Evette was almost revelling. Periodically she started bursting through my door to show yet another candidate around,

"And here's the surgery," she'd point. "And look – there's the new light fittings I was telling you about."

"Wow!" I had to watch each of them enthral. "Nice light fittings."

Yep – standard commercial light fittings – outstanding!

I was expected to sit there and smile like some dancing monkey but all I could do was keep checking the jobs I'd applied for. Refreshing my email I was getting nothing.

Click – I refreshed it again.

Click, click.

Still nothing.

Click.

Shit – I was refreshing like a madman. It was the end of the week and waiting for my last patient to arrive, I reloaded my inbox for the thousandth time. Suddenly I saw an email pop up from Mrs Shah.

"Call me," it read.

WTF?

She'd left only her number and gave no idea what it was about.

This sounded serious.

I checked my watch – it was 5.07pm

She'd soon be finishing work but desperate to call her, aware my patient would be arriving any minute, I needed somewhere private to find out what this was about…

Fuck it.

Rushing down the stairs to the disabled toilet outside the Sexual Health clinic, I locked myself inside figuring there couldn't be that many people in wheelchairs catching STDs.

I dialled her number.

Ring-Ring, Ring-Ring.

"Hello," she picked up, "Nav Shah speaking."

"Oh. Hi Mrs Shah it's Michael," I rushed quietly, hoping the big wooden door could soundproof me if anyone passed. "I got your email."

"That was quick," she lifted. "Are you still at work?"

"Well kind of," I had to turn away from a huge nasty skid mark someone had left in the pan.

"OK well I won't keep you. Firstly I just want to say I'm really sorry the board didn't go with your tender – I genuinely thought that they would but for some reason they changed their mind last minute. Anyhow," she went on, "I know this is all a bit sudden but I have something rare you might be interested in."

"Oh?" I waited intently wondering what the hell this could be.

"Yes you see we've been running a contract with an old dentist who is due to retire and the problem we've got is that these two Israelis are expecting to buy it off him. However, they've been so aggressive arguing with us for a premature transfer of it, we don't really want to deal with them anymore."

"Really?" this sounded good.

"Yes – I mean, we'd still transfer it to them if the seller insisted but given how well I saw you do in your presentation, I've suggested this dentist might want to reconsider by selling it to you."

"What!? That's amazing!" I exclaimed.

"Ha – I'd thought you'd like it."

I certainly did!

Since 2006, when the Government capped the supply of NHS practices, buying a practice in central London for a small timer like me had become nigh on impossible. Unlike private clinics, which were rendered almost worthless by the credit crunch, NHS practices had attached to them a kind of guaranteed income. Their values were skyrocketing so practices were being fiercely snapped up by heavily backed corporates. This meant that someone like me wouldn't normally get even a look in.

Now I was hanging on to Mrs Shah's every word as it sounded like she was providing me with some sort of in when,

"Scuse me, scuse me," I got a knock at the door.

Damn – someone was outside.

"Yeah just a minute!" I rushed.

"PLEASE I NEED THE TOILET!" the guy raised his voice.

"YEAH JUST A SECOND!" I repeated, covering the mic.

Trying to keep cool, I continued carefully into my cupped phone, "You were saying?" I spoke to hurry Shah up.

"Yeah so his number is 0..7.."

Fuck – no pen too – grabbing a green paper towel out of the dispenser I started trying, using the edge of my thumbnail, to scratch in each digit.

"Uh huh, zero... seven," I repeated back, "three... four"

"PLEASE!" the guy knocked again. "I KNOW YOU'VE FINISHED I CAN HEAR YOU."

Jeez – this guy just wouldn't shut up!

Pressing hard against the door to create a better seal I was doing my best to drown him out while trying to scribe each digit as quickly as possible,

"six, one... got it!" I rushed to Shah.

"You're welcome," she finished, still oblivious as to where I was calling from, the guy outside now fussing to himself. Mrs Shah then added one more thing,

"Oh I must warn you, just be careful. This dentist is not like any others."

"Careful?" I paused. "OK," I shrugged a little taken aback. "Anyway, thank you for this but I've got to go

– I've still got a patient waiting but thank you, I really appreciate it."

"Good luck," she finished.

Ending the call and wondering what the hell she meant by 'careful', I opened the door to finally face a pissed-off pensioner who was looking beyond me to the messy pan. His face changed to an expression of disgust. With nothing else for it – I simply returned him a huge grin, left him to it and legged it back upstairs to finish the last patient of the day.

Phew.

Heading home that night all I could think about was the lead.

Normally nothing worked out for me and even this was only a small heads up with no guarantees. Could I, however, really borrow enough to buy a practice?? This was nothing like buying a house as these businesses could go pop. Plus when it would come to raising money, I knew my parents didn't have any and my credit history was ropey. Furthermore, I doubted whether filling half of one of those pink pigs from NatWest would ever cut it.

Mulling it over, wet through from the rain, I unlocked the door to my gloomy basement…its grimness only underlining my lack of options…

Fuck it.

If this guy did choose to sell to me, I'd just have to worry about the finance later.

Pulling out the damp green paper towel I'd scratched the digits on, I picked up the phone and dialled…

13

JACK

Ring-Ring. Ring-Ring....
Ring-Ring. Ring-Ring.
Jesus – taking ages, I rechecked the paper towel.
Was that an 8 or a 6?
Not really sure,
Ring-Ring, it continued.
Suddenly the phone clicked and someone picked up.
"Hello?..." I called...
All I could hear was background chatter of what sounded like a pub.
"Hello?" I tried again. "Hello?"
Nobody spoke.
"Hello?"
"AghhhhhhAAHHELLO!" a grufty voice suddenly grunted down the line.
"Oh hi, my name is Michael," I said.
There was nothing again...
"Err," I decided to carry on, "I was given this number by Mrs Shah. She told me to ring you about your practice??"
Hearing only glugging now which was completely throwing me,

"She said you were err selling it?" I bumbled further.

"Arrrrrghhhhhrrr I'm with a beautiful woman!" the voice suddenly belched.

WTF??

"Oh ok," I didn't have a clue how to respond. "Shall I call another time?"

"Arrrrghhhhh meet me at the practice Saturday," he barked, "11 o'clock."

"OK... great!" I started scrabbling for a pen.

"Bye," the phone went dead.

My God??

Who was that???

As I stared at my blank phone, I suddenly realised that I didn't even have the address!!

After having emailed Mrs Shah for the location, I arrived in the area early the next morning with time to spare. I paced along the street in search of the practice. It was supposedly going to be somewhere opposite the tube station and by the corner of the beautiful Epple Park*.

Keeping my distance and not wanting to get too close just yet, I prowled along the far side of the road. Approaching the station I finally spotted a single beige door on the opposite side. It had the address number 7 I'd been looking for.

My immediate thought was that the outside of the place looked filthy.

Sandwiched between a cash machine and Tesco Express, the practice didn't have a proper front. With its tiny entrance set within a 1940s dilapidated four-storey brick building with three frosted windows on the first floor – all dirtied by the passing traffic – it look nothing like a dental practice. Above this, the rest of the floors

*Location name transposed to protect identity

appeared to be residential and were all sharing the same communal entrance by the bottom. This presented a bit of a weird mix but being opposite the station, it was a good spot nonetheless.

Having arrived a little early, I decided to go for a walk.

Twenty minutes later I returned to the site. Crossing the road, I saw by the door this time an old man with grey hair stooped and hunching over a crutch.

He was struggling with a large bunch of keys. Closing in, I guessed this had to be him.

"Hi," I waved just as he clocked me, "I'm the dentist, we spoke on the phone?"

The man half turned. I still couldn't be sure if this was some stranger.

Pausing a second,

"I knooooowww," he finally smiled, a slight song in his voice. "JACK," he suddenly jutted his hand out through the loop handle of his crutch.

"Oh Michael. Hi," I reached over to shake it, all very British.

It took him a minute to find the right key but eventually he unlocked the door. We ventured inside a gloomy hallway which was at the base of a steep set of stairs.

"Hold onto this." He passed me his crutch.

I followed behind as he precariously straddled each step. He pulled at the insecure wooden railing with all his weight. Keeping close behind I saw that the loosening rawl-plugs were wobbling like they were going to pop out.

Finally arriving at the small hallway on the first floor we stopped outside a heavy main door that was sided by two others, both looked residential.

"Aghh, wait a minute," he paused. "I don't know the code."

Rummaging in his coat, Jack pulled out a loose piece of paper to read the alarm numbers. Just as the hall light clicked off he managed to unlock the door before staggering in the darkness to the pipping buttons of the alarm. I followed him inside to an even narrower corridor when I was hit by a thick musk of stale air.

"Aghh go ahead," he grunted.

Bip Bip Bip, he clicked off the alarm...

Still in darkness he was fumbling for the light. Finally it popped on and the reception appeared by my side.

Jesus.

I thought the beauty salon was bad. This was a hundred times worse.

To enter the room properly, I had to step over piles of strewn papers that were laid everywhere. A random nitrous oxide cylinder was being used to prop the door open. This room connected to the staffroom ahead. Most of the tube lights were still tinkering on giving a strobe-like effect; it made the place look like some mad house.

Once the lights had stabilised, Jack stumbled his way over to the blinds and twisted them open to allow in the morning sun. With the rooms fully illuminated now, I peered through the old-style serving hatch that was positioned between the reception desk and the waiting room. Entry to the waiting room was through a door we'd just passed.

Staring through, I became even more stunned by what I saw in there.

Everything in the waiting room was proper old school and it could have been someone's out of date living room from a bygone time.

For decoration, the room contained a mishmash of partly ripped yellowing fibre wallpaper. In the corner there was a disused fireplace which had two overflowing bins beside it. Lining the walls were twelve badly worn wicker chairs, six on each side. One foot above each chair there was a dirty head mark forming an embedded line of circular stains where patients must have been resting their heads back for years. It was dire.

Hovering by the reception desk, I turned my attention up to the huge brown wet patch that had encrusted on three of the polystyrene ceiling tiles that were precariously hanging down in the middle. Jack caught me gawping,

"Aghhrr, don't mind that," he said. "It's just a bit of leaking."

"Sure," I smiled.

What was this place?

Finally making himself comfortable, Jack shifted an old defibrillator off one of the worn out reception chairs. Realising it was time to get down to business, I selected the sofa opposite which was covered with a dirty white bed sheet. He now leaned forward on his crutch,

"So..." he took a good long look at me. "Who do you work for?"

Shit.

Realising that this place was not far from Clive's, I figured this would end in one of two ways...

If Jack wasn't bothered about being given a reference, he'd either be impressed that I was working for 'Clive the Great' or, if it turned out that they were both friends, Clive would probably inform him that I was not to be dealt with under any circumstances.

Either way, facing this man as he stared, waiting for my answer, it was time to roll my dice…

"I work for Clive Hallam in Bethnal Green," I said.

"Never heard of him," Jack discarded.

And then, he blurted something I'll never forget.

"Aghh, I shagged a nurse in Bethnal Green," Jack readjusted the blind, "and she'd shaved her fanny."

"Huh??" I looked up at him not sure if I'd misheard.

Jack though, still talking blasé as you like,

"Yeaaah," he casually turned back, "I said to her what the fuck have you done to that, it looks like an elephant. Nowww, do you want a Stella?"

I was absolutely speechless!

14

THE DEAL

Taking me on a short hobble to his favourite pub, which was only down the road, Jack left me at the table with a morning pint of Stella and two years' worth of practice accounts.

This was fucked up.

Staying by the bar, he was finishing off some story with a barmaid he knew while I, not really having a clue what I was looking at, started trying to make sense of all the different columns and financial spreadsheets he'd given.

They were baffling.

Someone had once told me that as a rule of thumb, the real value of any NHS practice was roughly whatever its turnover was times 1.3, plus its 'assets' such as equipment. I couldn't imagine Jack's equipment was worth much and I wasn't sure what the profit was. His place, nevertheless, did come with a decent size contract of £330,000. Maybe I should go with this… I mean it wasn't like I had any other options.

About a quarter of the way into my pint I saw Jack hobbling his way back.

"Right," he settled opposite, hooking his crutch handle on the edge of the varnished table. "I'm selling the business for £340,000. Do you want it?"

"Yes," I blurted.

Shit – not even giving this a moment's consideration, I must have sounded far too premature.

Jack took a steady sip of Stella.

"The question is…" he changed to looking me right in the eye now, "can you afford it?"

Feeling my throat tighten as I realised my hastiness must have made him unsure whether he could trust me or not, I felt a wandering bead of sweat trickle down my side.

"Yes," I nodded carefully.

"Hmm," he still wasn't convinced. "Because if you need a financial advisor, you can speak to Neil a friend of mine. He sorts all my dealings."

"No no, it's fine, I can get the money," I sipped deeply into my pint.

Jack waited a second and watched.

"Well then. Is it a deal?!" he jutted out his hand.

Looking down at his outstretched palm, hovering over the practice accounts I barely understood, "Deal!" – I shook back.

My God – had I just agreed to buy a dental practice with no idea if I could even get the money?

Indeed I had.

"Good," Jack continued, "but before we continue, I must warn you of something – I'm true to my word Michael and straight with people so don't try to fuck me because I know dodgy fellas who break things."

"No, no," I reassured him. "I'm straight I'm straight."

And with that, sitting back, Jack's pint almost empty, "Aghh I'm sure you are," he nodded. "Nooow, drink up. The details we can worry about later. I'll get us another two."

Three hours later, I bounded out of the pub pissed out of my head. I couldn't believe what I'd done.

Half scared and still riding high on adrenaline, I had, amazingly just agreed to buy a dental practice in Zone 2 of London! His place might have been dilapidated but, with its NHS contract being the only thing that counted, (a healthy size of £330,000 and kept off the open market) it was no wonder that the Israelis wanted to bite his hand off.

£340,000 was a bargain!

We agreed we'd both speak soon and that I'd email his financial advisor.

The following Monday I happily arrived back in work when Clive had an announcement to make.

"We're having a meeting this afternoon," he leaned into my surgery.

"OK," I nodded with Tiesha.

I'd had an idea this was coming although his usual monthly staff meeting wasn't for another fortnight.

Later that afternoon, I sat in the waiting room where the rest of the broken souls had gathered. Clive clearly couldn't wait to tell us his news.

"Right," he began by performing a little wiggle of triumph on his seat. "Some of you will be glad to know that we've finally selected a graduate from Guys University who will be joining us very soon."

Oooo.

"So this means," he proclaimed while fixing a glare to me, "a few of you had better shape up because we plan to change things around here."

Fucker… obviously referring to me – I sat wondering how good it would be to make an announcement of my own. Needing his regular wage though for as long as I could and aware it would take months to sort out Jack's place, I decided I'd keep quiet. I hadn't even visited my bank yet.

"Anyhow before we come onto this," Clive was revelling he would have me in checkmate, "Kam, Penny and I have been doing some higher thinking."

'Higher thinking'????

"What we're now going to do is walk you all through our new marketing strategy," he parked a chair in the middle of the room and opened his laptop on it.

"…Penny?" he nodded for her to dim the lights. "To help you understand," he continued, "I've just invested £5000 to make a TV advert which is going to be screened on all the TVs in the huge bingo hall by the station."

Wow.

"And played hourly," Evette randomly kicked in, like this was some weird scripted brag, "to hundreds if not thousands of people. This could lead to us having queues out of the door," she stood proud.

"Yes," Clive nodded, reaching his sausage finger down to press play. "Here we go…"

With everyone huddling around his laptop the advert played out. We basically watched 30 seconds of a woman having her teeth whitened while Clive and his dream team, Kam and Penny, stood behind us all – so proud. They metaphorically patted themselves on the back as we all returned to our seats.

"Well?" Clive finished, waving to Penny to switch the lights back on. "What do you all think?"

Everyone just nodded like they usually did and I realised I'd been the only dentist excluded from this.

"Michael?" Clive turned to me. "How does this compare to that silly banner of yours, huh huh huh?"

"Oh yes his 'magic banner'!" Penny air quoted swapping a mocking look with Kam.

Dicks. Their smugness made me debate whether I should just tell the truth, when Clive teased me again.

"Any *'expert advice'* Michael?"

"Well err," I started puzzled. "There is something I'm not so sure of?"

"Yes?" Clive kept his smug look while Kam and Penny hung on excitedly ready to shoot down whatever I said.

"Isn't tooth whitening the most luxurious and expensive product we do? Yet you guys have decided to advertise this to a hall full of pensioners who firstly, won't be able to afford it, secondly will be too busy playing bingo or chatting to notice and thirdly, don't even have their own teeth to whiten in the first place."

Silence!

For the first time ever Clive and his posse were stumped.

Everyone was wide awake now while Tiesha threw me a smirk. Seeing the rest of the nurses and receptionists beam too, Clive turned livid.

"Michael can have a word?" he beckoned me with the finger.

Fuck – having to follow him immediately to his tiny office, away from the rest, my blip of cockiness evaporated. I could already feel the adrenaline start drying my throat.

Closing the door behind me.

"Michael, I was going to inform you of this later but our situation is clearly not working is it?"

Shit – say something cool, say something cool.

"OK," I just nodded.

Damn. With the adrenaline choking me, like some schoolboy caught in his first fight, I was determined Clive wouldn't finish me with the upper hand.

"So…" he continued, "I think it's best for all of us if you collect your things and leave here right now."

Come on tell him FUCK YOU! Tell him FUCK YOU!

"Do you understand!" he looked at me with a bullish face.

"Sure," I just swallowed again.

Bastard!

Losing my nerve as Clive stood waiting by the door, I'd become too choked up to say anything.

"Well then goodbye," he said.

"Bye."

I just walked out.

Gutted.

Collecting my bag and whispering to Tiesha I'd fill her in later, I felt that this wouldn't be the last of it with Clive.

Back on the main road and suddenly jobless once more, it was time to phone Jack.

"Aghhrr Hello?" he answered.

"Jack! It's me!"

"Aghh," he grumbled, not so chirpy this time. "What is it?"

"Hey, what's the plan to get this sale moving faster?"

The delay in his voice made it clear something was wrong.

"Aghh Neil says you can't get the money!"

"WHAT??" I jumped, shocked that Jack was already pulling away.

"Aghh, I'm sorry," he continued. "Neil's took a look at your accounts and says the bank won't lend you the money. You haven't earned regularly enough!"

Huh?

Only a day earlier I had sent his financial advisor all my statements in good faith. How could this guy be so sure I couldn't get the money?

What – are you telling me that in this short space of time – not even a full working day – he had tried all the banks?

"But this is bullshit," I protested. "I can get the money!"

"Well, Neil says you can't and I've known him for years."

"Jack. Come on I can!" I pleaded, even though Neil may or may not have been right.

"Look I'm sorry Michael," Jack sounded like he'd already made up his mind. "I have to trust Neil and he insists I should be selling to his Israelis who are willing to pay more."

"But listen, Jack," fuck – he did have a valid point, "I can get the money, I promise!"

"Wellll... I'm really sorry but Neil's been with me a long time and I don't know you."

My only salvation collapsing – think Michael, think!

"Jack!" I exclaimed, racing back to bits of conversation we'd had. "What about that Hamish dentist you told me about, your associate who left?"

"Eh?"

This shifted his attention.

"Don't you need cover for that?"

"Oh yeahhh!"

"OK well how about this – I'll cover at your practice as an associate," I rushed, "'cos with my PCT registration, I can help by working there straight away. And while your staff get to know me and stuff, we can make the deal smoother for everyone?"

"Aghhhh," he croaked, unimpressed. "I'm not so sure. Neil already has his buyers lined up and I just want to retire."

"You can retire Jack, you can!" I pleaded with everything I had. "My bank just has to arrange the money I promise!" I gave my last roll of the dice.

Listening to him grumble a second,

"You better not be fucking me here."

"Honestly Jack I'm not, you can trust me!"

"OK," he finished, having deliberated for what felt like ages. "Speak to Rachel at the practice. She's back next week and organises everything. You'll have to work out of Hamish's old surgery."

"Oh thank you Jack, thank you," I jumped. "That's top!"

Jesus.

Somehow, with my foot barely in the door I'd just about managed to jump ship.

Little did I know, however, that this would only be the start of an insurmountable battle that was going to involve court, bribery, intrigue and a whole load of other underhand shockers that I never thought conceivable.

Lurching ahead, I was about to take on the most fucked up tsunami of my life...

15

DAY ONE: GROUND ZERO

"Sorry but wuh cannit open the windaz cos'a poison"
Huh!

Two weeks later, having received the classic 'Thank you, your service is terminated with immediate effect" letter from Clive, I arrived outside Jack's. I wasn't really sure what to expect.

As a kind of half-baked plan, he'd told me that I should just pick up where Hamish, his previous dentist, had left off. I doubted things would ever be that simple. Firstly, I would be required to fix half completed treatments someone else had left, secondly, Jack had said that he wouldn't be around for the week and thirdly, he'd casually dropped in the fact that he didn't even have a receptionist!

This didn't make for an ideal start…

Heading inside and climbing the damp-smelling stairs, I re-entered his practice again. Nothing, however, would prepare me for the chaos that was to ensue.

Stepping into reception once more, I was reminded of all the junk. No one was around but all the lights were on, papers were still strewn everywhere and now a random set of stepladders appeared to be abandoned in the middle of the room.

"Hello?" I called out.

It looked like a burglary had taken place.

"Hellooo?" I shouted, wondering if I ought to find somewhere to hang my jacket or simply throw it on the floor in front of me.

Suddenly,

"Alreet," a Geordie in her early 30s, appeared from the back. "Am Rachel. Sorry 'bout tha clutta. You must be Michael."

"Hi, no worries," I shook her hand.

As a beefy hearty type, Rachel was donning that healthy northern overdose of orangey-tan foundation which managed to patch its way back to normal somewhere round her neck. Her bullish makeup wasn't the kind of thing I was into but, against pretty green eyes and modern silver glasses, she was attractive nonetheless.

"So, Jack says yer might be buyin' the place?" Despite her diluted Geordie, Rachel also wasn't afraid to be direct.

"Err? Hopefully?" I fumbled, not really sure how open to be.

After she'd folded away the ladders, I followed her through to the back. I noticed that just like the rest of Jack's 'it-be-reet' kind of place, the nursing top Rachel was wearing didn't have the right logo. In fact the logo displayed was from a different practice altogether and must have been from her previous job!

Anyway, kettle boiling,

"Well it's gan o'be a busy day," Rachel started heaping spoonfuls of sugar into one of the cups. "Oh an' if it feels a bit stuffy in hea', I'm sorry but wuh cannit open the windaz cos'a poison."

"Whaat?"

As she made us both a coffee, I listened to her explain. It turned out that despite all the hot air from the compressors and steam blasting off the autoclaves, we wouldn't be able to open a single window or the back door that led out onto the rear balcony this week all because of one of Jack's madcap plans.

Only days before, in a bid to fix a long-standing pigeon problem, him and his mate had suddenly decided it would be a great idea to spray poison all over the rear atrium at the back.

The neighbours upstairs had been making continual complaints about the pigeons but, after being repeatedly failed by their property management's pest controllers, Jack, who'd qualified in pharmacology before dentistry, had taken it upon himself to solve everyone's vermin trouble in his own special way. Instead of half arsing it like they had, Jack had used some illegal poison he'd kept stashed in his basement since the 60s – stuff so toxic just a spoonful could down a buffalo. This potency, however, was no drawback to Jack and he had sprayed it everywhere!

Gawping through the window now, even I had to agree that he'd certainly found the solution. Piling up on the old plastic netting that had been pinned across the atrium outside, were dead pigeons. They were everywhere making a right sight.

I was unable to help myself from staring at this pigeon Armageddon but I realised I was making Rachel uncomfortable. She decided it was time for us to get a move on. She took me down the corridor to meet the only other dentist still working here, Mr Chan.

"Hello." I stepped inside his surgery which, surprisingly, was quite nice.

"Good morning." the slim 50-year-old Chinese chap stepped from behind his dental chair.

Swapping a brief nod, he squared opposite me to formally introduce himself. I had no need to, but suddenly I felt uneasy as to what the protocol was for greeting old school Chinese. I wasn't sure if this was just an ignorant white-Western thing but trying to overcompensate on culture, and perhaps being overly enthusiastic, I first shook him back with both hands.

"Hi, hi," I even added a couple of needless nods.

With one of them almost folding into a bow, Rachel rolled her eyes.

"Howay," she'd seen enough. "Come, let's gan o'yer surgery."

"OK," I straightened up.

Eeee, feeling a bit caught out at having based my oriental introductions on Mr Myiagi and the Karate kid, I backed out of his room unable to stop myself giving him one last nod.

I liked Mr Chan. I mean, granted, the dude looked like a Bond villain and there seemed to be some unwritten rule going on that no one could ever address him by anything other than his last name, but as a pleasant, well-mannered man, he was super respectful. I could tell he was simply there to do his job and go home. No opinions, no Tank-Man, no fuss… just the Communist way.

He was nice.

Finally now being led to the room that I'd be expected to work in, I waited as Rachel fought and pulled to try to unlock the sticky door. I was in no way prepared for what she was about to reveal – this would be the worst dental surgery in Britain…

It might sound reckless of me, agreeing to buy a practice without actually seeing this particular surgery but, in the previous weeks I'd just gone with the flow. I'd figured that it was the NHS contract where all the value lay so, trying to play it cool, back when Jack was telling me about the finer points of shaven fellulahs and Stella Artois, I'd decided that one more room shouldn't make a blind bit of difference… right?

Well, that was my theory…

Standing beside Rachel now as she finally unjammed and pulled the door wide open, I faced what was waiting for me inside.

I was gutted – bombsite didn't even come close.

On opening, we were immediately hit by a wave of dank air. Filling the room were half broken, oversized chipboard cabinets which were all peeling and mismatched. They were supposed to be clinical not domestic but these looked like they had been dragged out of some 1970s kitchen and put together by Salvador Dali.

Hanging from the ceiling were more tube lights which were either missing or burnt out. Occupying most of the floor space – its centrepiece – was a huge beige, fake leather upholstered dental chair which had the main seam ripped down the front and exposed dirty yellow under-sponge that was trying to poke its way through.

I'd never seen a workplace in such a state.

Taking a closer look I spotted where the patients were expected to rinse after treatment. This made me even more depressed. Unlike a mini-sink, which I'd normally expect to see attached to the side of a dental chair for patients to spit into, there was just a huge corrugated industrial suction pipe, looking more like a piece of large intestine, which snaked its way up from the base of the chair. Attached to the top of this was a tin funnel held to it with rusty clamps. The idea was that this would be loosely raised to the patient's mouth who then had to do their best to hock into it!

It wasn't exactly elegant.

As I hesitated by the door, the collapsing enthusiasm for my career prospects must have been written all over my face.

Rachel bounded inside.

"Reet," she started clunking a few heavy switches on to power the place up. "Na time for gawkin', its five past nine," she checked her chunky G-shock watch. "And ya forst patient's already hea'."

Reluctantly I followed her into the room to start my day.

I lowered myself onto the dental stool.

What the fuck had I let myself in for?

16

THE MADNESS CONTINUES

I had to get used to this place, quick sharp.

Rachel rushed off to cover reception leaving me scrabbling through all the drawers. I was hoping to find just a simple examining kit. I couldn't believe what was actually in here.

Filled with hardcore tools like bone saws, jaw-breaking looking stuff and loads of other extreme shit I'd never come across before, the drawers started to freak me out. Don't forget, I still didn't have a clue what most of these patients were returning for – but there was no way I knew how to use any of this medieval shit.

"Yer good?" Rachel suddenly reappeared at my door.

"Err…"

Pressured to get a move on as she disappeared off to bring my first patient through, I still had my head buried in the drawers. I was not even nearly ready when someone approached.

"Morning doctor," a meek sounding voice spoke at the door.

"Hi just a second," I didn't even look up.

Shit – scrambling faster to find the right tools I'd need as the patient sat in the dental chair,

"What can I help you with?" I asked, stalling for more time.

"Err well," the man's mousey voice continued, "I had some denshures made off Hamish the Souf Afwican, and I'm not too shure wrabout them," he rolled his R's.

"Oh?"

Poorly indulging him while I knew I really should have been paying this guy more attention, "Why?" I asked.

"Well the teeth are wreally spikey," he continued bumbling in his thick Brummy accent. "And me fwends keep making nasty comments about them."

"Comments?" I'd just spotted the mirror and probe I'd need down the back of the drawer. "Like what?"

Then, for the first time, finally able to pull my head out from behind his chair, I turned to catch sight of the poor fella's issue.

Wow – faced with a pale dweeby guy, tiny pea-black eyes, they had to be the most horrific miniature plastic teeth I'd ever seen. This Hamish dentist couldn't have given the dude a more ridiculous look! Quite accurately, the patient then stated...

"I ruck rike a piranha"

Ha fuck me, he did! Tiny gappy teeth – all jutting forward and spiky – he looked exactly like a piranha!

Struggling to sit there while every part of me wanted to scream, "YOU DO MATE YOU DO," I needed to uphold the party line...

"Hmm," I strained a thoughtful expression. "Yes, we must make you a new pair."

"Fwankyou,"

Finishing off the rest of his check, I took new moulds expecting his osrdeal would be over. For this unlucky fish, however, it was about to get worse.

He was ready to spit out after his rinse but I had no clue how the ancient suction funnel worked. I simply lifted it towards his face. At the same moment, the poor fella, unwittingly dipped his head just as the unforgiving industrial suction motor jolted to life. All of a sudden,

Schlurrrrpppppppppppph

The bowl clamped itself to his face.

Shit.

WHRRRRRRRRRRRRRRRRRRRRRR

The motor whirred into immediate overdrive.

Fighting hard against the blockage now and belching out a massive screech, the funnel had started welding tighter and tighter to his face.

Sluppppphhhhhppppp.

Fuck!

Most people would have just pulled it off by now but this poor dude was thrashing against it looking like some epileptic fighter pilot and was only making it edge closer and closer towards his tiny pea sized eyes.

WRRRRRRRRRRRRRRR

There was little I could do!

The screaming racket was heard right the way through to the waiting room, alerting Rachel who, thankfully, rushed in.

"Sit still!" she shouted, "Stay STILL!!"

Gripping the guy she finally managed to prise it off.

Phew.

All was quiet now as we watched the poor fella sit back, his mouth left like a red, plucked beak.

"Sorry about that," I said, desperate to fill the silence. "Here. Have some free toothpaste."

Awkward as hell. I was determined to style it out when he turned to me again and spoke,

"But I don't have any teeth."

Fuck, he was right.

Full plastic dentures so no teeth – toothpaste was useless.

"Well for your friends then," I wasn't ready to give in.

Handing over as many free mini Sensodynes as I could, I cringed as Mr Piranha man received them in a daze.

"So see you next week, yeah?" I kept on smiling, trying to maintain that everything was ok.

"I guess," he finally exited by the door.

Shish.

What a start! Thirty more patients to go – this was going to be a long day.

Battling through the rest of the morning, I was thankful that most of Hamish's patients weren't actually too bad. There were still some odd ones, like one woman asking if I could extend her canines to look like fangs but apart from her, the day rolled on and things ran smoothly.

That afternoon, Jack rang to update me:

"Whoahh, great news!" he shouted. "Got you a new receptionist starting tomorrow!"

"Oh?" I answered, still trying to familiarise myself with everything else.

"Yeah!! You're gonna love her, whoah!" he rushed excited. "She's fantaaaastic!"

"Ha. Well we certainly need one," I replied, trying to be equally enthused.

"Tell me, how is your first day??"

I tried to be polite but forgot my place.

"Actually Jack I don't know how you normally have it here but this place could do with a good tidy, its chaos!"

Immediately brushing me off,

"Agghhhh. Relaaax," he said. "It can all be sorted. It just takes tiiiiimmmme."

"Well it really needs painting," I suggested, "and if its OK with you, I want to get rid of those dirty head marks in the waiting room tonight."

"Tonight? What's the rush?" he really didn't seem to care. "I know it needs a little sprucing up but take a rest. I'll get a pal to sort it."

Looking around at Jack's ideas of pals who can sort things – multiple dead pigeons sparked out on the net – I wasn't convinced.

"Yeah don't worry," I said, "I'll just get some paint and do it tonight."

"Suit yourself," he left me to it.

Returning from B&Q later on that night, I wondered if their staff in those crazy orange jumpsuits would fit in better here. With everyone gone home and all by myself, I laid the paint tins in the waiting room when the loud buzzer on the intercom rang.

BZZZZZ BZZZZZZZZ

"Hello?" I picked it up.

"Lemmi in!" the voice of some Scottish bloke yelled through the intercom.

"Who is it?" I was a bit worried given how late it was.

"It's Murray – C'MON LEMMI IN!!" the guy yelled again.

"Who?"

"Murray – Jack's mate!! FUCK!" he shouted louder. "Jack said y'needed 'elp."

"Huh?"

Reluctantly buzzing the door I walked to the top of the stairs to see who it was. Already kicking the bottom entrance open, a huge burly Scotsman barged his way in.

"Fuck me!" he looked up at me, a lit fag bouncing up and down between his lips. "Jack said you werratall lad but you're fuckin' well lanky! Ha."

Stomping his way up the stairs then, tattooed arms, lugging a bucket in each hand, he stopped at the top.

"Jesus," he laughed again. "I wouldn't like to meet you on a dark night, ha."

Dumping both buckets of paintbrushes right on my feet, he began to perform a mini shadow-box just inches from my face. I still didn't even now who the guy was!

"So where d'ya need me?" he looked on ahead.

"Err the waiting room?"

What a mad introduction. Following him through to the back, I realised that Jack hadn't even bothered to tell me he'd sent him. It was obvious though that Murray had been here before.

After taking two cans of Stella out of Jack's fridge, he lobbed one over to me, took a paint roller and got cracking.

I have to say, first impressions n'all, this guy was definitely rogue but, he helped me out and I was really impressed at how nice he was. Working hard, Murray explained how suffering with sciatica he was on benefits so didn't want paying in case it affected them. Instead he just wanted a few cans of Stella Jack kept stocked in the fridge.

I decided to join him. We cracked open a few more and worked tirelessly into the night. Showing me painting tips on how to make the corners look good, he shared stories of his days running a bar in Bermuda. It turned into a really good laugh.

I liked Murray and felt bad that I'd misjudged him.

A few hours later however, "Eh, Micky," he finally stopped me to admire our wall. "You know what would be great 'ere?"

"What?" I stood beside him, already pleased with what we'd done.

"Ma mate's 'ad it dun in his lounge," he stepped back, holding up his hands now as if beholding an almighty vision of what would guarantee an improvement to our masterpiece.

"What is it?" I asked excitedly.

Both staring at the wall, me waiting eagerly for his genius…

"TINFOIL!" he stated.

"Huh?" I suddenly didn't follow…"Tinfoil?"

"Aye, Tinfoil," he nodded, still focusing up. "It looks great."

"Wait a minute," I still needed some clarification here. "You mean tinfoil from the supermarket?"

"Aye, tinfoil," he repeated like it was obvious. "You just press it on."

"What? No glue or nothing??" I wasn't following.

"Yeah," he nodded.

Staring at him, I struggled to imagine patients sitting in a tinfoil covered waiting room while this 'pressed on' magic of his peeled off over their heads…was this Murray's recall of watching *Blue Peter* on acid?

Checking the side of his face again, I looked to see if there was any hint of a joke. This made him turn back to me. No idea why I was baffled,

"Hey," he finally spoke. "Can you pass me another Stella?"

Oh my…

17

TITS VS MASH

Yep, 'Tinfoil Murray' had meant every word!

The next morning, with the walls finally painted (not tinfoiled) and the place looking less like a *Little Shop of Horrors*, I bounded into work. Today was the anticipated arrival of our new receptionist whom Jack had assured us would be "Fantastic!!!"

"Fantastic" he'd said, "Fantastic!"

This made me happy…

Arriving early, my plan was to try to make the reception area less messy. With no one around, I cleared away some papers and bits of junk off the sofa. I reached under the desk to hide a huge shipper box of tuna that Jack had been given by his fishmonger mate. I felt the floorboards creak by my side. On backing my head out, suddenly I was confronted with a hot girl standing above me, her face poking out over the cleavage of her boobs.

"Allô," she smiled. "I am reception?"

"Oh hi wow!" I almost fell back. "Welcome."

My God she was fit! At 5'2 with massive knarks, I now knew exactly what Jack had meant by his word 'fantastic'.

Standing up and forcing myself to keep focused only on her face, I made some space between us.

"What's your name?" I asked, quickly brushing myself off.

"Aria," she answered in a beautiful alluring French accent.

"Cool, well err welcome Aria," I couldn't help but grin.

Not sure what else to say, I decided to show her around.

"Well this is your desk…" I pointed. "And here's some pens," I jiggled the cup… "Oh and here's some paperclips."

Jeez – I could already hear myself defaulting to that classic 'point and describe' tour people always hide behind when they're stuck. Aria was politely nodding but why was I being so dull?

Anyway, down to just a ball of elastic bands to critique, an awkward silence loomed. I was so enthralled with her looks, I'd failed to notice the major problem that was yet to emerge. Suddenly Rachel stomped in.

"Mornin'!" she said, dumping her bags by the desk. "Yer lab work is in yer surgery but yer still need'a write the ticket."

"OK sure," I turned. "Oh Rachel this is Aria, our new receptionist."

"Alreet," Rachel nodded, not half as bowled over as I was. "Welcome."

Leaving them to it I pranced off to my surgery buzzing. Our receptionist was fit!

Back alone in my room a moment, I couldn't help flexing my muscles in the window reflection to see if could make my biceps look bigger than those of someone who never went to the gym. Just as I was tensing at my most, however, Rachel burst through the door.

"SH' CANNAE SPEAK ENGLISH!!!!"

"Huh," I jumped, pretending my gun show was just me itching my shoulders.

"That fuckin' LASS back there!" Rachel mustn't have noticed my pose, "sh' can't speak English!!"

"You sure?" I'd moved down to itching my stomach, just to make sure I'd styled it out.

"Yes am fuckin' sure!" she shouted. "Sh' can't speak shite. When's Jack gettin hea?!!"

"This morning I think, why?"

"COS HE NEEDS T'SACK HER!!"

"What – but she's cool isn't she??" I was still in awe.

"COOL!" Rachel bellowed. "COOL???"

Facing her chunky eyebrows bouncing up and down now made it impossible for me to concentrate on anything else.

"Yer think am fuckin' daft don't you!?" Rachel continued. "Jack just wants t'see tits an' now you're actin' the same!!!"

"No I'm nottttt," I protested.

Eee – was I that obvious?

"Yeah y'arr!" Rachel yelled, "an'am sick o' it! No one gives a fuckin' shit about this practice an' am left t'do everything!!!"

"That's not tr-"

SLAM

Cutting me off mid-sentence, Rachel stomped out to the sterilisation room not happy at all.

I decided I'd leave it a minute before reopening the door. Once the coast was clear, I crept towards reception to go and see for myself.

Passing by the door of the waiting room first, I saw a patient had just come in and was already approaching the desk. Tiptoeing further along the side corridor to enter reception where Aria was, I pretended to busy myself around the filing cabinet behind her. I watched and waited.

"Good morning," the middle-aged lady proffered, leaning into the connecting service hatch where Aria was sitting. "My name is Pam Mullin."

"Allô," Aria replied in her beautiful French accent.

OK – so normal start so far...

Standing quietly, I tried to hide the fact that I was eavesdropping.

"I have an appointment with Mr Chan at 9.15," Mrs Mullin continued, rightfully expecting that this would move things along...

This time Aria didn't reply. Instead she just stared at her, blank-faced.

"Well???" Mrs Mullin had to ask.

Come on Aria say something.

Giving no indication as to what Mrs Mullin should do next, Aria buried her head in a pile of irrelevant papers on her desk. After about 30 excruciating seconds of doing only this, she then looked up as if she had suddenly found the answer.

"*Non*," she shrugged.

"No?" Mrs Mullin was confused. "No what?"

"Ummmmmm."

Taking another moment to reconsider, Aria just shrugged again, "*Non*," she said.

Shit.

Mrs Mullin was understandably irritated now and started stiffening up.

"I don't understand," she weighed in, "'no', my name's not Pam Mullin or 'no' I don't have an appointment!?!!"

"Ummmmmmmm."

Aria's lips tightened as if giving this deeper thought…

Come on girl…don't let me down.

"*Non*," she shrugged yet again.

Fuck.

Their eyes locked in stalemate, I needed to step in before this got worse.

"Hi Mrs Mullin?" I jumped between them. "9.15?" I scanned the ancient computer screen. "Yes please take a seat – Mr Chan will call you through shortly."

With the patient deliberating as to whether to stay, I froze grimacing at her until she finally sat down. Next, not wanting to expose our weaknesses but needing to check Aria's limitations, I ducked behind the serving hatch to finally confirm my fears.

"Hey," I signalled at the side of Aria beckoning her to copy me. "Come down," I whispered, needing her to lower her head to my level so that neither of us could be seen.

Aria obeyed, mimicking my movements as if this was some sort of game.

Finally out of sight and earshot of the patient,

"Can – you – speak – English?" I whispered to her slowly.

"Yes," Aria smiled.

"OK. What – did – Mrs Mullin – say?"

Still not sure why we were hiding, Aria simply nodded.

"Yes," she said.

"Yes what?"

"Yes," she repeated.

Damn. Displaying such spectacular knarks, Aria made me want to give her another chance. Maybe she hadn't heard me right...

"Aria. That – wom – an," I mouthed every syllable while pointing through the wall to where the patient was sitting, "what – did – she – say?" I gave her one last go...

"Yes," Aria just nodded the same.

Gutted. Rachel was right. This girl was just guessing and really was as lost as a peanut in a toothless mouth. Stupidly I'd allowed myself to be blinded by Aria's looks just as Jack must have done in whatever pub or random place he'd probably bumped into her and promptly offered her the job. It was no wonder we hadn't noticed this minor detail. I mean, obviously she could say a few things like 'hi' and 'yes', but being a receptionist unable to speak English – boobs or no boobs – we couldn't have this!! The practice was crazy enough!

"Right," I whispered, "stay here, I'll be a minute."

Standing up to leave while Aria's innocent puppy eyes followed me out of the room, I went off to tell Rachel. This was going to be a real shame. I know everyone loves a bit of eye-candy but Jesus...

Opening the door to the sterilisation room, "OK OK," I held my hands up to 'Chunky Eyebrows' who was now hauling steaming instruments out of the machine. "You're right. Aria can't speak English. A few words maybe but that's it."

"See!" Rachel lifted her brow. "See! A told yer!" she loaded more tools into the autoclave. "Well you can be the one to tell Jack t'get rid of 'er cos am not deein it!!!"

"What??" I protested. "Why me?"

"'Cos," Rachel barked, switching the autoclave to another cycle. "It's not ma job! An' besides I dee enough round here!"

Rachel was right.

She did far more than all of us but, short-strawing me to ask the boss to get rid of Miss Cleavage of the Year when she obviously made him so happy, wasn't going to be fun.

As the morning went on, Rachel, who was supposed to be nursing for me, tried her best in simplified Geordie to converse with Aria and show her as much as she could. It wasn't far off the blind leading the blind but I felt guilty as hell in the knowledge that Aria wouldn't be staying.

She was still a nice person… but in the few hours she'd been here, messing up loads of appointments, causing random gaps in the day list and already making bookings disappear all over the place… she was creating absolute havoc!

Thankfully, in the meantime, she could say numbers at least so Rachel had taught her a way to find bookings on the system. Aria was to ask patients their date of birth. Unfortunately, she latched solely onto this and it would become our curse.

At any moment that Rachel or I walked past reception, we would hear Aria answering the phones with,

"What is your date of birth?"

Then if the patient asked anything complicated like, 'Can I speak to the dentist?' or 'How long will my tooth take to recover?' Aria would insist, "Madam your date of birrrrrrth!!!??"

Even when they gave it to her and regardless of any further questions they asked, they would be met with Aria returning nothing but,

"What is your date of birth madam!!!!??!"

She'd then look around to make sure none of us were watching and just put the phone down as if the call had never occurred!!

Aria had a child-like cunning – I'd caught her doing this a few times!

Back in the surgery I heard a rumble of the door downstairs. Jack had arrived. It was time to tell him but I wasn't looking forward to any of it...

"Yer'd betta not pussy out," Rachel warned me as we listened to him thundering up the steps.

"I wont. I wont," I braced myself but I was not buzzin' off any of this, even though Rachel was right.

Waiting there as I tried to recite my lines,

BANG!!

Jack suddenly burst through the door.

"LOOK WHAT I GOT!!!" he let a huge box he was carrying crash onto the floor.

"Jeez what is it?" I was immediately thrown.

"A SHREDDER!!!" he hailed. "WE CAN USE IT TO TIDY RECEPTION."

"Ha cool," I bent down to have a look.

"Aghh, Tony my driver gave it us," he nudged it with a gentle kick. "It was being thrown out from some pawn brokers."

"Mint."

This was nothing like the type you'd find in Argos. Taking a closer look I noticed that the bin part was missing. Besides this, the thing was monstrous and, with its battered shredder head, it looked so industrial it could probably chop metal coat hangers never mind credit cards. It was hardcore!

As I kneeled admiring it, I felt Rachel's eyes burning into the back of my head to tell him what was up.

"Oh Jack by the way," it was time to do it, "I've got to tell you, it's about the receptionist."

"Woah. She's fantastic isn't she?!!!!!"

"Wellll," I stalled, ignoring Rachel now glaring right into my face. "She's cool 'n'everything... but we're not too sure."

"What?? Patients will love her!!" he hailed.

Much as I wanted to agree with him I had to persist. Before I could speak though,

"Jack!" Rachel stepped in, "sh' can't speak English!!!!"

"Course she can!" Jack continued messing with his box.

"Yeah, she can say a few words," I stood knowing I'd better join in, "but as a receptionist she needs to know more. All she can do is ask people's dates of birth."

"Aghh stop complaining," this was only making him irritated, "she'll pick it up."

"Jack sh'can't pick up a huurl language!" Rachel tried, "an' if the conversation gets too difficult sh' just puts the phone dowwn!"

Gathering pace it sounded like we were ganging up on Jack when, "LISTENNNNN!" he stopped us, "it's her first day so relax. Everyone has to find their feet." Her feet were useless here.

"Yeah, but I could find someone else," I protested.

"ENOUGH!!" Jack barked. "You two forget, I've been doing dentistry for over thirrrrty years, so quit it. Aria's fine and is staying. Now open the door!"

As he dragged off his mammoth shredder to reception, Rachel and I were left dumbfounded at how we'd just lost what should have been an unlosable argument. Stuck facing each other feeling like we'd been Jedi mind-fucked somehow, we couldn't say a thing.

Before we knew it, Jack was hobbling his way back to the pub. Little did we know that he had left Aria in charge of what was soon to become a ticking bomb. What happened next would cause me to have a near heart attack and the term 'lost in translation' would be an understatement…

That afternoon, after taking a short break, Rachel and I had returned to the surgery hoping to perform a complex molar root canal (something I already hated having to do) on a patient. This would take about an hour. With the patient in the chair, mouth open, we commenced the delicate procedure. We were forced to leave Aria to her own devices throughout. Not long into the work, we heard a sound coming from reception…

Niiiieeeeeerrrrrrddddd

I swapped a brief look with Rachel.

Delicately balancing metal hand-files over the patient's mouth now and taking extra care not to drop any sharp instruments down his open throat, Niiiiieeerrrrrrddddddd the shredder belched out again.

My God.

Subject to it grinding some more while we were both trying to concentrate.

Niiiieeeeeerrrrrrddddd.

Niiiieeeeeerrrrrrddddd.

WTF was she shredding back there?

Nieeeeerrrrrrrrrrrrrrrrrrrrrddddddddddd ddddddd.

There wasn't that much junk!

Trying to focus, my worry grew as we heard another 30 minutes of Aria chopping and grinding with the shredder like some sawdust factory.

Nieeerrrrrrrrrrrrrrrrrrrrrrrrrrrrrrdddddddd.

Niiiiiieeeeeeerrrrrrrrrrrrrrrdddddddddddddddd.

It was driving us mad. The noise wouldn't stop.

Nieerrrrrrrrrrrrrrrrrrrrrrrrrrrrrrrrddddd.

Impossible to concentrate, I was gritting my teeth having to hear her force-feed this thing as if she was making *foie gras*…

Nieerrrrrrrrrrrrrrrrrrrrrrrrrrrrrrrrddddd.

NIIIIIEERRRRRRRRRRRRRRRRDRDRDRDRDRDRD RRRRDRRDRDRDRDRD.

Right – fuck this.

Leaving the patient in the chair with rubber-dam on his face and cheek clamps in his mouth, I headed out to find out what the hell this crazy Frenchie was up to….

Marching down the corridor, paper dust clouds already looming in the lights, I prayed this wasn't coming from anything important. I braced myself and opened the reception door.

Oh fuck!

Finally stepping in, eyes peeling, I couldn't believe what she'd done….

All the notes were gone.

All the medical files were gone.

All the papers had vanished and looking down at Aria, who was now on all fours, about to load yet another batch of patient files into the shredder…

"ARIA!" I shouted. "WHAT-THE-FUCK-ARE-YOU-DOING?!"

"I mash!"

Niiiiieeerrrrrrrrrd. She shoved them right in.

NOOOOOOOOOOOOOO!!

Having no idea of the significance of what she'd done, Aria had shredded everything!

"Aria STOP!" I had to shout as she reached for even more. "STOP! STOP! NO MASHÉ!!! NO MASHÉ," I yelled in my guessed attempt at French.

This was a disaster!

Standing there in complete bewilderment surrounded by bags and bags of what was now patient record hamster bedding (legal documents that the crazy bitch had shredded) I knew that as a practice we were now fucked...

18

CHAOS

As I held my face in despair, the phone rang. Aria picked it up.

"Allô dental practice," she said. "What is your date of birth?"

Head in hands, I was still standing in disbelief.

"Monsieurrrrrrrr!" I barely registered her. "Your date of birrrrrrth!!!!"

Wait a sec – half catching the voice on the other end – this wasn't a patient.

Shit. "Give me that," I snatched the phone from her. "Afternoon, dental practice," I took over, "how can I help?"

"Oh hello," the stern voice started. "It's Nicholas Beaty here. I'm calling from the PCT."

The PCT!!! – what did they want?!

"Is Dr Jack Brocks available?" his manner serious. "I've been trying to get through all morning."

"Errrrr."

Glancing at Aria, I pictured how she'd probably been badgering this dude for his date of birth every time he rang. This was not good. Besides handling contracts, the main job of the PCT was to police dental practices and shut down any that weren't professional. Closing my mind to our poisoned pigeons, the shredded medical records that I was surrounded by and a crazy French receptionist who was incapable of speaking English,

"Oh, I'm sorry," I answered, trying to sound calm, "Jack is unavailable at the moment. I'm his associate. Can I help?"

"No," the voice cut. "Would you please inform him he must contact me urgently."

"OK," I finished.

He ended the call. This was definitely bad.

I darted straight into the back needing to get Jack on his mobile…

Ring-Ring. Ring-Ring.

Come on man pick up.

"Ahhhllo," Jack finally answered to the background chatter of a pub.

"Jack! Aria's shredded all the records!!"

"What?" he paused, sounding like he was taking a sip. "Oh dear," he quietened.

"Yeah! I told you she's a liability. What did you tell her?!!"

"Aghh I just told her to get rid of all the junk lying around but relax."

"Relax?!" I couldn't believe him. "Jack – I don't think you realise, Aria's shredded all the patient records which means we're fucked!"

"Aghh, I'm sure we can sort it."

"Oh yeah??!! Well you'd better get here man cos the PCT have been phoning for you too and this is serious!!!!"

Just then, feeling like I was about to lose it on a boss who clearly didn't have a clue, I heard Aria pipe up behind,

"Madame what is your date of birrrth?" she started again in reception.

"I've told you already!" some woman barked.

Shit.

"Jack – a patient's arrived – gotta go!"

Racing back to reception I was confronted by a smartly dressed woman in her 50s, wearing driving gloves. Standing at the desk, it was clear from her expression that she was already pissed off.

"I've told you my date of birth!" she was barking at Aria. "Now where is Hamish?!"

"Hi Mrsssssss errrr?" I stepped in.

"Round-Turner," she glared across, "and you are?"

"Michael. Hi, I'm the new dentist. I've replaced Hamish."

"Good," she interjected. "So you'll be able to do the treatment he promised won't you!"

"Um, certainly."

Fuck me – how long could this chaos last?

No medical records, no idea what treatment was required and definitely the kind of patient primed to complain. This was dangerous. If she reported anything and the PCT found out how we'd just shredded everything, we'd be done for.

I was left with no choice but to keep smiling like an idiot.

"Please," I grimaced, "take a seat. Won't be a sec."

Parking her in the waiting room, I raced back to the surgery trying to maintain that everything was normal.

I burst through the door. Rachel was still balancing clamps in my other patient's mouth.

"Right," I leaned over him. "Sorry about that but I think we're going to have to let this tooth settle. It seems you still have some infection," I rushed, trying to hide that I was freaking, "so we'll temporarily fill it and book you back in ok?"

"Okayyy," the patient murmured.

Ignoring Rachel glaring at me knowing that this was just a blag and with no time to explain, I quickly patched his tooth and booked him back before finally going to collect Mrs Round-Turner…

As I escorted her from reception along the corridor,

"You know I'm still not happy with what Hamish did," she griped.

"Yes sorry about that," I blindly apologised as I sat her in the surgery. "Oh before I fetch your file," I had to tread extremely carefully here, "can you remind me again what you've come for?"

"'Come for???'" she snorted. "This back filling of course. It's never been right since Hamish did it and this is the fourth time now so you'd better get it right!!"

"Absolutely."

Phew – giving her a smile – it was just a filling – easy.

Resting her in the chair to start the routine of injecting her gum, I picked up the dental syringe. As I began reaching it towards her mouth, however,

"Erm EXCUSE ME," she suddenly knocked it away. "What on earth do you think you're doing?!"

"Huh?" I lay it back down, "I'm just numbing your tooth, why?"

"Because I'm here for sedation!!"

Sedation?

OH FUCK!

This was even worse!

Sedation was a specialist qualification that required advanced training. There was no way I was certified for this – nor was Mr Chan!

Long gone Hamish might have been but Midazolam was the drug of choice and the same stuff that killed Michael Jackson. Administering it without proper training was very dangerous. Then again, in our current state, we couldn't exactly risk her complaint.

"Sedation?" I gritted. "Of course."

What the hell was I doing??!

I indicated to Rachel to follow me out of the room. Round-Turner must have clocked the strain on my face. Before I left she asked,

"You do do it don't you?"

"Yeah, certainly," I lifted, "I've just got to get the equipment." Straining again, I had Rachel glaring at me as if to say 'are you fucking nuts?'

She followed me out silently.

We headed to the tiny stockroom where I was hoping she could give me a crash course.

Like most basic dentists, I was half aware of the theory but having observed sedation only twice during an introductory lesson at Uni, I was hardly equipped for the job. I really should have being paying more attention. Instead like a dick, I'd been too busy watching my Nigerian mate EB, who, unable to pronounce "th" in 'teeth', sounded like he was asking each and every patient, "Hello can I see your tit?"

Their reactions were amazing but this made me miss most of what I was supposed to learn. The pass mark was only 50%. Why couldn't this have been this 50% I'd listened to?

Anyhow, no time to Google it and Rachel starting to panic at what I was asking her to do,

"This is fucked up ye kna'," she protested grabbing the gear from the drawers. "Yer've never done this 'av yer?"

"No but if that woman finds we've shredded her records and reports us to the PCT we'll be ruined!"

"Well this is wrong."

Shaking her head in disapproval while rummaging in the drawers, she pulled out pipes, arm drips and loads of other equipment I wasn't even familiar with. Taking three minutes she gave me her best description on what she'd seen other dentists do. I reckoned I could do this.

I mean I know the training normally takes three months in the safety of a training hospital but if a smackhead could do it – how hard could it be?

Cradling the gear I prayed that it would all work out.

"Right," I took a deep breath. "Just act cool."

We returned to the surgery trying not to look like we were both panicked.

"That took a while," Round-Turner scowled.

If only she knew!

Assembling the packaging in front of her and straightening her elbow on the arm rest, I got the IV line ready and hoped I could just get this right...

Tapping into arm veins was nothing like injecting gums added to which, her veins were thin and tiny making this procedure ever the more precarious.

"OK here we go," I said. "Just relax."

Lining up my best, I plunged the needle straight for her vein.

"Oww!!" she yelled.

"Oops. Sorry about that."

Shit. Too deep.

Another try...

Plunge.

"Oww," she yelped again.

Damn – missed it.

Her skin was starting to bruise now as the few veins I'd found were already beginning to collapse.

"Are you certain you know what you're doing?" Round-Turner glared.

"Yes absolutely," I nodded.

Sweat forming on my brow now, I could feel her scrutinising me, doubting my every move. No choice I lined up for a fourth.

OK. Here we go...

"OWW!" she yelled again, this time loudly. "Right that's it," she barked. "I've had enough of this!"

Just as she was about to lose it and me thinking it couldn't get any worse, we all heard a loud crash of the door downstairs. This was followed by the noise of Jack grunting his way up...

Shit – this was all we needed.

He'd just come from the pub. Rachel rushed out to give him the heads-up but it was all happening too quickly. Jack came bursting through our door,

"Aghh what's going on?" his presence silenced us. "YOU NEED A VEIN? ERE GIVE IT 'ERE."

Fuck! Fuck! Fuck!

Wobbling towards us and scarily unbalanced, he swiped the needle off the tray. Both Round-Turner and I recoiled.

Apart from the beer, the very reason Jack was so unstable and needed a crutch was because of a scuba-diving accident that had been caused years earlier by his mate.

Diving deep, his buddy was leading the way and wanted to sink even deeper. Jack kept telling him it was time to surface but he refused to listen. The friend seemed intent on swimming to an early grave.

Almost out of air by this point, Jack realised the guy must have been suffering the hallucinogenic effects of narcosis. Sacrificing his own health he dived even deeper to grab him. The situation became so desperate that they both ran out of air on the way up and had to surface as quickly as they could. Rocketing to the top catastrophically resulted in the two of them suffering from 'the bends'. Jack's cerebellum was seriously damaged which was why his coordination and balance were now shot. His mate, who suffered a similar fate, however, was saved.

Of course none of this was of any consolation to Round-Turner. To tap a needle into the tiniest bruised vein, something both Hamish and I had failed to achieve already, was going to be impossible. So faced with a swaying man now who was hazardously shuffling towards her with a needle in his shaky hand, she froze.

Jack looked like he was about to fall on top of her. As he went to jab her, I braced myself waiting for the scream. Within seconds though, he'd plunged the needle, tapped her vein and almost immediately, eyes rolling back, Round-Turner was gone.

OMG!!

Beep Beep Beep

He'd done it! What a legend.

Sedated now with the Pulse Oximeter beeping to let me know she was safe, I knew that Jack had nailed it!!

"Wow – you did it man you did it!" I looked at him with a newfound respect.

"Agghh, told you," he just shrugged. "I could find a vein in an orange peel!"

Leaving me in awe, he shuffled off as if it was all just another day.

Soon after, I finished replacing the filling. Thankfully the side effect of Midazolam is short-term memory loss. Round-Turner was happy and she eventually left the surgery having next to no recollection of the event. Waving her goodbye, the day finally over, I went to go and see Jack.

He was in reception checking through the filing cabinets. Aria had gone home.

"Aghh she hasn't shredded that much you know," Jack said assessing the damage. "We still have the patients' notes we need and most of the others she shredded haven't been for years."

I, however, was already humbled by what he'd just done.

"Thanks for saving me back there," I mumbled, tail between my legs. "I didn't know what I was doing today."

"Welllll," he said. "You shouldn't really be doing stuff like that on your own but we all make mistakes."

"Thanks man," I said gratefully.

Jesus.

If it was Clive he'd have nailed me but Jack just handed me my jacket.

"Aghh you forget Michael, I've been doing this business for a long time and you still have a lot to learn."

"I know," I murmured.

Giving a smile he noticed where I'd hidden his tuna.

"Nowwww," he finished, "do you still want me to throw Aria out or can she make a mistake too?"

"I suppose we could help her."

"Good," he nodded. "Glad you agree. Now get some rest."

"Ok."

Waving goodbye as I headed home I couldn't help but think, what a chaotic day…

19

PROGRESS

I survived the first few weeks at Jack's and soon the days were flying.

It actually started to feel like we were making some real progress. I was now in charge of finding an extra receptionist. Aria was messing up only a couple of appointments an hour and since she'd learnt to do more than just ask people their dates of birth, even Rachel was beginning to tolerate her.

Well, that's assuming her chunky eyebrows weren't trying to tell me something else.

Anyway, happy with the way things were falling into place, I headed up North for the weekend on what felt like the umpteenth stag-do that summer when Jack rang.

"Agghh, I finally spoke to the landlord about you getting the place," he started chirpily. "He wants you to introduce yourself."

"Oh yeah?"

I still hadn't bought the business yet but as part of the initial stages we needed to organise transferring the lease of the building into my name, a routine legal requirement for any sale.

"Yeah and he's a nice guyyyy," Jack continued. "He's been my landlord for over thirtyyyyy yearrrrrs."

I listened to him amble on as I pulled up to Doncaster Paintball. It turned out that, after enjoying their long catch up, Jack and the landlord had decided to have a random bet on the football against each other. Jack naturally bet on England and had already won.

"Whooaah, so he's taking me to his members' club in Mayfair," Jack roared on. "He says the food there's fantastic!!"

Ha. Smiling to myself at the last time he used the word 'fantastic!!'…

"Yeah and you think the steak at the places I've taken you to is good," he continued excitedly, "whoaah, this'll be something else!! Anyway Michael, make sure you ring him 'cos I'm hoping he'll let you come along."

"OK, cool. I'll do it now."

Thirty minutes later, having checked in with the rest of the stag party who were struggling into muddy overalls, I figured why not call him from here. The back of a paintball safety area was probably not the best place to phone my future landlord but he sounded friendly enough.

With the rest of the stags barging on ahead while I finished getting changed, I dialled the number.

"Oh how nice of you to call," the landlord hailed when he finally picked up.

"Hi yes," I said. "Nice to speak to you too."

God he sounded posh.

I'd been told that as a wealthy aristocrat, the landlord owned polo horses and played international baccarat. In contrast, I was now struggling to muffle out the noise of a screaming air horn as twenty blokes started suddenly swearing and shouting behind me over some stupid red flag. Yeah perhaps it wasn't the best place to try to level with this guy. Nevertheless...

"Jack tells me you're also very polite," he continued.

"Oh thank you," I flirted back.

Jeez – even Lloyd Grossman would sound a chav next to this fella but doing my best to keep him on point,

"Well, I'm really looking forward to buying Jack's practice," I said. "I guess we just have to start getting all the legals organised."

"Hmm?"

Suddenly he stopped like this was of significant interest.

"Yes. Tell me," his tone changed, "how much are you paying for his business?"

"Err..."

Woe, this felt a bit direct. I mean, I know this was the landlord and everything but I wasn't sure if I ought to be sharing this kind of information.

"£340,000," I felt compelled to say.

"I seeeee," he pricked up...

This made me feel a bit taken aback but in the light of the friendly bet he'd just made with Jack and the fact Jack had practiced dentistry from his building for over three decades, I had to assume this must be his general way of chitchat. Besides, his business rent was fixed for the next four years so, as long as I confirmed I could be a reliable tenant to continue Jack's building lease, surely it didn't matter what I said here – did it?

My first business mistake!

"And tell me," the landlord delved further, "how keen is Jack to retire?"

"Um, well," I was still naïve in friendly mode, "he barely works there so soon as possible I guess."

Following a series of probing questions, the landlord went on to ask how much dental practices normally sell for, the profit they make, my situation with the bank, why NHS businesses are in demand whereas private ones aren't and many others which, at the time, I couldn't fathom had anything to do with the lease.

Thinking that I was just being helpful though and well on the way to forging a trusting relationship, I continued to fill him in on all the gaps.

"Marvellous," he said. "Well I'll look forward to meeting you in the near future."

"Great," I finished proud I'd done a good job. "Thanks."

"Yes, bye for now," he ended the call.

Despite never getting the invite to this fancy Mayfair meal he was treating Jack to, I was elated. Feeling confident that I'd convinced the landlord that I knew the dental business inside out and would therefore pose no problem in taking on his lease, I switched off my phone excitedly and joined in the game. Little did I know, however, that from this moment forth, from the seemingly irrelevant information I'd just passed, a cascade of events would set off which would later railroad Jack's practice right to the brink of extinction…

Roughly one week on while I was busy working back at the practice…

"WHAT THE FUCK DID YOU TELL THE LANDLORD??!!" Jack phoned me from a taxi.

"What – why?" I said shocked, quickly having to duck out of earshot of a patient.

"Aghh I've just been taken out for that fancy Mayfair lunch with him," Jack barked, "and he's demanded either you or me now have to give him 68 grand cash otherwise he won't sign the lease into your name – which means the bank won't release your purchase money – which means the sale is completely fucked!!!"

Motherfucker!!

It turned out that as soon as the landlord had finished drawing his information from my call, he'd wasted no time in strategically inviting Jack out for their magic Mayfair lunch. All his toff pleasantries, even bringing his new Filipino wife along to sit opposite Jack and help make the whole event appear to be nothing but friendly, had just been a devious guise for him to strike his supremacy when it would have maximum effect.

At the table, exploiting his newfound knowledge, the landlord demanded either Jack or me now pay him 20% of the sale price up front, in cash, otherwise he'd do everything in his power to block the sale!

Bastard.

This was completely illegal. Unless there were extenuating circumstances, which there weren't, the landlord had absolutely no legal right to refuse to assign the lease nor could he claim any monies for the privilege.

This, however, was my first wake up call to the reality of business.

A blatant bribe! I soon realised it is dangerous to believe that, in business, there's any such thing as a moral code or that its practise is ever restricted to the parameters of the law.

What's right or wrong, fair or unfair does not apply here. When it comes to making money, there are simply no rules. All that matters is the ability to predict and counter-predict what someone can do to you, whether it is illegal or not.

Look at Clive blocking me from winning the bid – and now this fucker!

I'd come to learn, as a rule of thumb, that when trying to advance yourself in any career, project or business, if your next move involves a step up in relative status or money, especially if it's on the radar of someone who is status driven or who cares about a similar success, you need to watch out big time!

To egotistical people like Clive and now this landlord, another's success (even if it's independent of theirs) will invariably make them feel like they're missing out or that someone else in life is winning too easily. As a result, regardless of whether it benefits them, if it's yours they will try to screw you, block you, steal your idea or not settle until they've had their piece of the action. And to keep you down, boy will they fight…

To test this theory, just observe the unique reactions of an experienced businessperson. See what happens when you try to compliment their success or charm them with generosity. Instead of soaking it up like most people would, they will, instead, glaze over in order to block its weakening effect. They know more than anyone that that's usually the time they're about to get fucked!

"Aghh, so Neil (the financial advisor) says I should fuck you off and sell to the Israelis or you pay the bribe!" Jack hit me with another shocker right at the end.

"What?!"

Shit, I couldn't afford this! I knew Neil's Israelis might be able to blast the cash but against my skimpy finances and the fact that I was still waiting for my loan to be approved by the bank, I was defenceless.

"Jack I can't afford the bribe but this is bollocks!"

"Aghh, well then I'm sorry Michael," he was already pulling away, "I'll have to stick with Neil as I've known him far longer than you, and to be fair, he's right – you have fucked things up and his Israelis did offer to buy it first."

My God.

Stuck against Neil, his so-called 'friendly financial advisor', who was now jumping all over this to wedge his Israelis back in…

"Please Jack," I scrambled, "you don't need to sell to them! I've got a top lawyer who can sort this!"

I didn't, but trying it anyway…

"Agghh well... he says they'll just pay it no bother and as I warned you before I just want to retire."

Fuck me. I couldn't believe how this was falling apart. Neil must have been chewing Jack's ear off to reclaim whatever secret intro fee he had, no doubt, prearranged with these Israelis behind Jack's back.

"Please Jack," I pleaded, "no one needs to pay any bribe!"

"Aghh…" he was losing all confidence in me.

I raced for something more but what else could I offer?

From what I'd gathered, the only reason Jack had been happy to sell to me, apart from Mrs Shah's tip, was that, unlike these stiff Israelis, he saw me as someone to have fun with and relive his youth through.

Now though, the landlord had made me look like some blabbing dick and because of this, Neil had managed to blindside Jack causing him to believe that I should no longer be trusted. Spiralling fast, I was stuck for anything more.

Fuck.

Racking my brains on how not to lose him – come on think…

Oh, wait a second, there might be one thing I could try…

20

IT'S ALL ABOUT TRUST

"Jack!" I had an idea. "Do you need me to take your tooth out?"

"Eh?"

Yeah this distracted him.

"Your lower 8," I rushed. "Do you need me to take it out?" I said remembering he'd been on about getting it sorted.

"Oh yeahhhhh," he lifted. "It's been bloody annoying!"

"Alright well how about this; Friday we go for a nice meal at Chez Bruce," I knew that this was his favourite restaurant, "and afterwards, I take your tooth out but beforehand, we visit my lawyer to fight this bribe. How's that?"

"Aghh," Jack retracted again, unconvinced. "I've told you I've got my own bloody lawyer, I just don't need the HASSLE!"

"It won't be a hassle Jack, honestly" I pleaded. "You'll be well impressed – these lawyers specialise in business people so the bribe won't even be an issue. Please."

"Wellllllllll..." he vacillated... "I do need my tooth out.... aghh... book the table but we'll have to see."

Jesus. With him ending the call on what felt like his sourest tone yet, I knew I'd let him down big time. I'd have to cling on…

Friday then and despite the short notice, I luckily managed to find a lawyer who was available for an appointment but only because I'd stupidly gone with a shiny red flyer that I'd been handed outside the tube.

'Honest Advice' the flyer promised. 'Caring service' it went on. 'Highly recommended… blah, blah, blah.'

It sounded good to me but I didn't know what I was looking for.

The lawyers were located on the edge of town at the back end of Colliers Wood and my plan was to meet Jack there. Arriving early I knew that I needed to do everything I could to impress. If I could just win Jack over and persuade him with a classy service to fight this bribe, it would hold off Neil and his rich Israelis from offering sums I could not possibly compete against. Furthermore, the move would mean I could avoid paying a bribe I simply could not afford. Hopefully then, my purchase of his practice would be back on track.

As I stood waiting for Jack to arrive, I realised that I couldn't have picked a worse place. Despite the flyer's classy promises, I found myself huddling from the rain under the lawyer's canopy amongst a load of chavs who were annoyingly there just to smoke. Listening to two of them arguing it felt like I was watching a Jeremy Kyle show.

"Fuck off Chantelle," the bigger one shouted, "they're my fags!"

"Nah you still owe me one," his girlfriend barked. "You cunt."

Nice.

This wasn't exactly the awe-inspiring impression I'd hoped for.

I sidestepped to the main entrance cringing at the huge bright green and golden slogans they had plastered all over the automatic doors.

'Where there's a blame there's a claim' the left one said.

And 'We fight for you!' boasted the right.

I was gutted. All this screamed the exact opposite to what I was desperate to convey. Nevertheless, too late to change things and expecting Jack would be approaching any minute, suddenly my phone rang…

"Hello?" I pressed answer.

"Good morning it's John Corrigan. Is that Michael?"

"Speaking."

It was the bank.

"Yes sorry I've not had chance to get back to you," he started. "I've been busy in and out of meetings."

"Oh no worries," I shelled, even though it had been torture that the guy had been dodging me all week.

"Yes well, I thought I'd better inform you," he continued, "about your loan before sending it in email."

"Yeah?" I murmured, still not sure whether this was going to be good or bad.

Just then I spotted Jack and Tony, his burly Barbadian ex-bouncer driver, pulling up in the people carrier only yards in front.

"Yes, as you know," bank man rolled on while I had to wave at Jack already locking eyes with me from the passenger side, "we did say we could probably provide you with a competitive rate but, as you've probably seen in the news," Jack started opening the door, "banks are having to reduce their lending risks which means unfortunately..." bank man kept going, "we cannot offer you a loan.."

Snap.

"Jaaaack!!!" I shut the phone off reaching to shake his hand. "Great to see you!" I smiled through a grimace.

This was all I needed.

Dying inside, I helped Jack out of the people carrier. I'd have to worry about the bank later.

"Aghh this better be good," Jack griped already in a bad mood.

"It will be, it will be," I said trying to distract him from staring at the abandoned fridge.

We ventured through the double automatic sliding doors.

The waiting room was packed, filled with enough sick people to make the place look more like A&E. This start was not good.

I'd promised Jack that these lawyers were purely business specialists. Just from looking at the clientele, they were obviously, though, nothing of the sort. Jack would not be happy. He wasn't a judging man but as a straight-up bloke who did everything on a handshake or taking people at their word, he hated the kind of exploitation where every accident had a currency and people no longer took responsibility for themselves. A service like this wasn't his style.

Standing in the queue victim after victim followed in behind us through the double electric doors. I cringed seeing that they were all clutching the same red flyer of hope that I'd picked up, seemingly convinced that by coming here they would win something regardless of the odds. Waiting around I was beginning to sweat.

The longer we stood there the harder it was to pretend that these shyster lawyers were any better than the daytime TV types who make money by targeting vulnerable idiots and persuading them to sue hospitals for things like slipping on their own piss or tripping over their own shoe laces! Worse, I could see that this was also becoming abundantly clear to Jack.

"Owwe cum I godda pay if it's no win no fee?!" a brawny cockney bloke was already waving his broken arm, arguing with reception. "I can't afford this!"

Just then,

SLAM SLAM.

Having come in some way behind us and causing a huge bashing of the automatic doors, a 100-year-old Zimmer-frame dude, limited to shuffling only millimetres at a time, had somehow managed to trap himself right between the blind spot of the inside and outside sensors.

SLAM SLAM SLAM

It looked horrific and too immobile to move any faster than a plant pot, the frail codger, unable to get out of the way, was now having his body along with his fingers bashed off his frame one by one.

SLAM SLAM SLAM

Gutted. Stuck clutching on for dear life and no match for the heavy-duty doors, that twatted against him trying to reset.

SLAM SLAM.

I buried my head. None of the staff passing nearby him seemed bothered.

"Can someone help him?" Jack shouted, just as Zimmer-framed Yoda managed to jitter himself free.

I was relieved he was through but my prayers that this would be business-types only, not ill folk hoping to win cash, were left unanswered.

What kind of place was this???

Following our long wait in the queue, a receptionist was eventually free. I approached the desk to see she was chewing gum and gawping like she didn't give a damn.

"Hi, we have an appointment," I smiled at her from the other side.

"Ticket machine," the twenty something girl just dismissed us like we were both pieces of shit. "That box!" she pointed behind us.

Wonderful!

Jack followed me as we trudged back to the entrance to rip off a ticket.

"Thought you said this place was shit hot," he grumbled.

"It is, it is," I said, determined to keep up the façade.

For fifty more painful minutes we had to sit watching staff rudely order people around like they were cannon fodder for their machine. No sign of us being called. Jack kept checking his watch…

"How long is it going to take??" he said, his tone letting me know that any remaining confidence he may have reserved for me was rapidly evaporating.

"Any minute," I persisted. "Honestly Jack, they're good."

Just then, when I thought it couldn't get any more dismal, the receptionist made an announcement over a speaker.

"Just to let anyone 'ooze askin' 'noh, the lawyers 'av broke for lunch so for anyone waitin' its gonna be at least another 'ower."

"Right that's it," Jack grabbed his crutch. "This place is bollocks and I'm leaving!!"

"Jack wait!"

Fuck.

Scrambling after him as he lurched for the exit, I'd blown it.

If Jack hadn't been sure whether to believe in me over everything Neil had said, he definitely had no sensible reason to now. In my efforts to impress, I had shown poor judgement and against the Israelis, I must have looked amateur yet again.

Sliding open the long side door of Tony's people carrier, I helped Jack struggle his way into the front. I sat anxiously in the back.

As Tony quietly drove us to Chez Bruce, the awkwardness between Jack and me was hell. I was aware that I still needed to take out his tooth.

Finally pulling up, we entered the beautiful Michelin-starred restaurant right on Wandsworth Common. We sat by the window opposite each other. The sommelier came to take our drinks order,

"Gentlemen. Good afternoon," the slim, suited connoisseur bowed to each of us. "Welcome again. Now for drinks today we have a fine selection of wines–"

"Aghh, just beer," Jack cut him off.

"Very well." he nodded. "Today we have Coopers Pale Ale–"

"Coopers sounds fine," Jack cut in again.

"And for you sir?" the sommelier turned to me.

Now, given how much I'd fucked up and already lost Jack's trust, I figured I'd better choose what any sane patient would expect of the dentist who was about to take out their tooth.

"I'll just have orange juice," I smiled.

Jack suddenly looked at me with a glare.

Oh shit – stopping everything, was this wrong???

Jack glared now like I was committing a mortal sin –

"Err actually?" I retracted, "I'll have the Coopers too please" I gambled.

Jack relaxed back with a nod.

Was this what it was going to take to get him onside???

"Jack," I leaned in once we were alone, "you do realise I'm taking your tooth out?"

"Yearrrhhhhhh," he grunted, "but you'll be fine."

My God. This was almost like some random rite of passage or maybe it was Jack's mad attempt to see the truth in me? In any event, drinks were served and we were soon pissed out of our heads.

This whole scenario seemed nuts but in a way I guess I kind of understood. There's something about sharing beers with someone that forges a hidden bond you can never establish while sober. It's like a deeper truth where you get to share the more honest side of each other, something that is almost impossible to achieve in an office when sipping tea.

The meal soon passed. I'd had way too much to drink and still wasn't sure whether I'd actually regained enough trust. Last two in the restaurant, he waited for me as I staggered back from the toilet, the staff waiting to clear up.

"Right come on," Jack blurted. "Let's get back and see this dentistry of yours."

"What??"

So the crazy bastard still wanted me to pull out his tooth!!!... In this state!!!

Driven to the practice and blatantly plastered, we climbed the stairs. Rachel saw us at the top.

"Canny meal was it?"

"Yeah, is the surgery free?" I slurred.

"Why?" she asked.

"Cos I'm taking his tooth out."

"AGHH I'LL GET MORE BEER," Jack pushed past us.

Just shaking her head, Rachel left us to it.

I set everything up in the back as Jack returned with cans of Stella. Carrying out a dental procedure whilst under the influence is dodgy as hell. If the GDC (General Dental Council, who regulate all dentists) saw me, I'd be struck off in a second but there were more important things at play. Shutting my mind to this I cracked open my can and turned up the radio.

'All That She Wants' by Ace of Base was blasting – great tune.

"Aghh, come on," Jack eventually sat back in the chair. "Stop fannying about."

Putting my partly finished can to one side, I numbed him up. I gripped the forceps onto his tooth and started working it in figure of 8.

Suddenly there was a knock at the door.

"COME IN!" I shouted.

Just as I ripped out the molar, music still blaring, a girl entered from the other side.

"ZARA!!!" I hailed, waving the blooded tooth in the air like a scalped trophy.

Zara was the new second receptionist I'd hired who'd only come in to drop off her paperwork. Staring at us in astonishment, radio full volume, beers lay about and the two of us pissed as farts, she was, understandably, speechless. This wasn't exactly a usual intro.

"AGHH, GREAT JOB!" Jack clambered down from the chair pushing straight past her, "I'LL GET SOME MORE STELLAS," he said, oblivious to her reaction.

"Cool," I continued glugging the rest of mine.

Watching Jack turn at the door then, he added one more thing,

"Oh yeahhh," he nodded, "don't worry about the bribe Michael… I'll get my barrister on it."

Boom–

Finally I'd done it. Finally we were friends!!!

Staring down at his blooded tooth as I returned to my nearly finished Stella, I couldn't help but think again, what a fucked up way to have got there!

21

DODGY DEALINGS

Monday lunchtime now and sitting in the Indian restaurant which was down the road from the practice, I was being handed some serious looking contracts to sign.

"… And just autograph this one dear boy."

Having come especially, Neil insisted he wanted to hand deliver all the documents I'd need and be my aid when I signed them.

"… And just this one needs initialling…"

It had been weeks since I'd taken Jack's tooth out and although I'd been lucky winning back his trust, I just knew that against Neil's lurking influence, it would only be a matter of time before the snake sitting before me would find another way to fight his Israelis back in.

"And this one by the tabs…" Neil smiled.

Fucker.

Just the two of us and still in the delicate stages of the transfer, I figured that the only way to slip a parasite like this off my back, especially given how much he seemed to own Jack's trust, would be to cut him in.

A few days previously and hidden behind the guise of efficiency, I'd hinted to Jack that I'd be happy to let Neil set up my loan for me but only if it made things easier for everyone. Obviously I'd never mentioned how my own bank had just denied me. Hoping to kill two birds with one stone, however, if I got Neil to organise my loan, his hunger for the bank commission he'd receive should at least make him less inclined to keep sabotaging my efforts –

"And just another one here…"

Well that was my theory.

Sitting now in the awkward silence of the empty restaurant opposite Scrooge faced Neil in his stale grey suit, I realised that the bastard had brought far more documents than I'd bargained for…

"So what's this one?" I had to stop him as he handed me yet another contract.

"Oh it's just red tape," he waved, "only boring nonsense. You just need to sign it by the tab."

Hmm. I doubt brushing off 25 pages of small print was nothing!

Neil must have plied this line a thousand times but was adamant I must sign every tab. Aside from the main loan he was setting me up with, he also sprung on me that I needed a payment protection scheme, a private pension investment and a whole load of other hardcore contracts I'd never anticipated.

"Shouldn't I read some first?" I picked the thicker one out of the pile. "They look pretty serious," I tried scanning as much of it as I could.

"Oh. No no," he dismissed, reaching his hand to block the page. "All that is jargon. It's just for fools who've got nothing better to do with their time. Besides," he pointed his finger over the dotted line, "I've done all the hard work by reading them for you."

Dick.

Acting as if he was my new best friend while refilling his glass and bitching about how meagre the wine menu was, I doubt he was aware that I knew the number of times he'd fought to persuade Jack to dump me.

Nevertheless, leaning in as I tried to read more,

"Oh come on," he became impatient, "it's only your autograph," he urged passing me his pen.

No pressure then.

Legally, financial advisors are required to explain their terms and declare any commission they're going to take. Clearly not happening here though – I expected to be bled of some commission but to this swindler the offer of an inch meant taking a mile and this felt dodgy as fuck.

"Oh come on!" he pressed.

While hovering the pen over his dotted line my mind was racing about what to do.

If I committed blindly, these extra contracts could be full of tie-ins and commission clauses that could sting me for thousands. If I didn't give in and play into his hands though, from this point forth I could be storing up a future attack I may not see coming.

Facing his eyes screwing tighter as he waited.

Fuck it.

Deciding it was better to have my enemies onside I took his pen and scribbled my signature initialling each and every page.

"Excellent," he finished, immediately tucking the contracts back into his briefcase. "Well, must dash."

Scarpering off Neil left me feeling that I had just committed to some snake-oil scam. I had to tell myself that this was a necessary evil for the bigger picture and would just have to pray that whatever I'd signed wouldn't turn out to be as consequential as the bribe being forced by the landlord...

Four weeks later and onto tackling this bribe, Jack had arranged for the two of us to visit his barrister in his chambers in Marylebone in order to get the lowdown on what would happen if we took the landlord to court.

Right from the off, stepping inside I saw that this place was amazing and nothing like the one I'd taken him too. Missing were the double electric doors, ticket lines and Zimmer dudes getting bashed about at the entrance. I crossed their huge marble floor into reception and stared up in awe at their ornate ceiling.

"Ah Mr Brocks," a well-dressed lady welcomed us through. "How have you been?"

"Alriiiiight," Jack answered her, clearly having been here many times before.

Making ourselves comfortable on the green leather sofa and enjoying the plush surrounding of the waiting room, I was drawn to the dark mahogany table where they had a whole array of Bourbons.

Man – this was incredible.

With the cheap northern trait I couldn't avoid, I sneaked an excess of biscuits into my mouth, enough for even the crumbs to give me diabetes. My cheeks bursting, Jack's barrister suddenly appeared from the side,

"Jack!" he reached to shake his hand affectionately.

"Roberrrrt," Jack pulled on him to stand up.

The two of them smiled as friends then both turned to me – mouth full with surplus dry biscuit refusing to go down.

"And you must be Michael?" the charming barrister smiled.

"Mmmm-hmm," I had to nod, throat locking on me! "Mmhello," I finally managed.

Wiping my mouth, I followed as he led us through to his office. The barrister opened with a story about Jack and him. Reminiscing about the first time they met, it turned out it was to help Jack back in the 90s after he'd just been arrested by the armed police.

"What!?" I asked.

This was classic!

With both of them laughing as the barrister brought me up to speed, the story went that years back, Jack and his mate were finishing a BBQ at Jack's house and were waiting for a taxi to go out on the town. It took too long to turn up, however, and both became so bored they decided it would be a good idea to pass the time by getting Jack's real Magnum out and start firing empty Stella cans off his pond wall.

Literally, they were having a blast. With bullet bangs ricocheting off neighbours' windows all the way down the street, the two of them had no idea of the commotion that was being caused.

Trying to ring Jack's house, it unfolded later that the taxi company was trying to relay an urgent message that their driver couldn't get onto the street as it had been cordoned off... while simultaneously, and to the complete surprise of a pissed up Jack, a fully armed response unit had charged over his back fence to arrest them.

It was crazy.

Jack's face was pressed against the floor at gunpoint while he handed over his hand cannon to shocked officers but Jack still thought what he'd done was OK.

"Aghh, it was my garden," he pitched in now, just as the barrister finished telling me.

"What!"

I had to laugh at his excuse but the arrest, today, could have been serious. Luckily, being pre-911 and with his gun fully licensed, Jack was merely given a massive fine with an order to relinquish ownership of all remaining pistols and rifles still left in his house.

"Yeaaah, real shame that," Jack reflected. "It was a good gun."

I guess part of me should be shocked but having been to his house and played with his real Samurai swords (worth a fortune) and whole arsenal of the other daft weaponry he'd bought, it all made sense. Jack was the eternal bachelor and it was the kind of daft shit only he'd bother to buy!

Anyway getting down to business, I sneaked a couple of Jammie Dodgers the barrister kept on his side as we listened to him advise us about the bribe.

Luckily, he was in agreement with what I'd been saying and didn't support us paying the bribe either. He warned that if we did pay, there would be nothing to stop the landlord coming back for more.

The flipside of course was the slow and expensive proceedings the court route would take to force the landlord to transfer the lease into my name, a requisite for all banks. This would take several months to get to trial.

The costs of using legal representation of this kind would be around £45,000 and, assuming the landlord's defence bills would be similar, whoever lost would be forced to pay for both sides northwards of £90,000.

Shish… legal figures this big sounded scary.

Nevertheless, the barrister concluded that we had a reasonably strong case as long as the landlord couldn't find a reason to withhold the lease and if Jack, when required to give evidence, could present himself well in court and display he'd been a flawless tenant. He reassured us we should all be fine.

Hmmm. I think if the judge just witnessed the previous ten minutes of nostalgic conversation about shooting Magnums pissed as a fart, Jack might not come across as quite the responsible angel we needed him to be.

Nevertheless, with the preliminary meeting over, Jack and I were resigned to the fact we'd just have wait it out for our big day in court. Shaking hands and saying goodbye, his observant barrister handed me a napkin! I headed back to the surgery while Jack headed home.

As things stood, if the Israelis didn't try to trump me on anything before the court case, and the new bank that Neil had set me up with would still release the loan on the lease transfer, all I had to do was just sit tight and make sure everything else stayed on track.

Thank God everything was finally going to plan.

This, however, wouldn't be for long…

22

CLAWS IN

A fortnight later and with me still buzzing that everything was working, Jack phoned with an absolute shocker…

"Aghhh I've been struck off."

"What??!"

"The GDC!" he barked. "They've just struck me off!"

"You're fucking kidding!" I jumped. "Why???!"

It turned out that Jack had been struck off for letting his Continual Professional Development (CPD) hours lapse.

This was unbelievable!

A few years back the GDC (General Dental Council) which regulates all dentists, had introduced a continuing professional development programme whereby dentists were required to study 250 hours of further education by the end of every five-year cycle.

Way before the first five years was due to take effect however, Jack had been planning to retire and sell his practice to Hamish, the piranha-sculpting dentist.

Unfortunately, just as they were about to close the deal, Hamish's wife ran off with their neighbour and hit poor Hamish with a divorce causing him to have a nervous breakdown.

Jack tried everything he could to help him out and keep the deal open. Despite this, Hamish found his situation too upsetting and was unable to cope. He eventually dropped out and retreated back to South Africa where he came from.

Meanwhile time had crept on for Jack.

As a man who loved reading the papers but, ironically, hated paperwork, Jack had been distracted by all the shenanigans and had overlooked the deadline.

He then dropped his second bomb, as if his first wasn't stressing me enough,

"Aghhh, so the Primary Care Trust want to meet us both Monday."

"What?!" I recoiled. "The PCT!!"

This was even worse!!!!

The job of the PCT, Primary Care Trust, was to monitor everyone's NHS contract. Jack was the principal and therefore the signed 'contract provider'. His getting struck off meant that from a legal point of view, the PCT could declare our whole NHS contract, the entire lifeblood of the practice, null and void…

"Jack!" I freaked. "This could wipe us out!"

"Aghh. Relax," he said calmly. "It's all bollocks! I know what I'm doing in dentistry and besides they never bothered with this CPD shit in my day."

"Yeah, but you don't understand," I couldn't seem to make my point, "if they want to meet, it must be serious!"

"Aghh, listeeeeeennnn," he was never one to panic. "You worry too much. The PCT know you're buying the place and I don't even treat patients anymore so I'll just smooth it over when we talk to them."

Wholeheartedly unconvinced, I could feel we were walking into a shit storm…

The following Monday, 3rd November, having put on my same old interview suit and given myself a pep-talk, I headed out to the Primary Care Trust headquarters which was located not too far from The Tower of London and the River Thames*. I made my way by tube.

Jack said he would meet me there. Nervous and already sweating into the armpits of my jacket, I approached the main road. On arriving, I realised that Jack was nowhere to be seen.

Damn.

After waiting a while outside their huge corporate building I rang his mobile.

Straight to answerphone.

Maybe he was inside.

I decided to check in. I approached the guard just as a huge black Mercedes was allowed out from the electric gate he was manning.

I signed the book and was handed a visitor's pass. This all felt very intimidating.

We had been summoned by the big boss, a man neither Jack nor me had ever met, a man we would, somehow, have to convince that everything was A-OK. Finally I stepped into their huge stone floored lobby but still; there was no sign of Jack.

This was all I needed.

Of all the days for him to be late – I was frantic to go over what we could and couldn't say. Running out of time now as deliverymen signed off boxes at reception

*PCT and its location have been changed

and delegates marched in and out, I knew the director would be coming for us any minute.

Anxiously, I began grimacing at every single suited person who exited the lift just in case it was him. With my guest pass around my neck, I realised I must have looked like one of those frantic dogs tethered outside the supermarket who looks at everyone desperate for its owner to return.

Come on Jack – where the hell are you???!!!

Minutes ticked. Suddenly a young delegate surprised me from behind

"Good morning," he shook my hand. "Are you with Mr Brocks?"

"Hi yes," I shuffled, "I'm Michael, Jack should be here any minute."

"Very well," he nodded. "Please come this way."

Fuck.

I had to follow this guy as he passed instructions to reception about where to send Jack if he arrived. Collared on my own, I did not like this one bit.

Chaperoning me to the lifts, the delegate pressed for the third floor and informed me that due to schedule changes, the director upstairs wanted to commence the meeting as soon as we arrived.

My mind racing, we ascended to the top passing each floor.

When those doors opened, I knew I'd somehow have to think up every way I could to defend Jack and best portray our practice should they ask.

Ding

We'd arrived.

My worry was rising as I was led along to their big office at the back but it soared when he opened the door to the conference suite and I finally saw inside. This was a fucking ambush.

I was confronted by a lawyer, a minute-taker and the 50-odd-year-old austere Chief Director. They were all waiting at the table like they'd been planning this for some time.

"Good morning," the director started. "Please take a seat."

Laid before him on the table was a pile of reports which, I saw, had our practice name on. Performance assessments had already been circled in red.

"I'll cut to the chase," the director stood before me, pacing as if heading up his own version of an SS squad... "We've had to call this meeting as we have grave concerns about the practice."

I stayed silent.

"The GDC, which we'll come on to shortly, has informed us about Mr Brocks," he glared. "However, we also have very serious concerns about the practice's overall performance and professionalism."

"Ohhhh?" I fidgeted under the table having flashbacks to Aria shredding patient records while I attempted unlicensed sedation.

"Yes!" he snarled, probably expecting me to elaborate instead of just pitching that confused but concerned face, the kind you feign at school when your teacher busts you for something you're not yet ready to accept...

"PERFORMANCE REPORTS!" he shouted. "Your submitted UDA quotas (units of dental activity) warn you are below target and have no chance of achieving enough treatments by the end of year to reach it!... Also your Vital Sign Stats," he bowled on, "track that you have critically low levels of new patients registering which means you currently breach all the access guarantees promised in the government white paper!... And finally," he paused, firming both arms aggressively on the desk. "Most serious of all, the GDC has reported Mr Jack Brocks, the principal on the contract, as being STRUCK OFF!!!"

Fuck! Throwing the book at me, it felt like I was being pasted on *Dragon's Den.*

"Well?" the director tensed while his lawyer and minuteman watched ready to document my response.

"Err"

Shit. I had to be careful here. Revealing too much would be suicide.

"Shouldn't we wait for Jack?" I tried to divert them.

"Well the reason we summoned you too," he continued, "is that Mrs Shah has informed us you are in the process of taking ownership so we also want to know what has happened to completion?"

Obviously this was just as important. If they were worried about our professionalism, however, any revelations about the bribe or court would make us look even worse.

Deciding I'd skirt around it and give the most non-committal answers I could blag, Bill Clinton – *I did not have sexual relations with that woman* – style.

"Yes err," I tempted delicately, "regarding that, we have had a few hiccups with the practice but we're just in the final process of the landlord signing the lease over and expect completion promptly."

"Hmm," the director paused, not too impressed.

"Look," I sensed I'd better say more, "I appreciate our situation may conflict with some of your protocols," I noted lawyer and minuteman were scribing down everything I said, "but if we could perhaps just take a moment to discuss this without the lawyers?... I only say this because I don't have one myself."

The director took a moment to sit down. Intrigued by what I might say, he indicated his lawyer to step outside.

"Thank you," I leant closer, partially relieved. "First of all I just want to thank you for taking the time to call us here and communicate your requirements," I bumbled at little. "And I agree that there have been minor disruptions of performance in the practice which naturally can only be expected as we improve and streamline our services."

Jesus, could regurgitating the same corporate lingo back at him really baffle his brains?

"However, moving forward," I was gathering pace now, "and speaking on behalf of Jack as well as myself, I can assure you with the upmost confidence, we take everything you and the PCT say very seriously, as professionalism IS and always will be," I stressed, "at the forefront of our care."

Just then, at the very moment the director was starting to believe me (almost on par with Monica Lewinski handing back her jizz-stained dress) Jack, with his incessant gift for destruction and his disastrous sense of timing, burst through the door clutching a humongous bag of lobsters...

WTF!!!

"AGHH – SORRY I'M LATE." he bellowed.
FUCKER. FUCKER. FUCKER!!!!!
I wanted to die!!

23

WHEN PUSH COMES TO SHOVE

Catching his crutch on the way in and holding up his ridiculous boil-in-the-bag lobsters as if they were prized trophies, "YEAH SORRY I'm late," Jack continued, "I was held up at Borough Market getting these off a mate."

Oh sure – cos that would be important wouldn't it!!

The boss froze dumbstruck at what the hell was going on. Jack meanwhile had completely killed my spell.

Promising professionalism??? He had ruined everything.

"Err, I'm Mr Melican," the boss tried first, not sure how to react. "I'm Head of…"

"JACK!" Jack jutted his hand out in his usual way before the Head could even finish. "PLEASED TO MEET YOU."

Dumping his stupid shellfish on the desk, he'd flummoxed the guy who now had no idea where to pick up.

"… err, well, we, err.." the boss faltered… "We were discussing your practice and performance indicators…" when Jack, screwing us again…

RING – RING

His brick phone began blasting out.

RING – RIN-

My God.

"TONY, HANG ON!"

He even answered it.

"YEAH. I KNOW TONY," Jack continued shouting into his mobile so big it might as well have been the Nokia One, "YEAH PASS YOUR PHONE TO THE GUARD – I'LL SORT IT."

Jesus.

At that very same moment the guard must have come onto Tony's phone, I was stuck watching Jack turn to the boss...

"AGHH MY DRIVER'S ARGUING WITH THE GUARD DOWNSTAIRS," he bellowed and thrusting his own brick mobile into the boss's face, "CAN YOU JUST TELL THEM TONY ONLY NEEDS TO USE THE STAFF CAR PARK FOR TEN MINUTES!"

Unbelievable!

Through years of drilling teeth, Jack was half deaf which caused him to shout constantly. Even in normal situations people didn't know how to take him. But now, when first impressions were crucial...

"Hello it's Mr Melican speaking..."

It was shocking. The boss, our about to be annihilator, was being forced to take Jack's call, "... Yes I know this in an exception but please can you..."

Just like he'd done to me many times, Jack, through sheer lack of insight, had Jedi mind-fucked someone yet again.

Passing me his crutch next and taking all the time in the world to settle in the chair by my side, Jack began shuffling himself closer to me. I, on the other hand, buried my head.

"Hey," he nudged me.

Now staring forward I said nothing.

"Heeyyyy!!" Jack nudged me again whispering so loudly he might as well have spoken out.

I continued ignoring him.

"HEEEYYY!!" he said even louder, forgetting the boss man was still handling the call.

For fuck sake, "What?!!!" I hissed.

"Johnny gave you these," Jack dumped two of the bagged lobsters onto my lap. "He wants a filling off you – says you can microwave them in three minutes."

Desperate to push them back and do everything I could to maintain the image that we were still professional, "Jesus Jack," I whispered. "Chill."

Completely oblivious as to how serious this really was though,

"Aghh take 'em," he forced them straight back. "They're good!"

We were still scuffling amongst ourselves over bagged lobsters just as the boss finished dealing with the guard. He turned and caught us both. He regained his composure but was not impressed.

"Mr Brocks!" he said, handing back Jack his brick phone. "We've had to hold this meeting as a result of a severe breach of regulation at your practice."

Oh no, here we go.

"Yessssssssss," Jack looked up at him as if this was all still a minor matter of fact.

"So as a severe breach," the boss gritted… "As a severe breach…" he had to repeat, finding it was impossible now not to be distracted by Jack readjusting his chair, "we cannot have anyone unregistered as Head of Contract!"

Jack was still totally unfazed and answered again like this was all one big joke.

"Nooooooooooooooooooooo," he replied.

"NO!?" the boss stopped.

"Nooo," Jack lifted. "Because you can transfer it t'Michael!" he almost sung each word before throwing me a wink.

This only made the boss madder.

"Well. Unfortunately for you, Michael tells me your lease has not yet been signed into his name!"

Tension was mounting now but the relaxed Jack continued as if he had some killer of an ace card up his sleeve. Switching randomly to a Scottish accent this time,

"Nooooooooooooooooo..." he even grinned, "because-that's-why-we're-going-to-court-to-stop-the-landlord's-bribe," he tapped the desk to each and every word.

Fucking hell.

Besides the behaviour, Jack had just revealed the one and only piece of the jigsaw that I was desperate to conceal. The boss's bewilderment turned to immediate anger. But just as he was about to speak, Jack jumped in again.

"You know, before he worked here," he turned to mutter to me right in front of the boss, "we used to do these meetings in the pub."

"MR BROCKS!!!" the boss finally exploded...

Jack, still had no idea he was the blind mouse playing between the lethal paws of a cat. Carrying on he even revealed how we had to wait a few months to take the landlord to court and that we couldn't transfer the lease into my name until then.

Stone me. I was ready to kill myself.

Having just spelled out everything I'd been so determined to hide, Jack, in five minutes flat, had inadvertently demolished our professional image, made me look like some lying bastard by disguising major legal problems as 'hiccups' and handed the PCT the exact chess piece they could use to wipe us out!!

It was devastating and now the boss was ready to make his own move.

"Mr Brocks," he said, indicating to his lawyer to come back into the room. "We were not aware of this extra situation with court but this now puts us in an impossible situation which, unfortunately, has only one ending."

Oh shit, he was closing in.

"As you know," he poised, "regulations strictly dictate that the contract provider must be both GDC registered and provide services from a location which is legally licensed to that contract holder. Otherwise," he made sure his team were taking note, "the NHS could effectively be supporting services provided from all sorts of unlicensed premises. You yourself have just confirmed that your landlord refuses to transfer the lease or allow sublets. This results in either Michael heading the practice with no legal lease or you, Mr Brocks," he pointed his finger, "heading our contract with no dental registration!"

There goes our ace card.

"Either way," he positioned himself for the kill, "the soonest you hope to achieve a lease transfer is still months away which now makes your entire NHS contract, I'm very sorry to say, completely invalid."

"But this is bollocks!" Jack shouted. "I don't treat patients so what's the bloody difference who leases the building!"

"I'm very sorry," the boss wagged his finger clearly enjoying having the upper hand. "Rules are in place to protect the public as well as our accountable NHS."

"But it's ABSOLUTE BOLLOCKS!" Jack shouted louder.

"No it is not 'bollocks'," he returned as if silencing a child. "And I'm very sorry to end it like this but your practice contract will now have to be…" he nodded to his documenting lawyer, "terminated."

"AAARGH"

"WAIT!" I shouted, my mind racing for anything we could clutch onto that could rebut this decision. "You have a death policy right?!"

"Excuse me?" the boss stopped not sure what I could possibly say.

"Your bereavement policy?" I bowled on. "It states that when a contract provider dies or is incapacitated, their family or next of kin are given three months to pass over the contract to another provider in order to protect their inheritance."

Watching the boss become visibly weakened now I kept going as fast as I could, "Therefore, Jack being deregistered is technically the same as him being incapacitated which means you, the PCT," (I didn't have the guts to point my finger back) "are obliged to provide us with an interim period to sort it!"

"Yeah!" Jack parroted. "An interim period!" he nodded next to me, despite being clueless as to whether this was true.

The boss looked stumped while the young lawyer just shrugged.

Clearly, no one was sure whether 'incapacitated' could be interpreted this way but not wanting to give them the time to think, I steamed on.

"Thus, irrespective of our current performance indicators," I continued, "which, as you say yourself are just 'indicators'; as long as we fulfil all other targets by the end of the contract in March and with Jack's deregistration occurring October 28th, you are now obliged to give us a three-month window from this date to transfer the lease."

"Yeah," Jack jumped in again. "A three-month window!!!" he joined me as my true partner in crime.

Seeing every one of them flummoxed, I realised it was time to get the hell out.

Gripping Jack by his arm, I hurried him to his feet,

"So January 28th," I cemented, "we'll have it for you then," I handed Jack his crutch, "by which date everything will be transferred."

Grabbing his stupid lobsters we scrambled for the door before they could catch us on anything else.

"Aghh thanks folks," Jack added on his way out.

My God!

Finally exiting and back outside in the tranquillity of the car park, "Aghh that was brilliant!!!" Jack hailed. "But how did you know about bereavement?"

"Because, all weekend," I helped him into Tony's car, "I studied the 300-page contract, just in case. Now please Jack," I stressed, "get that barrister to book court ASAP!"

"Aghh will do," he saluted me as if he had a newfound respect.

Phew.

We'd hung in but with today being already November 3rd we had only 12 short weeks to fix this.

The clock was ticking…

24

THE MAKING OF A NARWHAL

Do you ever have one of those days where the pressure becomes so relentless you could just explode?

For me, this was today and even though it would end in a stroke of pure luck, I was about to lose it in more ways than I could ever imagine.

Let the stress begin…

Arriving back from the PCT having left Jack to contact his lawyer, I headed to the surgery to finish the rest of the afternoon when I saw Rachel waiting on the steps.

"Mista Pearson's hea' again," she said, ready with my dental top.

"Jesus. What's he want this time?"

Returning later than expected I still had a full list of patients to see.

"He says that fillin' yer did is too short."

"Again?" I scoffed. "Pfff. I've changed it for him four times now!"

"A know," she followed me marching through to the back. "But he says he wants it longa' this time."

"What!"

The guy was an arse!

Longer, shorter then longer again; he was driving us mad.

Mr Pearson had to be the most annoying miser in the world. Weeks back I'd spent ages restoring his upper second incisor to perfection. The result was flawless. It was so good in fact you couldn't even tell it had ever needed dental work. I mean not one to blow my own trumpet here but when it came to dental aesthetics and reconstruction at the front of the mouth, I was exceptional.

Against all my advice, however, and insistent he wanted yet another stab at the filling dimensions himself, Mr Pearson was now demanding that I made his tooth even longer.

I just couldn't get him to appreciate that if I extended it against his backdrop of crowded teeth, his incisor would stick out like a sore thumb!

"I tried tellin' him this," Rachel shrugged, "but he insists yer lengthen it right now!"

"'Right now?'" I scorned again. "Oh really," I said irritated at how we were still pandering to his whims.

"Well he's in reception. I'll get the surgery ready."

Rachel disappeared. Leaving me to get changed, my mobile rang – it was Jack.

"Arghh, bad news," he grunted.

"What?" I said fighting to put my clinic trousers on.

"I just spoke to the barrister. He says the earliest we can get a court date is March 16th."

"March!" I yelled. "MARCH! That's over four months away – that's not even close! I thought he said it'd be two max!"

"Aghhh, I know. Apparently they're still fixing a massive backlog after summer and you know how Christmas always sets things back."

"But this is a disaster!!" I couldn't believe what he was telling me. "Jack don't you get it??! We need court before January 28th otherwise we're screwed... FUCK!!!" I let out another yell.

Still on the line, "Aghh don't worry," he quietened. "I'm sure something'll turn up."

"Oh yeah!! Like what?!!!"

Ending the call I was livid.

No bones about it – if we didn't get a court date before the January doomsday, the PCT would terminate our entire contract.

"Excuse me. Excuse me!" I could suddenly hear someone barking now at Aria on reception. "This is ridiculous! When's that dentist coming?!"

Recognising the voice through the door, I realised it was Mr Pearson.

"I've been waiting here ten minutes!!" he berated her.

Dick. Checking my watch I saw that it could only have been five.

As a favour arranged by Rachel, Mr Pearson had been squeezed between booked patients and warned that if he insisted on tuning up without an appointment he'd just have to hang on.

I marched into the waiting room, other patients present, and forcing my professional smile,

"Mr Pearson?" I greeted. "Thank you for waiting, please come this way."

"Oh finally!" he couldn't stop himself from playing to the gallery. "I was just telling your receptionist I'm norrappy with this tooth you've done."

"Yes I am very aware," I had to grit, my comments restricted by medical confidentiality. "Please come this way."

Leading him through to the surgery I tried to remain as polite as I could. Normally, I could tolerate the pushy types but enraged by Jack's news while this guy had conveniently forgotten the number of times we had fulfilled his every wish, I was ready to snap.

"Please take a seat," I plonked him in the surgery chair.

He turned to Rachel, "Is this your nurse still?" Pearson looked her up and down condescendingly. "I've told her too. It's too short here look!"

"Yes. Hang on," I said. "Just rest back and we'll take a look shall we?"

Having indulged this ballbreaker far too many times I knew that this was the kind of patient who'd never be satisfied.

In dentistry, everyone comes across a moaner like this. They're about one in three hundred and reading his notes, I saw that Pearson had already done the rounds with four other dentists before me. His file was an inch thick so his gripe had to be about more than just the treatment.

In healthcare, we have to suffer more and more types like this. They think it's ok to take out their life frustrations on staff. They're horrible and the pattern's always the same; changing demands, moaning here and blaming there while never contributing anything positive. They're impossible to satisfy.

"Please hold still," I said getting the injection ready.

In the past, we wouldn't have had to take this but the blame culture has taken a real grip. Unfortunately it's starting to dictate the shape of healthcare today and not in a good way.

Professionals are now too scared to stand up to these idiots and the subtle message from our regulators has become: "Dentists are pieces of shit no matter what" while "the patient always, always, always knows best."

It pisses me off.

Not only are we not given any respect for having any sort of intelligence, our professional expertise is being constantly undermined by our regulators who now ensure that we turn out a soulless service. Feeling pushed to the brink with Jack's news, I thought maybe today I should just accept them at their rule.

Yeah fuck it – if this Mr Pearson insists I lengthen his tooth despite my advice, then today's his day he's gonna fucking get it!!!

Rachel laid out the tools. I got busy with the drill and white filling material. Soon it was time to give this dude exactly what he'd asked for.

For the next 20 minutes, with Pearson lay in the chair, I set about lengthening and constructing the most monumental extension of his tooth that I could manage. Sculpting away to his demand, I kept a straight face while Rachel, having to pull her mask over her mouth, looked on in shock at what I was building. Finally, after shining the blue setting light, I'd finished bonding to his incisor what could only be described as a mini tusk.

He looked ridiculous – In fact he looked like a Narwhal!!

"What do you think?" I passed him the mirror.

"Errrr"

Pearson's eyes almost popped as he faced what he'd asked for – his tooth so big he could also have been a bucktooth rabbit.

"Do you want me to make it longer?" I prompted.

"Err??"

Still clutching the mirror, his face white, he was completely speechless.

"Cccc-caaan you make it a bit shorter?" he asked nervous now at the huge white tent peg hanging over his lip.

"Shorter??" I was still livid. "I can make it shorter if you want."

"Yeah, shorter please," mouthed Pearson.

"OK sure," I shrugged. "No problem."

Firing up the drill again, I gently touched it onto the surface of his tooth. Mirror down, with him unable to watch me properly, I made it appear that was trying to trim off loads when instead, despite all the water spray and noise, I was only just skimming a slither. Just for effect, I was even working my elbows in an exaggerated fashion.

"How's that?" I waited for him to pick up the hand mirror again to marvel at his unchanged tusk.

"Errrr..."

Now, I don't want you to think I'm a bastard here – I probably do sound like one but I was never going to leave this guy worse off. I'd simply had enough of all the times he'd talked down to me and treated the staff like minions but this didn't mean we couldn't have a little fun.

"Ccc-caaan you make it shorter again?" Pearson was squirming now.

"What – EVEN shorter??" I laboured to Mr Narwhal, making sure to copy the same condescending tone he'd used on Rachel.

"Y-Y-Yes," he quivered.

Following two more attempts of skimming hardly anything while Pearson sat with the worry that he might have to permanently confront his new alter ego as some sabre tooth fool, I smiled until finally buckling under his own arrogance...

"Pppplease can you just make it how you had it before," he asked.

OHHHH. Now you want to listen to me huh?!!!

Still fuming, I returned his tooth back to how it should have been four appointments ago. Letting him out of the chair I nodded as Roger the Could-have-been-Rabbit left, tail between his legs.

"Rightt," Rachel turned to me clearing away the tools. "That was fucked'up. What's really pissing yer'off?"

Having seen my frustration, she realised something far bigger was going on.

I finished off our list of much nicer patents and ended the afternoon. Time to de-stress. Rachel and I sat in the back to have a cup of tea and share a microwave lobster.

Ding.

Three minutes to cook – Jack was right.

Using the compressor as a dining table, I watched Rachel drain the boil-in-bags. We sat, just the two of us with only plastic forks to tuck into the most random meal of the year. I explained how we were now screwed...

"So why can't yer just pay the bribe?" Rachel asked after listening, not sure how to start on the claw.

"Well," I said, helping her with it having watched it on YouTube, "because..."

I explained further that having visited Jack's barrister a few weeks ago, we had instructed him to get the ball rolling by threatening the landlord with court action.

Far from shying away, however, the landlord had apparently responded with glee.

This was because years back he'd bullied Jack into a legal battle in order to impose an extortionate rent increase. Only he lost. As a gambling man, however, and a high net-worth property crook, winning and controlling people meant everything.

For him, this was no longer about money. This bastard was on a power trip to simply screw us which is why we couldn't pay the bribe now even if we wanted to!

"Jeeeeeeezas," Rachel sat back staggered at our predicament. "But why can y'not just rent another shop?"

Shrugging my head, "Again this is also impossible."

One problem was that we were still bound by the landlord's lease for four more years and even if there was an available premises to let, which there wasn't, we were right on the border of the PCT's boundary. Moving just 20 metres to the left would mean we'd fall outside the borough's jurisdiction which wasn't allowed.

Alternatively, if we wanted to relocate in the opposite direction, apart from the street being residential only, that move would take us closer into town. This was also prohibited because of the "competition clauses" with other NHS practices.

"Fuuuccckk," Rachel slumped in her chair realising how this had become a time bomb set for us all.

"Yep," I finished. "And apart from this, trying to change the commercial usage of any shop (A1/A3 usage) to permit dentistry (D1) takes several months of processing with the planning authorities which means that by the time we find one we'd be breaching our deadline anyway. See – the PCT have us nailed in a coffin!"

I wallowed in my own self-pity as Rachel took a moment to reflect. I stared into my little lobster's face and wondered if it would just be less stressful living under the sea like Ariel the mermaid.

Suddenly Rachel thought of something that was so obvious I'd completely over looked it.

"Hea'," she jumped. "If we'v' got 12 weeks, can't Jack just do the CPD?"

BOOM!

I'd forgotten all about this option as we didn't have the time before! With the PCT having given us the bereavement window, Jack could now just make up the 250 hours he'd missed out on and get re-registered by the GDC!

"Ha! You bloody legend! Mwah," kissing her on the head, I grabbed my phone to ring Jack.

If he booked a load of fast track courses and hammered out forty hours a week for the next few months, it would enable him to re-register with the GDC. The PCT then wouldn't be able to stop a thing… targets aside.

"Aghh right-o I'll get on it!" Jack answered, chuffed we'd found a solution.

Brilliant!

During this time, the way CPD hours worked was crazy. The point of the hours was to provide continuing education and training to qualified dentists. Each month, the British Dental Association (BDA) website offered two new hours of CPD through their journal. In order to acquire these and prove that they have studied the journal, dentists simply logged on and answered their multiple-choice questions. This could be done in seconds. There was no pass mark and even if dentists had not studied the paper but had merely ticked answers randomly and even if they attained a zero score, they were still awarded the full two hours. Over the year, these hours could easily be accumulated to the required number without any meaningful further education. The system was clearly flawed, the object being defeated. Sounds simple; all Jack had to do was log on. Unfortunately, as it turned out for him, the hours had an expiry date and it was impossible to backdate the procedure. Too late for him to take advantage of this trick, he'd have to do it the normal way. Nevertheless, it is still a typical example of the ill-conceived ideas that come from the powers that be!

"Hey fancy a drink?" I said to Rachel believing we'd finally cracked it.

"Aye, lets."

We headed to the pub with our spirits lifted but we were not out of the woods yet, not by a long shot.

Jack's next news was about to make those woods even darker and I was about to react...

25

BOILING POINT

The whole evening soon passed with Rachel and me drinking in the pub, perhaps letting ourselves go a little too much. After sharing loads of Jägerbombs, it wasn't long before the two of us were plastered.

We'd had shitloads.

Hearing last orders at the bar and hungry, I had a surprising second urge for fish. Rachel said she knew a chippy that might still be open. She dragged me down a load of backstreets I'd never seen before while I stumbled behind her like some pissed-up zombie.

"Keep up," she shouted.

"Coming," I followed, lowering my attention to her arse.

Mmm – ogling through my misguided beer goggles – it looked sexy.

I mean, in her big blue jeans her arse looked bigger than most but I liked it.

Mmmm yeah – even her perfume smelled sexy. I wonder if she'd be up for some…

Nah – bad thought. This was work. Keep it professional.

Feeling like we'd trekked miles despite it probably just being a few hundred yards, we eventually arrived outside what appeared to be the most illuminated chippy of all chippies; The Golden Bowl. Gawping through the windows of their bright, huge steaming vats to see displays of battered all-sorts, I was immediately drawn in.

Starving and suffering cravings more ravenous than a stoned Cookie Monster, I slapped my pocket full of accumulated change onto the counter. I ordered three battered cods, a battered sausage, mushy peas and as many chips as I reckoned I could stuff into my face. I was being gluttonous but I didn't care and I attempted to munch my way through the lot.

Soon the Chinese owner had to shut us back out onto the street where I continued forking more greasy cod into my mouth. After a while of this, it dawned on me that Rachel was standing a lot closer than usual.

"Good fish?" she asked.

"Yeah," I nodded, half propped against an overflowing wheelie-bin.

"Mm," she murmured, glancing differently into my eyes.

Wait a minute – catching myself momentarily lucid, was she flirting?

Rachel leaned in to steal another chip from me as I ogled down at her cleavage. I was certain her knarks were showing more than normal.

Nah. Drunk thinking. Professional. Professional.

Curbing my thoughts, I paused again as she scooped some mushy peas with her finger now – this time her stare drifting onto my lips.

Maaaad – she defo was flirting!

Letting her take a few more chips, I stayed put when out of nowhere she lunged in for a kiss!

WTF!

I never expected this. I mean I'd had my suspicions that she fancied me but swaying before her like this, wrecked and with flecks of green mushy pea sauce streaked all over my face, I probably looked more like some deranged version of a camouflaged Rambo – plus I felt getting it on with staff was not cool.

I know Jack used to do it in his younger days but how awkward would it be the next morning at work?

"Oh hi, did you get in all right?"

Argh fuck it. Too drunk to care, I decided to reciprocate and try to pleasure Rachel with all the tender sophistication I could muster. Starting by inching my greasy hand under her top, I finger crawled it up and over the firm wire rim of her large bra to try to gently caress her nipple.

Now, I'm aware here that some women might be expecting a *Fifty Shades Of Grey* moment but with the two of us wrecked by the side of a dirty wheelie-bin-come-recycling point – this was going to be nothing of the sort. I could barely stay upright let alone pleasure someone else.

Just about managing to balance my chips in one hand, I used my other to initiate the squeezing and soon offered her my best.

Unfortunately, 'my best' involved about as much coordination as a broken beanbag.

"Uhh," Rachel still let out a noise.

Hey – at least she liked it!

A few minutes on, our tongues continued riling in each other's chip grease when I suddenly felt her hand start venturing downwards towards my penis.

Shit, it was currently limp.

Do something, do something!

Fretting, I could feel her fingers inching purposefully closer–

"Uhhhhhah," I decided to reciprocate with a porno style moan.

Damn!

This only encouraged her closer but my limp dick just wouldn't pick up.

Come on fucker, please-

Only seconds away now, Rachel's fingers were already working to unzip my pants.

Come on shitty dick do something…

Any moment she'd be catching me out.

Please Cyril you lame dick – rise!

Imagining all-sorts I flashed through everything I could think of;

Jennifer Lawrence naked.

My hot neighbour.

A threesome with my ex.

Fucker! Fucker!

Despite trying every guy's failsafe – which is to never think of the person they're actually with – nothing was helping. I could now feel Rachel's fingers creeping cringingly inside.

Come on Cyril, last chance – I beg you!!!

Finally reaching in, Rachel pinched my flaccid truth.

Gutted, it was too late.

Letting out a breath of disappointment she respectfully tapped my limp member to confirm it was dead.

"Hm," she sighed.

"Don't worry it can still come," I pleaded but our moment was gone.

Standing there – a single shade of red – I felt awkward as hell. Thankfully, breaking the silence Rachel's mobile rang.

"Aghhh, is Michael with you?" I heard Jack's voice as she picked it up.

What could he possibly want now?

Rachel had to pass it over. She was not impressed.

"What's up?" I said, wiggling my pants back up.

"Aghh I've been trying to get hold of you!" he barked. Flipping my phone I saw it was flat. "I spoke to the GDC and it's not good."

"Why what's happened?" I didn't want to panic.

Jack, however, promptly announced his killer line....

"Aghh, they say I'm not allowed to re-register for ten months!"

"WHAT!" I yelled. "WHY NOT??"

It turned out that Jack had been classed as 'Erased' from the GDC and not just 'lapsed' out of membership – neither of us had known that the two things were very different.

Jack had ignored all his correspondence. Amongst this was an important letter from the GDC relating to a complex root canal case on which he had been unsuccessful. The letter also outlined the conditions that the hearing committee had imposed as a result of the case. One of the stipulations was that if his CPD hours were not submitted by a specified time he would be 'Erased' and not just deregistered. Once 'Erased', the GDC rule was that no one could reapply for a minimum of ten months. This meant that we were screwed and there was now nothing we could do!

"FUCK!" I screamed out.

I hate the GDC with a passion. I know they offer some regulatory function and, to be fair, Jack should have carried out his CPD but most dentists are aware of how full of shit the GDC really are behind their façade.

As a clear example of hypocrisy, they claim to be non-profit making but just so happen to locate themselves in a huge plush building on Wimpole Street; one of the most expensive prime real-estate areas in central London.

They refuse to relocate to anywhere cheaper such as Birmingham, Milton Keynes or even just a little further out to Zone 2–4 where access is just as good. To save money many bank headquarters have had to move but the GDC, instead, keep themselves wastefully next to Oxford Street where they continue to blast resources like it's *Brewster's Millions*!

They're scandalous and while everyone else's purse strings are being tightened, the GDC cohorts still manage to lavish themselves with fancy soirees and huge hotel expenses on top of paying themselves extortionate wages.

As another example of how they abuse resources, in 2014 the GDC, just like that, pretty much doubled their annual registration costs (something dentists are legally obliged to pay) ranking them now as the most expensive self-charge-setting dental authority in the world, way beyond America's and even three times more expensive than their equivalent in Australia.

But what could be the GDC's justification for such a hike?

Their fees are linked to Zimbabwe's inflation rate perhaps??

No, the official party line was – "We need more money to handle this sudden surge of complaints."

What the GDC failed to mention was that, in order to generate this sudden surge of complaints, they actually blasted thousands of pounds on national press adverts to encourage the public to complain about their dentists.

How undermining and self-interested is that?

Not just affecting dentists though, behind this GDC's cleverly jigged guise of "Our number one priority is care for the public", scaremongering tactics from such an inappropriate source only encourages our country's healthcare litigation culture, which, wider afield, is now massively savaging our NHS.

The GDC!

I wonder what the 'C' really stands for???

Anyway, back on the street finishing the call with Jack, his news leaving me as an overheated pressure cooker, I felt ready to explode. I just couldn't accept that after everything we'd tried and the fact Jack had no intention of even treating patients, the GDC regulating us and PCT handling our contract were finally going to destroy us with petty small print.

It was devastating. The unfairness of it had suddenly overwhelmed me with rage. This would turn into the moment I lost it…

"FUUUCKK!" I shouted in front of Rachel. "THIS IS BULLSHIT!!" I screamed with boiling frustration. "GDC CUNT WANKER FUCKS!!!"

Launching my chips against the wall I was blowing off like a banshee, "I'm the only one that does anything for this fucking practice," I yelled. "NO ONE ELSE DOES FUCK ALL!"

My blind venting in front of Rachel, however, caused her to immediately snap back.

"Err. Fuck off," she followed. "I'm in this too you kna, it's not just you!!"

"Oh yeah? What do you do?" I couldn't help myself. "You do fuck all!"

Shit, I really didn't mean that but too late to take it back, the words had escaped and we continued to take it out on each other.

Rachel shouting even louder,

"A do just as much as you yer fucking shitty limp-dick PRICK!"

Oooooooo.

Spiralling fast and only fuelling the frustration.

"Fine," I barked. "Fuck off then!!!"

"A will, you fuckin' tiny bent dick!!!" she waved her little finger.

This was getting way out of control but amping each other up had filled me with the wrath of a demigod.

Rachel marched off as I was about to attempt, for my own release of pent-up anger, the most ridiculous idea that had ever come to me.

Stomping over to a parked Micra, more livid than the Hulk, I had a plan to throw this and all the other cars in the street, over.

Yep – looking back it was ridiculous but too enraged by this point to care, I genuinely believed that this would unfold like some scene out of *The Avengers.*

Sadly, I couldn't have been more mistaken.

Gripping the rim of the wheel arch tightly, "Yeah, you'll be sorry," I muttered in the direction of Rachel trailing off into the darkness.

Taking a deep breath, I was ready to unleash my fury.

Here goes…

Hhhhuhhuhhhhhhddddd I strained trying to lift with everything I had.

Nothing.

Huddddpff I tried again.

Come on fucker.

Huddffffffhh

Shit – my body was effectively humping against the side of the car now, leaving me looking more like I was trying to shag it.

Hddhhhhhhhhhhh I refused to give in.

Hddddhfff

Come on.

Hdf

Hd

Hh

Fuuuuuck!

Almost bursting a blood vessel maybe I'd lifted the car slightly on its suspension but really it hadn't moved an inch.

Gutted.

I let it go.

The car relaxed back making a sympathetic squeak. This is when it hit me – I wasn't actually a superhero.

Soon defeated, I realised even more embarrassingly that Rachel had already turned back and just witnessed the entire thing.

"Did you just try n' pick up that car?" she smirked approaching.

"No," I backed off subtly trying to wipe the tyre grime off my hands.

"Yeah yer did," she cupped her mouth barely hiding her laugh. "You just tried to pick up that car didn't you?!"

"No did I fuck!" I adolescently denied, my voice jumping to a high pitch. "I didn't!"

But Rachel knew that I was lying and walking off, immune now to my slurs, finished,

"Whatever, King Kong."

Left abandoned by the car, "So?" I yelled, determined to get the last word in, "I don't give a fuck!!" but she had gone and it was game over.

Everything was lost; my dreams were over, the practice was fucked, even Mr Floppy had let me down… this felt like the worst day of my life.

Without invitation, however, my stomach decided to join in…

Oh shit,

"Hurrrrrrrhhhhhh," I suddenly chundered.

"Huurrhhhhhhhhhhhhhh," I bowled over on the pavement,

"Huurhhhhh," I blasted again.

Huuuurrrhhhh. Hurrrrhhh. Hurrrrrhhhh.

Vomit even catching my shoes, I wiped chunks of fish off my nose as the tears streamed down my face.

Yep. Now it was the worst day of my life.

Staying half bent over I started stumbling home trying to find my way back off the estate. Eventually I was down to just a dry heave. I decided it was time to take a rest.

About a hundred yards on I could see a church bench.

I took a seat as I wanted to recover and reflect on where it had all gone wrong. After some time I picked myself up. Stiffening a moment, I gazed over at the church to see a message that woke me right up.

OMG… catching what was written in the window, I couldn't believe it.

Marked in big letters on a poster – as if written by the Almighty himself, it said:

FOR SALE

Hallelujah!
We were saved.

26

THE FIGHT

For reasons I will never quite understand, churches and places of worship, unlike café's and shops, have exactly the same planning status as dental surgeries (D1).

It's bizarre.

This small failing church was being auctioned off on January 12th for conversion into flats or commercial space. It was located close enough to the practice, it was well within the PCT boundary and it was already licensed for dentistry!

The dates were tight but with immediate completion available, if we could buy it, we could register the lease into my name and transfer all the equipment over. This would allow us to legally fulfil all the PCT's requirements and although we'd still have to rent the old place, our lifeblood contract would be saved.

Jesus I love you!

The next morning, waking to feel like my head was in a vice, I got straight on the phone to Jack. Obviously, I still needed to patch things up with Rachel but, right now, if we didn't win this church, none of us would have a job.

Dialling him up,

"Argrhh sounds fantastic," Jack hailed after I told him.

Jack was always gung-ho about things.

"Yeah but can we borrow the money?" I said with a little more caution.

Checking the specs online I saw that the church had a guide price of £1.4 million. Clearly, there was no way I could afford it. However, maybe at a stretch, I hoped that Jack, with his second house investment and longstanding bank history just might... Praise be to God.

"Aghh leave it to me!" he finished.

Onto the florist next and spending a small fortune for the immediate delivery of some 'sorry' flowers to Rachel, I asked them to write on the card:

"From the biggest arsehole in the world
To the best person in the world."

OK – so perhaps this wasn't the most imaginative apology but I was hampered by a killer hangover and irritated at having tokeep repeating my message to their disinterested cockney on the other end of the line. Simply put, it was the best I could do.

Time to retrace my steps to the church.

Starting from the chippy, everything looked different now. I soon found myself shuddering my way past the infamous Micra I'd tried picking up only eight hours earlier. What the hell had I been thinking?

I must have looked a right dick.

Tracking old bits of splattered fish like some weird bulimic version of *Hansel and Gretel*, I continued following the path until eventually I arrived at the church.

Wow – stood there imagining it as a converted dental practice – it might look a little strange but it was still a reasonably modern building and nothing like the classic Goth churches made of stone. This was definitely doable.

Its box shape building was made of two floors. Peering through the windows I could see on the ground floor there was enough room to set up a couple of surgeries and, if we converted the top floor into a separate flat or two and sold them off, we might even be able to recoup most of the initial investment money.

Yeah, if we planned it right, this was definitely doable.

As I took a walk around the sides to check out the rest of it, my phone rang. It was Rachel.

"What the fuck did yer mean by that message?!!" she dived straight in.

"Huh?" I said, her persistent anger shocking me.

I figured that she must have received my flowers by now and I knew she had every right to still be pissed off at me, but Jesus, give me a break.

"Callin' me an arsehurrl!" she balled.

"What you on about??"

Rachel's accent always became stronger when she got angry. Talking further, it transpired that my attempts to repair my actions from the night before (one being an absolute weirdo for trying to hump a car) I'd thrown another spanner into the works. Rachel had correctly received my massive bouquet but the apology instead read:

"From the best person in the world
To the biggest arsehole in the world."

Great!

She must have been well confused. My fake porno moans, my Mr Floppy, my behaviour with the car and now the 'apologetic' message had left her totally bewildered.

Luckily, she saw the funny side once I'd explained but I had to stop the call as my phone started pipping again with another.

It was Jack.

—— SWITCH ——

"Arghh I've just spoken to Neil," he said all excited.

"Oh yeah?" I shrank at the mention of the financial advisor's name.

"Yeah, he says we can get the money and he wants to buy half!"

Gutted.

Neil was the last person I wanted to be going into business with.

Since the last time he'd visited me in the Indian restaurant and made me sign all his contracts in a hurry, I'd discovered how much he'd actually rinsed from the pension he'd set me up with and I'd had to bite my tongue.

Out of the £6000 investment he'd made me put in, Neil had hiked £4000 in undisclosed commission, while The Pru, taking their cut, had left me with just a grand. It was outrageous. None of this had been disclosed, which in itself was illegal and I couldn't even access the remainder until I was 60!

Double-dealing twat.

As a side note, commission hikes like this are far more common than you might think but it's not just in the private sector. Staff in the NHS are being ripped off too.

Doctors who have been paying into this system their entire working life signed a contract that promised them they'd receive their pension at the retirement age of 65.

Fair enough right?

Suddenly, in 2015, this 'contract', legally binding as it was, counted for absolute zip as the Government, for some inexplicable reason, was able to unilaterally change the terms and make doctors work another five years before being able to claim... just like that.

Now, when they finally are allowed to claim, not only will they have eaten into their precious years of healthy life that are increasingly scarce, but, hitting them as a double-whammy, they will have even less years to claim!

Not nice eh??

Anyway, opinions aside let's get back to the story...

With Jack still blindly trusting Neil, (that much was obvious from his phone call) I knew I was in no position to start a war. So if this was the only way we could win our House of God, I guess it was time to roll dice with the devil...

27

HAMMER TIME

Monday January 12th and finally the morning of the auction.

Jack and I arrived outside the steps of the Berkeley Hotel in Knightsbridge where it was being held.

In the run up to hammer day, I'd anticipated that there would be some competition. With no control over finances, however, and having no real clue as to how this would go, I'd done everything I could to put people off.

You'll either love me or hate me for my attempts…

One tactic was to try to make the area around the church look dramatically crime-ridden. Strapping bunches of cheap flowers to the trees outside and posting bogus pictures of my Nigerian mate EB, I'd attached gang eulogies saying,

"We miss you blood" and, "A bullet never kills…we fight on."

Yeah – perhaps this was a little immoral and could, no doubt, be deemed racist by those full-of-shit righteous rioters of London but given the circumstances, we didn't have the luxury of being politically correct. Besides, within days of posting, some weirdo had added his own bunch to our shrine for no discernible reason. My Tupac volunteer found this pretty damn funny considering.

Cheers EB.

Anyway, Neil was now left in charge of finances and had told Jack, in the run up to auction day, that he'd found a bank ready to lend the money. Knowing how his grubby finger would be foraging in the pie though, I wasn't convinced.

Aside from the main pension scam which he'd already set me up with, Neil had tried to push both Jack and me into buying some off-the-market semi-built flats in Barbados. For a £100k loan, he said that the developer was promising an amazing £40k return in less than a year.

Wow – it sounded exciting.

Hearing later that the developer had mysteriously gone bankrupt soon after, I started to realise the hustle that Neil had just tried to pull. Like a true con artist preying on greed and naivety – two traits widely abundant in London – he basically hooks you into the idea of making money fast.

Over some posh meal and lots of wine, Neil, and scammers just like him, will offer you an exciting offshore investment – something you can't easily see or verify. Complimenting your intelligence to make you feel suave, he will reveal how the deal is so fantastic that he's investing too. As you sit there discussing this, usually being lavishly wined and dined in a Michelin-starred restaurant, surrounded by what appears to be other elite, it's easy to be plied and coaxed into believing you're suddenly better than the hometown you came from. At the very last moment, however, when all deals need to be signed and sealed and you've been proficiently led down the garden path, the scammer will conveniently back out from putting in their own money, blaming a family drama or something while urging you to go on ahead.

It's a smooth move.

But, while you drink the champagne and become swept up in the belief that you must be doing the right thing, you stupidly invest, allowing the scammer to safely hike commission from both sides of the deal before leaving you rinsed in an offshore scam where no one is accountable.

The work of a true bastard!

"Arghh, Neil's not been answering my calls since yesterday," Jack murmured now, as we hung near the edge of the auction hall waiting for him to show.

"What?" I jumped.

Shit.

Maybe I was only just beginning to piece together Captain Swindle's tricks but, for today to work, we absolutely needed Neil to confirm that the bank's funding was in place. Otherwise, come church buying time, we couldn't bid for a single crucifix.

"Have you called him?" I rushed, having to step out of the way of people herding past us to get into the hall.

"Aggh, I've already tried," Jack barked. "His phone's off."

Fucker.

With time closing, I had no doubt that Neil would skank me but, given the large pension and mortgage renewal commissions he must have been bleeding from Jack every year or so, what would be the benefit of him not coming to this?

Looking at the clock, and realising we had no choice but to start joining the crowd and head through to the banquet hall, I was still clinging onto the hope that Neil would appear. Taking a seat, we saved a spare chair by our side.

The auctioneer soon stepped onto the stage. Causing 200 people or so to reduce their noise to a quiet mumble, the little man hammered on his gavel to command everyone's attention.

Bang Bang Bang.

Silencing them all, he explained the house rules. He signalled to his delegates, who were standing around the sides, to be ready to record the biddings. He then rang his large bell.

Driiiiiiiiing

The selling had started.

Shit.

"Lot number 1," the auctioneer announced just as a huge picture was projected up onto the screen. "A commercial pub in Doncaster. Do I have three hundred thousand?"

Ours was lot 57.

Come on Neil.

"Three hundred" someone shouted up front.

"Very good... Three-five?" the auctioneer pointed.

"Three-five" another nodded...

"OK, four?" Do we have any takers on four?" The auctioneer checked. Nobody budged.

"OK, three-seven?" He looked to see there were still no hands. "Three-six?... Three-five?... Three-five!...OK I have £350,000. Going once, going twice – three times" Bang. "SOLD to the gentleman in the corner."

"Lot number 2," he immediately rolled on. "A high street bank in Chepstow.. Do I hav..."

My God, this was moving fast… but where was Neil?

"Sold!" he shouted in what must have been less than a minute.

"Lot number 3…" he said next.

WTF.

"SOLD."

Oh my, this would be over in no time.

"Lot number 5," the announcer called soon after. "A card shop in Swindon."

"Sold…."

Jesus. Where the hell was Neil?!

"Lot number 10," he called. "SOLD."

"Lot 18."

"Lot 22."

"33."

Fuck Neil come on.

"39."

"41."

My God.

"48"

"52"

Motherfucker come now you cunt!

"56"

Finally, arriving at the lot we needed to win.

"OK. Our next lot," the auctioneer hailed. "Lot 57 – The church."

Shit.

This was it!

This was our church and still no Neil!

"Bring up the pictures…" he signalled to his staff.

With giant images of the church screening high up on the walls, a sea of commotion passed through the crowd.

I was gutted – clearly my *Boyz n the Hood* scene hadn't put off anyone.

"OK, quieten down, quieten!" the auctioneer hammered on his gavel.

Down to only a hubbub now, everyone was ready to start.

"OK. Do I have offers of say, One point one million?" he teased the pack, casual as anything.

"One," a punter shouted.

"Thank you. Do I have one point two?"

"Two," another fella shouted from the front.

"OK let's pick up the pace – One – five?"

"One – five," another group shouted .

OMG.

Burning through the hundreds of thousands now like this was confetti, we had to do something quick,

"Jack," I whispered. "Can't we bid?"

"No," he waved me down as if I was a child. "We need Neil!"

Fuck. Stuck sitting at the back together like abandoned ducks, it was torture.

"One point eight million?" the caller raised next,

"One-nine.."

With the bids soon racing passed £2m, developers were jumping over each other like this was a game of Yahtzee. It was clear by now that, even if ten Neils turned up, we were about to be fucked.

"Two point five," the caller pointed.

"Two-eight?"

"Three million?"

"Three-one?"

"I have three point one million in the room," the auctioneer finally paused, "Any advance on that? Going once, twice…"

Fuck.

Not even waiting for the hammer to strike, I got up and ignoring auction etiquette, I headed straight for the exit.

"SOLD!"

I waited for Jack to catch me up as the next lot rolled on without incident. We turned into the foyer. Suddenly Neil sprang out in front!

Mother-fucking-fuck-face!!!

"Oh there you are!" he hailed, "I've been trying to get hold of you. Did I miss it?"

"Yeah," Jack barked. "Where've you been?"

Huh?! Where's he been??? Fuck asking him this – let's strangle the bastard!!!

"Oh sorry chaps my phone stopped working," he flashed it. "I've just come now. I've been chasing the banks all morning and trying to reach you to say they've dropped out. You didn't bid did you?"

What!

This story didn't add up. What a coincidence that, out of all the listings, Neil just happened to arrive less than a minute after our lot was sold. More likely that the bastard had realised that Jack couldn't borrow all the money and needed his half. Plying his last minute commission trick of, "Oh you go on ahead and buy without me," wasn't going to work this time. Appearing like this, looking all innocent, though would be Neil's only way of keeping Jack sweet.

"Aghh it just sold for three point one million," Jack stated.

"Yeah but glad your phone's working Neil – that's the main thing eh!" I butted in ready to kill him.

Immediately blanking me to give Jack all his attention,

"Oh dearie," Neil tutted. "Well that's way above the asking price! Looks like we never would have won."

"Aghh, something'll turn up," Jack murmured, already happy to accept it.

WTF.

"Well chaps," Neil again, "there's a wonderful bistro opposite. It serves glorious lunches – shall we head over?"

"Aye lead the way," Jack started marching.

My God. I couldn't believe it!

In seconds, Neil had managed to sweep under the carpet total lies about abandoning us, while Jack – being Jack – was already resigned to the fact we'd somehow be fine!!!

This was insane!!

Having poured all our best-laid plans into this church, and the fact that our PCT clock was ticking with only 16 days left, whether we were screwed or not now – one thing was for sure – I was seething at the way Neil had just blagged Jack into being his best buddy again...

Fuck this – I was going to have to expose this fucking parasite once and for all...

28

PAYING FOR IT

We arrived inside the quaint English pub to see the place was empty. We took a table at the back by the fireplace and Jack veered off to the toilet. I sat opposite Neil while the waitress came to take our drinks. Playing it cool, I searched for some sure fire way to blow this whole charade sky high – but how?

Neil had spent years professionally wining and dining punters like me and although he had a shapeless body and burst nasal capillaries as a result, he was still cunningly sharp and capable of all sorts. I had to be careful.

I just needed an angle.

I ordered myself a Carling. Jack was already returning and having no idea of the mutual hatred between Neil and me, he innocently sat by my side. To my amusement, instead of sharing Neil's bottle of wine as he usually would, he cheerfully copied my choice of beer.

(Yeah – and it wasn't even Stella)

Now to anyone else this wouldn't mean a thing. To Neil though, this was an alarming break in loyalty since the last time they drank. Pecking orders were threatened and he obviously didn't like it.

"Hmm," he retracted opposite. "Beer instead of wine?" Neil scorned at me to start. "Tell me, how is it being a student these days?"

"It's cool," I ignored his jab.

I knew he wanted to get a rise but I was determined I wasn't going to bite. Neil tried again.

"You see Jack, Michael's just a dickhead who wants to drink beer!"

Motherfucker, I couldn't believe his brazenness – talking about me as if I wasn't even present. This comment made Jack look up from his menu.

"Oh but we love him don't we!" Neil quickly backtracked, realising he'd overstepped his mark.

Twat.

"Aghh, nothing wrong with beer," Jack muttered, returning to reading.

Ha.

Neil's preliminary efforts to oust me had clearly not worked. As we drank the first round, tensions progressed. Jack stepped away again to get better reception for a phone call, when Neil switched tack.

"Listen," he leant forward, glancing over my shoulder to check Jack couldn't hear him. "I have a special deal you might be interested in."

"Oh yeah?" I stayed calm.

"Yes. It's a large NHS contract I can sort for you," he expected me to light up.

I figured this was just another control tactic of his so playing my 'silence' trick, I forced him to say more…

"You probably don't care do you?" he goaded, turning momentarily to drink more wine. "You're just a student who wants to party right?!"

Remaining uninterested, I started to toy with the bubbles in my beer before finally drifting, "Well… everyone loves to party."

Ha.

The fact that I wasn't begging to know more must have been killing him and unable to help himself,

"It's a £5 million contract!" he blurted.

Five???

What a dick!

If Neil had picked the average contract size of £350,000 maybe I'd have believed him. I mean, even the top-end NHS contracts which were rarer than hen's teeth, were no bigger than about a million; but five?!

This guy was such a nob.

Sticking to my village idiot routine while he waited eagerly for me to respond, I decided to play out my indifference with a long slow sip.

"Man this beer is strong," I teased, pretending to be completely mesmerised by the bubbles in my pint.

A look of either disgust or confusion formed on his face but I waited as Neil, the ever-determined scammer, tried to hook me once more.

"It's a £50 million NHS contract," he jumped.

Fifty this time!! Fucking hell!!

He seemed to think that I'd misheard him. Either that or he was just shocked that his ever successful spell of greed was not working on me the way it must have done on countless other clients. It was hard not to laugh. Able to see right through him and wanting to keep this going, I wondered how long it would take for him to increase the amount and say, with that little finger of his, Dr Evil-style…

"One billion dollars!"

Dick.

We soon saw Jack heading back from taking his call. Neil clearly wanted to drop the subject. The food came next and tucking in we got progressively more pissed. Jack started regaling us with his stories…

Opening first about guns, the dangers of marriage and chlamydia, his antics were crazy and I had to laugh. Sharing one about his days when he was doing really well in dentistry – he'd bought a Ferrari and was invited to a prestigious raffle of theirs.

Buying a couple of tickets, which in the 60s were £200 each, he just so happened to win a second Ferrari, exactly the same as the one he already had, except this one was a different colour.

Imagine that!

"So what did you do with it?" I asked.

"Aghh I sold it didn't I," Jack shrugged. "It was no use to me,"

"Ha. And what did you do with the money?"

"I bought a speedboat!" he said, downing the rest of his pint. "It was a fast one too – whoaah – the women loved it – it had four engines – so I could take them to France for lunch, shag them and get pissed on good wine."

Haha. Enjoying his madness the conversation moved around the table. It was Neil's turn next. He tried, and failed, to match Jack with boisterous antics of his own but despite the opinion I'd already formed about him, one revelation was still able to shock me.

He started by describing how months ago he'd come out of the toilet on a train and was confronted by a man asking if he'd seen £65 in there.

Saying he hadn't seen a thing, Neil returned to his seat in first class. The man came back insisting that Neil must have taken the cash as he was the only one who'd followed him into the toilet straight after. Despite Neil's protests, the transport police took him off the train at the next stop.

It turned out that the victim was a shopkeeper and the money stolen was mainly in £5 notes. Sure enough, when they checked in Neil's jacket they found that he also had £5 notes of exactly the same amount. Neil explained that this was just a coincidence.

He said that having not had any time to go the cash machine, he'd borrowed the money from someone at work. Luckily for him, the police were too busy to check his story and he was allowed to go.

Hmm. I could tell from the way he was talking that he had managed to convince himself that he was innocent. No doubt, he'd told this story many times and now believed it himself. To me, however, it had the hallmarks of Neil's particular brand of bullshit all over it. He finished off with how much he hated the cops and railed at the injustice of it all.

I mean, I know the guy was a scammer but listening to him regale basically having deprived a man of his earnings (denied by him of course) and for such a small amount, left me with a bad taste in my mouth. Strangely enough, as the waitress began loading us with more drinks, I noticed for the first time the pain behind Neil's eyes. It was pitiful.

Through years of lies and deception, even to himself, this ogre of a man had obviously become entirely disconnected from society. And after losing sight of whatever dreams he must have been darkly clambering towards in his youth, it was clear his days of sharing any real happiness or forming a worthwhile connection with anyone were well and truly dead. What an empty life.

Still, with the meal over, copious amounts of alcohol drank and the bill waiting patiently on the table, Neil was still a twat and I needed to know exactly what this prick planned to say about me behind my back.

Time then to pull a move of my own…

Setting my mobile to Dictaphone in my jacket pocket, I hung it on the back of the chair. I left my share of the bill and standing wearily to exaggerate my drunkenness, I waded off to the toilet.

Now, if you ever you want to discover what someone really thinks of you, it's this moment – just as you disappear out of sight – having irritated them a little – when they'll spill what's truly on their mind.

Biding my time, I hung around in the toilet lazily watching piss dry around the urinal. I knew Neil would be spilling his guts about me out there. Once I knew what he'd said, I'd be able to plan a counterattack with the element of surprise.

Time check – right – ruffling my clothes in the mirror to keep this drunken persona going and keep Neil off guard, I decided it had been more than long enough to head back out.

Here goes.

I started approaching the table – damn – expecting to finish off my plan, I saw nothing was as I'd hoped.

Jack was fast asleep while Neil, sitting quietly, was occupying himself reading the back of the wine bottle. The young waitress returned to collect payment but what happened next left me appalled.

She picked up the leather bill holder in which I'd left my £50 note. When she opened it in front of us, however, to my horror the £50 note I'd left was no longer inside.

Motherfucker!!

"It's £147 please?" asked the waitress.

Neil said nothing.

"£147 please," the waitress repeated, embarrassed this time that no one was offering.

Livid, I realised that having seen me stagger to the toilet, Neil must have assumed that I was just as pissed as Jack and stealing the money right from under me, thought I'd be too drunk to notice.

The cunt!

Immediately ducking my head under the table, I pretended to tie my shoelace in order to force him to deal with the waitress. I waited to see what he'd do next.

"Jack!" he barked,

"Agghh, what?" Jack started stirring from his sleep.

"The bill!" Neil commanded. "It's £147. This lady needs payment."

With Jack still half asleep though and wreaked, "Agghh," he grumbled. "I thought it was your turn, I got the last two."

"No it's yours!" Neil gritted.

Bringing my head back up I saw Neil donning that sickly smile of his to the waitress as Jack croaked back.

"Aghhh it's your turn," he said.

"No, it's yours!" Neil raising his voice this time, as if disciplining a child.

With adrenaline surging though my body now, shocked at Neil's audacity, I watched as Jack buckled like a hypnotised parrot.

"Agghh, it's my turn," he muttered.

Fuck.

Neil was playing us both as if we were puppets.

"WELL WAKE UP!" he shouted next. "And pass your card OVER!"

Fucking cunt. I wanted to kill him.

Watching Jack slide his bankcard across the table as the waitress took the full payment, I became gripped by an overwhelming rage.

Fuck it – I was going to strangle this bastard.

This wasn't me but I was going to strangle Neil right across the table, empty his pocket and reveal my £50.

"Thank you," the waitress left.

I watched Jack take his card back as I positioned myself to thrust at Neil's neck – I'd never done this before. It was mad but teetering like a novice on a high diving board and trying to gamble the right beat…

… come on…

… I launched off my seat to lunge at him when suddenly,

"Alright guys!" Tony, Jack's driver appeared from behind.

Fucking hell!

Recoiling straight back.

"Aghh you're early," Jack said, waking up.

"Yeah. I'm on yellows. How long are you going to be?"

Jesus. Completely startling me, Tony was right behind.

"Aghh, five minutes," Jack said.

Luckily, nobody had noticed my flinch but still going to do it as I waited for Tony to go –

"Hey I've got some airport jobs if you want," Neil said to him next.

"That'd be great," Tony hollered, still hanging about.

Come on man, do one.

"Splendid," Neil nodded. "I'll give you a call about them in the week."

"Aghh. Where's my crutch?" Jack now.

"It's here," Neil passed it.

My God.

With all this stalling, the sensible part of my mind started racing through the consequences. Neil knew our lease situation so if I choked him here and now, just to spite me, he'd definitely tip off the landlord about how our lease affected our NHS contract and just how beholden to him we really were.

"Aghh great meal guys," Jack said.

Fuck, what should I do?

"Yes excellent food," said Neil

Fuck it – I'm still gonna do it…

Rocking again… the edge of my seat…

Nah. Fuck. I can't.

Ahh.

Owing it to Jack it was too dangerous.

Bastard… Slumping in my chair a second and zipping up my coat. "Jack," I said, "I gotta go man, but thanks for the meal."

"Aghh, it's no bother," he tapped warmly on my arm. "Speak tomorrow, and hey, don't worry about the church, we'll sort something."

"OK."

Stumbling into the bright daylight, I'd never felt so violated. I wanted to kill Neil. Sweating and shaking like I'd just been mugged, I couldn't believe someone could do that.

Waking the next morning, I saved plotting my retribution for this prick as right now I had a much more imminent situation to fix. My phone was ringing. It was Mrs Shah. I'd sent her an email on the way home the night before.

"Sounds like you're in trouble?" she called.

"Yeah, thanks for getting back to me," I said.

With less than 16 days to go until the PCT shut our contract, nothing else for it I had decided to reach out to see if there was any way she could pull strings or blag us just a few extra weeks until we could at least get a court date to transfer the lease.

Mrs Shah wasn't the boss and if he found out about me telling her this we'd likely be screwed but, as a sympathetic hand, I was hoping she could help.

"Listen," she rushed, "I can't talk long. I'm covering ophthalmics, but here's the news. You're termination is still set but because we're understaffed here until March end of the contract year, they're going to extend it until then."

"Oh thank you that's great… right?" her silent pause made me sense there was a catch.

"Well – they're also planning a formal inspection in about two months for which you have to be acting boss. You'll receive a letter in a few days outlining the details but listen, I have to go and wish you the very best of luck."

Despite her strange tone, she finished on what was surely good news. I got back on the phone to tell Jack.

"Aghh, that's fantastic," he shouted. "It's about time you ran things."

"Yeah thanks."

"Oh – by the way," he paused. "Did you give me £50 pounds yesterday?"

"Huh?"

"This morning," Jack muttered. "I woke up to found a £50 pound note in my pocket. Was it yours?"

My God!

It turned out that back in the restaurant, while I'd been waiting in the toilet scheming, Jack had picked up my money to pay for both of us on his card. Because he'd fallen asleep though in a drunken stupor, he'd forgotten everything.

Fucking alcohol!!!

29

WAR BREAKS OUT

When I arrived at work on Thursday morning there was a sinister brown envelope waiting for me.

Without even opening it I could tell it was serious. Tearing off the top, I saw the title 'PCT Inspection Notice'. Reading each point, however, I soon realised our situation was worse, far worse, than I'd imagined.

The PCT were demanding to see a huge list of improvements and performance requirements which, given the way dentistry normally operated, would take a team twice our size more than a whole year to achieve.

We, on the other hand, had until March 13th, just eight weeks and one day to suddenly find thousands of extra patients, overhaul the practice with equipment we couldn't afford and somehow shift our entire annual performance average to a level that would take driving demand beyond any other dentist in London.

It was impossible.

While I was freaking about whether there was any way of asking if they could reconsider, Mrs Shah phoned.

"They sent you the letter right?"

"Yeah," I said, trying to keep polite, "but it's not what I expected. I mean these targets aren't exactly doable – can't they give us more time?"

"No. Listen," she urged. "I shouldn't really tell you this but the PCT have been getting pressure from central government to cease contracting to small practices. It's for their New-patient Campaign. They're still way behind so, to fix targets, they now want to break small contracts where possible and divert funding to all the bigger practices which are able to boost stats."

"What – but Jack's patients have been coming here for years!"

"It doesn't matter," she rushed. "From what I've heard the boss will close you on the lease issue if it drags on but politically it looks better if they use an inspection to finish you off."

"Aw but come on, we're set to win court!"

"I'm sure you are but if you could somehow make these targets by March end then, along with your lease, they'll be legally forced to renew."

"But please, this timeframe," I begged, "it's impossible!"

"I know and I'm sorry," she sighed. "I wish I could help really but jobs here are changing like crazy too and this boss is doing everything to switch funding. My advice is just do what you can and you never know…"

"Yeah but."

"Michael I'm sorry – I've got to go."

Fuck.

Ending the call I realised just how much we were on our own. This was bad. The PCT was clearly lining up to burn us. I was sickened to comprehend we were just a pawn in their far bigger game but no way were we getting this far without a fight!

Fuck 'em.

With my mind racing as to how to rally the troops, I knew that we would have to blag everything we could. If this was war they wanted, we'd be prepared. From this moment forth – whether legal or not – we would have to make moves more fearless than a fucking shark.

All out – it was time to go guns blazing!!!

30

THE MASTERPLAN

First on the PCT's hit list was performance.

The practice needed to be rammed.

We needed to register loads of new patients and achieve more 'units of dental activity' as they were called. To do this though we needed money – lots of money for marketing – which we simply didn't have.

Twice a year recall letters were sent to patients reminding them that their six-month check-up was due. However, I decided to pull this short by a month. Immediately I ordered Aria to send all the recall reminders saying, "It's your six month check-up time again.." even though it had actually been only five months.

It was a cheeky move and sure, we'd lose a few patients who spotted the prematurity but bringing future bookings forward like this and disregarding patient's comments of, "Doesn't it come round fast?!" boosted us instantly by 80%.

Next up: ramping the website.

Jack's website had been made years ago by some nurse of his and was now well out of date. Trading favours with IT students, I had them copy Apple's super slick website which looked great. Still way down on Google rankings, however, we needed ours to be top of everyone's search.

Marketing companies said they wanted £8000 a month just to guarantee we'd be in the top three but we couldn't afford that! Listening to them bang on about how their biggest hurdle was to overcome Google adjusting its rankings based on the different numbers of IP addresses that logged onto a particular site, I came up with a better idea...

Being on the tail end of a credit crunch and armed with the same skills I'd learned bending my CV at Clive's, I knew the job section of sites like Gumtree would be rammed. So, posting an outstanding job in their most popular section I advertised:

"Receptionist Wanted. No experience needed, part time/full time, training given, bonus given, flexible hours...£35,000 to £40,000 basic, friendly team... Click on www.(our website).com for details"

The job was entirely fake and although Rachel was dead against me doing this, in less than 24 hours – the ad, standing proud as an outstanding opportunity – drove 9000 people to click on our site.

My £25 investment shot us instantly to number one.

It was brilliant and although Gumtree later busted us and froze our account for posting this and many others that went way too far, and while Aria who, having learnt a few new words now, had to keep telling every other caller "No job"; the domino effect was won.

By day five we had established a permanent upsurge of real traffic through search optimisation. This generated even more bookings which kick-started the money needed for phase two.

Desperate to expand, I was able to take on two more dentists who luckily already had PCT performer numbers allowing them an immediate start – Lana, a Swiss woman and Sergio, a proud Spanish dentist in his early thirties. Both were ok but Sergio strutted around with his open collar, hairy chest and clothes so tight he presented more like a matador – the guy was oblivious to how he came across. We all liked him and he was a good dentist, but sometimes I had to tell him, "Hey man – stop scratching your balls in front of the patients!"

I think his itch was being caused by his tight elasticated polyester pants…

Anyway, styling aside, taking on two extra nurses and finally being able to save Tiesha, the Jamaican from Clive's, resulted in a top team. Clive didn't know she'd come to me but she was on borrowed time there with her fake national insurance number and I knew if she got caught without a visa, both her and her child would be deported.

Employing someone illegal, however, was a big risk for me but fuck it – her kid was in school and Tiesh had suffered a pretty tough upbringing. Also, she was the best nurse I knew for handling the workload ahead.

Next was street presence. Although our practice was opposite a tube station – hidden amongst residential flats and above a Tesco Express, nobody knew we were there.

First thing then, and despite the flack I'd taken for this back at Clive's, was to get a massive banner made up, just like I'd seen work for the beauty salon. The canvass was so big, not only did it cross our three sash windows, it also covered the tops of the lettering of the Tesco's sign underneath. Luckily, I was friendly with the till girls there who didn't give a damn so we were able to hang it long enough to give us the impact needed before the Tesco's site manager visited.

Rachel and Zara manned reception and took on even more bookings. This left Aria free to help me with something else. This is where it got daft.

Aria told me she could sew and was happy to do anything. I therefore got her to stitch up a giant tooth costume and start flyering the streets. Initially her efforts were amazing and generated loads of extra walk-ins. I was really impressed. After a few days of attracting new patients, however, I noticed that a lot started coming in commenting on the fact that they'd just received a flyer from our ghost.

"Ghost?" I asked.

Having never actually checked what Aria had been up to, I decided to go outside. I spotted her flyering at the entrance to the tube and immediately understood the 'ghost' comments.

From long days of standing around in heavy rain, the coat hanger she'd used to support the tooth's head, which was made entirely from white bed sheets, had now collapsed around her face.

She looked ridiculous!

The draping eyes she'd drawn on in black marker pen were also streaking down the wet cloth. Aria just looked like some weird-arse ghoul.

It was absurd!

Nevertheless, Madame Casper, probably not our best mascot, was attracting patients. This proved we could scale up. Hiring a Professional Musical Theatre costume company to construct six giant weatherproof teeth, we moved to the next step. To tap up something no one had thought of…

When it comes to advertising, you might notice that high-street dentists either don't advertise, believing they're above it or, if they do, they'll try to push only the expensive stuff like tooth whitening or implants.

What they don't seem to realise though is that this appeals to only the rare 1% of the population who are price matching and who don't have an issue with trust. For the rest, what nearly every patient wants initially is just clean teeth and on that much simpler premise, requiring minimal trust, they are more likely to visit a new practice.

This relatively easy procedure is far more attractive to them than all the fancy work that could be carried out. For everything else, trust can be built from this.

A scale and polish, however, is free on the NHS. I recognised affluent Londoners didn't value anything free and the generic language used to describe most dental treatments sounded horrific. Therefore I invented a new leaflet and decided to completely rebrand the traditional Scale and Polish. Printing thousands of leaflets I called it:

"Mega Clean
1/3 off
Now £40 instead of £60

It was pretty much the same product. No doubt there'll be scores of uppity dentists who, reading this, will be throwing hissy fits at me for making professional treatments sound like something you could order at McDonalds, but it was how we also distributed the leaflets that swung it.

Anyone who has done a paper round as a kid will know that no matter how big or honest a company says they are, ultimately most of their flyerers deliver a few leaflets before dumping the rest out of sight. I needed something special and people I could trust. I had to be inventive.

I was still living with Justin my jobbing-actor housemate, who knew a load of stand-up comedians. I figured that they would be perfect for the job. The reason for this is that comedians are often intelligent and decent people. Starting out their careers involves gigging at night for low money so they would need something that was flexible in the day to supplement their shortfall.

Furthermore, unlike actors, most comedians know each other through the very small comedy circuit and are part of a heartfelt tribe offering deeper loyalty, which was key.

Justin recruited as many as he could and we soon formed an army of comics so tight that, if any newcomer tried dumping our mailshots, everyone else benefiting would spread the word on the comedy circuit never to trust the spoiling bastard. For them it meant risking their more important gig offers which meant no one messed us about.

It worked! Hiring 23 comedians in total and paying them well resulted in them becoming so good that nothing like them existed in any other marketing company. Besides helping to push Facebook and social media, the leaflets they posted would also depend on the type of house they saw, ie:

"Free Scale and Polish..."

if it was a council house or...

"£40.00 Mega Clean..."

if the house looked posh.

The boys were epic.

We even let Tinfoil Murray join them because he needed the cash. Except for his blunder where he had handed out flyers at schools with free adult toothpaste which some kids ate by mistake, he added to the assets of our team which was now nailing it.

We had a whole army of giant teeth jumping outside the tube stations each day while even more were coordinated to mass leaflet every house. Anyone near the infamous park at the time would definitely have known about us.

From this alone, we were starting to register 180 new people daily, all rushing to book their McMega Cleans. In comparison normal practices were registering an average of one to three new patients a day. Our sort of performance was unheard of!

(It's funny because a lot of comics used to regale their adventures on stage each night and years later I smile to see some of them are now on TV with one even starring in his own sitcom! Well done boys.)

Anyway, with our advertising fully set and the patients flooding in the door, my next challenge was to turn the mediocre dentists I had into Formula 1 performers.

To do this would require something even more twisted…

31

THE MASTERPLAN: PART TWO

The PCT's timeframe required nothing short of a miracle so I had to hope our team could somehow outperform every other dentist in the county.

To do this though, we'd need a killer move... but what??

On the NHS, an enormous scam (still being used and abused nationally to this very day, especially during the contract catch up months of February and March) is to give patients claiming benefits a bite guard to prevent them from grinding their teeth.

I'm not into it but if you've ever received free dental care you may have had one yourself.

The reason dentists are so eager to offer this is because it's the only treatment that is non-invasive, takes minutes to make and costs them only £12. The best bit though is that it is counted as twelve units of dental activity (UDAs) which is four times the equivalent of providing multiple fillings, plus the NHS reimburses the practice £300!

It's a ridiculous hushed up loophole though dentists can't lean on this too much. When a Uni mate of mine was falling behind at a practice, however, where his boss kept threatening to sack him, ever desperate to use this to reach his target, he tried persuading an African lady on benefits to have one, only this is what he asked:

"Do you grind your teeth?"

"No," she answered him in bad English.

"OK," he said frantic for a 'yes'. "Do you ever, like, bite hard when you're eating?"

Answering 'no' again, she caused him to scrape the barrel even further.

"Fine," he pleaded this time. "Do you ever... you know.... your teeth – do they ever just... touch in the middle – ever?"

"Well yeah?" she shrugged confused.

"Right," he clicked as if suddenly solving it. "You need a bite-guard!"

Ha – he was such a fucker! But while the puzzled woman left not knowing why the hell she'd been handed some free gum shield thing she'd probably just throw in the bin, my mate met his target and kept his job.

Admittedly, it would have been great to fit a few of these ourselves but being on the PCT radar already, there was no way we could risk it. Before my time, other dodgy scams existed too like the "Australian trench". It seemed that back in the 60s Ozzie dentists, working their two-year visas, used to just run drills right along the patients molars from back to front, causing them to require fillings that were hitherto unnecessary. Sack that; for me faking disease was crossing the line.

Having hired even more dentists though and still short on the cash needed to meet the PCT's refurbishment demands, we needed something ethical but radical and quick...

Enter 'The Claw'...

In the UK, most people have long been conditioned to accepting cheap and nasty (mercury) amalgams which, unlike the pricier white fillings, not only look rubbish but also require dentists to bore out larger holes to hold them in place. Of course explaining this in the usual way barely makes an impact on the patient's decision. Needing our wealthier clients to elect the more expensive options, however, I soon realised how the timing of key words combined with expressive body language could make all the difference.

Training each dentist, I had every one of them scripted to say,

"Yes for the **Mercury** filling we have to **drill hooks** or under**cuts** to hold them in place."

Simultaneously labouring the sharp sounding words to explain, more importantly each dentist would now screw their hand into a claw shape just inside the patient's peripheral vision. Jarring this subtly towards them, as if this represented the nasty hooking of the drill, the patient's subconscious would now register the association of a sharp aggressive claw action with the horror of choosing amalgam.

Then after leaving a pause to let the patient's mind hunt for a better option, the dentist could offer light relief...

"Alternatively," they'd soften, "the **best option** and the one that **everyone is going for**," the dentist would switch to flattening their hand this time, "is a **nice white**

filling…" which, swaying it from left to right as if drilling decay, was suddenly the same as spreading butter…

"Yes," they'd finish, "we can simply lay it where the decay was."

Now, after this kind of choice – the T-Rex Grapple vs. Gentle Butter Hand – who would be crazy enough to want Amalgam?!

"Oh yeah, I'll have the Mercury one please! Just hook that shit into my face."

No way!

Thus, amongst far more detailed scripts which I won't go into, our pitching methods became so effective that the success of selling high-end treatments, which dentists would only choose to have in their own mouth, jumped twenty-fold. Generating vital funds for refurbishments, we were soon able to upgrade the equipment and even convert the spare rooms into two extra surgeries, allowing us to treat more patients still.

It was great.

In addition, we opened at weekends, stretched to 12-hour days and shift-rotated the dental chairs with staff to be operational even over lunch. These moves almost tripled the effective use of our four-surgery practice and for the NHS side of things, we were soon powering six times our annual contract pro-rata!

We were doing excellently but still needed to keep the pace going and make up for lost time. It wasn't too long before the newer and less concerned members of the team began acting up…

Lana was the first dentist I'd taken on. As an attractive 28-year-old blonde Swiss, she had started pulling sickies and pretty early on I could sense she was selfishly refusing to contribute anything beyond a plod. It was annoying – especially given how much the rest of the team relied on her.

However, she was not slow enough to sack and it was too late to replace her. We were all desperate for her to work harder and keep things going. Rachel and I had tried all sorts. Plying typical management spiel we tried being nice, being harsh, we tried creating internal competitions against other dentists, agreeing new targets; man – we even tried swapping her to the best and newest surgery at her behest. None of this worked!

For the sake of everyone else and needing her to work harder, what I did next, although incredibly manipulative, was to play on what every single dentist denies they ever live for…

Status and Materialism!

Instead of arguing now, I agreed with Lana, who'd nicknamed herself 'Princess Best', that she was as rightfully impressive as she would have everyone believe. I began letting her assume that her performance and therefore her resultant wage would be far higher than she'd actually achieved.

In this country, dentists, broadly speaking, get paid 50% of their gross private treatment income and £10 per NHS "units of dental activity" – 1 unit being a check-up for example and 2 more units being a filling. Both the boss and employee are supposed to track the totals.

When it came to Lady Lana's first pay at the beginning of February, she'd not even worked more than a fortnight but I blagged that I still hadn't had chance to calculate her wages. For an average dentist, their monthly wage would be around £7k or £8k a month. Uncommonly pre-paying her upfront I overpaid by her £4000 saying that we'd sort out any differences later. Grinding through February and approaching the beginning of March when her next pay packet was due, I told her that 'silly me still hadn't calculated even her first wage'. I knew she wouldn't have bothered to do either. So agreeing that she'd surely done even better this time, I overpaid her again by £5000.

Leaving it just long enough, however, for her to make that fatal mistake of lording it over everyone as to just how much more than them she was earning while lavishing her lifestyle to suit, I then broke the news.

Reining her pride right back with a few weeks still spare, I printed her real performance which left Lana facing two options; either pay back the extra money or earn it by working harder.

So after all the preaching and bragging about how loaded she was – which option do you think she chose?

Lose face?

No way.

And, although I felt horrible for having to do such a thing, sure enough – tail between her legs – Lana soon picked up pace and for the final two weeks, she worked just as hard as everyone else…

Meanwhile, jeopardising the rest of our team, Lana hadn't been the only one.

Zara the east London half chav who'd regrettably seen me drunk while pulling out Jack's tooth, wasn't helping either. Always texting some boyfriend instead of answering the phones, she was now leaving Rachel and Aria to carry her laziness and was generally being a dick.

"Why you disrespecting me?"

Oh yeah, like some Jimmy Choo-wearing, Prada-flaunting Jenny from the Block, she also used the word 'disrespect' a lot which I fucking hated.

Anyway – down now to just a day left before our inspection and with too many other newbies slacking off, I realised with me being too friendly, they clearly saw me as far too soft a boss. I decided to call a meeting.

"Right," I said to Rachel, determined to command authority and regain respect. "Get all the staff seated," I told her. "And I'll march in and tell 'em what's what."

"On it," she nodded.

I loved Rachel, she was loyal.

As she left me to psyche myself up, I decided, stupidly, having never held a meeting as boss, to hit it totalitarian. This, however, was a shocking approach.

In preparation to lay down the law, I watched some *Godfather*, tried shadowboxing, downed four Red Bulls and even did some weird looking press-ups on the street.

Yeah – I was pumped!

Everyone was soon waiting for my grand entrance while Rachel, lining up all the staff in the waiting room, had pre-warned them that I was about to unleash hell. Having geared myself up way too much – I stomped straight in…

"RIGHT!" I gritted, brimming with biblical rage. "I just want to say that some of you here are fucking dihhhhhhhh…"

Shit.

Suddenly I found myself choking up on all the passionate adrenaline I'd built.

"Your fuckin dihhhhhh……." I tried again.

Trying to spit out the word 'dickheads', I'd become way too overwhelmed with emotion.

"Fuhhhh fuhhh," I struggled again.

Fuck. The adrenaline was gripping my throat.

Barely able to breath now as I faced shocked staff just sitting staring at me struggling like Gareth Gates, I was crippled.

"Fuhhh," I tried again. "Fuhhh…"

"Hrrrr…r"

My God. I'd even added a wincing sound this time making the silence beyond awkward.

"Chhhhhhhheerr," I kept at it. "Chhhrrr…"

The tears started to stream down my face.

"Chhhhh."

Nope! Still fucked.

I must have looked like I was having a stroke.

Luckily, I was sitting next to Rachel who realised she'd better jump in.

"Yes well, I think what Michael's trying t'say," she rushed, tapping her papers on her lap like some newsreader, "is that some of you have been slacking off."

"Yeah, fuuuuhhh in tehhhl 'em," I flailed my arm.

"And," she glanced at me again before sensibly powering on. "It's certainly not good enough!"

"Yeah tehhllmm."

Shit.

With Rachel having to wrap it up for me I was just left to face stares of complete bewilderment. My big bad meeting couldn't have gone any worse!

I soon walked out ashamed and teary-eyed feeling like the most pathetic boss in history. Lesson learned – for anything important… never big it up beforehand in your head!

With the inspection only 18 hours away, I wished we could just function tighter as a team. It turned out, however, that more randomness was heading our way and I wouldn't be the only one about to make a super misjudgement…

32

OVERSIGHT

Hiding away on the back balcony, I thought about how far we'd come and what we still had to do for tomorrow to get through this inspection. I was still nursing my shattered ego while, lunchtime over, everyone returned to work. Rachel came out to join me.

"Thanks for sorting it out in there," I muttered meekly.

"It's no worries," she shrugged, lighting her cigarette. "Yer just tryin' a'sort the place and the real team kna that."

I loved Rachel. As my second pair of eyes she was über loyal.

She filled me in next on who I should and shouldn't trust when speaking of the devil, Zara, who Rachel had hated right from the start, suddenly appeared at the door.

"Help me! Help me!" she shouted.

"Shit! What is it?" I turned, shocked to see her shaking and raking her nails down her raw neck.

"I, I, I, I've just had this banana off a patient," Zara stammered, her skin pulsing now red and white. "And

I I've not had one since I was six and an' I think I'm having an anaphylactic shock!"

What the fuck!!!

I swear this place is cursed.

"OK. Don't worry," I rushed, freaking as I noticed that her lips were swelling too. "Go into the first aid room and I'll come through in a sec."

Watching her disappear off, I turned momentarily back to Rachel who, far from panicking, was still enjoying a long slow drag on her cigarette. Without even skipping a beat she then expelled it calmly and in response simply shrugged...

"She's fuckin' lyin!"

Yep! Laugh or cry I could read exactly what was going on in Rachel's head.

I mean, granted, Zara was a bitch and I completely understood Rachel's resentment towards her for slacking but, given the swollen lips 'n'all and flushing red skin, I think it was safe to say this time, "Zara might be telling the truth you know!"

Rachel, however, still flatly refusing to swing this girl any benefit of the doubt, just shrugged again and coolly blew a smoke ring into the quiet frosty air. I, meanwhile, darted inside after Zara...

As I searched for the first aid box in the back room, I saw that Zara was getting worse.

With her standing behind me, shaking and frantic for my help, I pulled open the dusty green case but, just like my first day in Hamish's surgery, I freaked that there was a load of hardcore kit again.

Shit! I raced to confirm everything that was needed for anaphylaxis.

Like all dentists, I'd attended plenty of first aid courses but I'd never actually done it live before which made everything 1000 times scarier and riskier to mess up. Rachel, reluctantly, came in to help me pick out the adrenaline. Rush-reading the mini instructions, I couldn't make a single mistake.

Holding the needle up, as stupid as it sounds, that infamous scene out of *Pulp Fiction* began playing in my head. I knew that stabbing the heart with the needle was absolute bollocks, unless you intend to give someone open-heart surgery, but the idiot part of my brain was still debating as to whether I should just stick it into her chest. Blanking this from my mind, the instructions said I needed to inject 0.5 mg 1:1000 Adrenaline, IM (intramuscular) which meant the upper outer quadrant of her arse.

OK. I can do this.

I filled the needle from the vial.

"Sorry," I turned around to Zara, quietly trying to calculate how many liquid millimetres this converted to, "you're going to have to drop your pants a little while I inject."

Zara was obviously terrified. In contrast, sceptical Rachel who was convinced Zara was still putting on an act, crossed her arms and just leaned against the doorframe to watch.

I lined up the needle behind Zara and took a moment to breathe.

In all the first aid courses I'd attended, they'd never actually taught what happens when you give adrenaline… I mean would Zara stop shaking? Was she going to chill out? I wasn't sure what to expect…

Anyway standing behind her now as she bent over and frantically kept looking back, it was time to inject...

Plunging the needle, I squeezed about a quarter of the barrel into her bum cheek and waited....

Shit!

Nothing happened.

I glanced over at Rachel.

Arms folded – she just shrugged.

Yep, nothing but hate.

Feeling fairly alone on this one I decided to inject some more.

Here goes...

Another quarter...

FUCK – still nothing!

Praying for something, with the name 'adrenaline' you'd expect fireworks or at least something epic, right??

I stared along Zara's back to her frantic face. She was still struggling for breath and understandably panicking.

Fuck this – tripling the dose this time, I decided to empty the entire barrel.

Yeah – that ought to do it...

Standing behind a few seconds, realising I'd probably just administered enough to stun a baby elephant, I saw Zara was showing no discernible change.

"You know what?" I tried pretending I was calm. "Maybe we should just go to hospital."

Yeah! This felt a more sensible idea. Grabbing her coat with Rachel staying behind, tracking her out of the room like prey, we jumped in a taxi together. Zara and I raced to A&E.

Luckily, by the time we'd arrived, the adrenaline had kicked in and she was actually starting to improve. Her face was still blotchy but her lips were beginning to go down and thankfully we were taken straight through.

Phew – she was in safe hands. However, it wasn't quite over yet.

Sitting in the waiting room as I watched random people, some with breathing apparatus on their face, I was still wondering how we could get a tighter team. Another hour passed before the answer would present itself.

One of the doctors came marching out.

"We want to know who you are to be injecting medical adrenaline!" the brash white coat started interrogating me straight off the bat.

"Huh!" I said shocked. "I'm a dentist," I tried to explain.

He was being super-arsey with me. I was still holding Zara's jacket and half way through having to defend myself, the stupid ring tone of her mobile began to blast from the pocket – Drrr-tkd-drrr-tkd-drrr-tkd-drrr.

"Hang on," I paused.

I pulled it out to silence it pressing on the stiff Diamanté case and couldn't help but notice the first two lines of her unread text.

From Jiddy, presumably her boyfriend, it read:

> "Ha t lanky rasclat. Wots dat jordi bitch up 2! U still playing them fools? ;-$"

Dick!

Apart from the weird emoticon, the text was clearly relating to Rachel and me. Still in heated debate with this doc, "Well Zara's asking for her phone to call her mum," he finally finished. "Can I have it please to take it through?"

"Here," I handed it him.

Passing him Zara's coat too before he left me, I got straight on my phone to Rachel.

"Do me a favour?" I rushed. "Log on to the server and see who's done what with those files."

I'd discovered only this morning that the thousands of patients' files we were each supposed to have computerised, hadn't been done. Zara's text made me want to see if it was her who'd been pulling us down.

"Ok give me ten," Rachel said.

Ringing me back while I'd moved to outside,

"Right," Rachel started reeling off the news, "Aria's done 3483, Tiesha's done 4960 and Zara's only done 420."

"420?!!" I snapped. "You're fucking kidding me!"

If we screwed up just one demand, they had us.

"What's she been doing?" I felt stupid now having also just bought this girl some overpriced Ferraro Roche from the hospital shop.

"I divven' kna," Rachel recoiled suddenly turning shitty towards me. "Probably playin' on Facebook. What difference does it mek?"

"Huh?" I didn't understand this abrupt attitude. "What's that tone supposed to mean??"

"Well everyone thinks yer just lettin' her get away with stuff cos she saw you drunk that time taking Jack's tuth oot!"

"What!? That's bullshit!"

OK, so maybe Rachel did have a point.

"Well that's what everyone thinks."

"Fine," I said.

Ending the call, the news making me livid, I stomped straight through the double doors to where Zara was on her bed.

"Awe are they for me?" she looked up from texting.

"Yeah," I automatically handed her the chocolates despite what I was about to say…

"Zara, you fuckin' let me down!" I blurted.

"What?"

"I sorted you out with this job and you promised to do those files but I've just found out you were the one fucking us with the notes!"

"No, I did the notes, it was the others!" she protested.

"Bullshit!!" I returned. "We just checked them. Everyone's done thousands and you've only done 420 and that's with extra sessions! Man you know this is vital for our inspection but you clearly don't give a fuck do you!!"

"I do," she slumped.

"Well, I don't believe you so I'm sorry," I firmed, not nearly as controlled as Alan Sugar. "You're fired!" I said. "Rachel'll post everything with your final wage."

Boom! That told her but wanting to add some more before I walked back out,

"Oh yeah," I paused, turning to reveal that I'd discovered it from her text… "Ennnjoy reading!"

Fuck!

Stomping off prematurely I was meant to say, "Enjoy reading that text off Jiddy!" Choking up again, however, on my own adrenaline right before the end, I instead exited and just left Zara clutching chocolates and completely confused at the most random comment ever!

Back at the practice eventually with only hours to spare, I joined Rachel and the rest in a race to computerise the unfinished files. Having sacked Zara I felt sad but, once everyone heard the news, we were strangely brought much closer together as a team which made me oddly thankful for the random banana.

Anyhow, finally we were ready.

I booked an agency nurse to replace Zara and switched Tiesha to cover reception. All we needed now was for everyone to do what we'd rehearsed for when this PCT examiner arrived tomorrow.

Deep breath....

33

D-DAY

March: Friday 13th

Apart from the fact that it's recently had a slight restructuring and been renamed the 'Area Team', there are two things you should know about the Primary Care Trust. The first is its staff.

As a monitoring body responsible for handling contracts, it is usually made up of disgruntled ex-dental nurses or clueless government workers who, despite wielding huge power, barely have any insight into how dentistry actually works. The second is, the way they make decisions for a practice or a patient's fate. This can be frightening.

Take the current dental banding system for example.

You'd like to believe that when it comes to big decision-making, commissioners and governing bodies in charge would assess healthcare from a neutral position, base their findings on relevant evidence and only then draw sound conclusions or strategies.

Unfortunately, not too dissimilar to the way the Iraq war was kicked off, its often the other way round. What occurs instead is an immediate decision is formed based on something they've either superficially seen or heard, then in reverse, they conjure whatever statistic is necessary to back this up…

Look at the NHS charging system as my case in point.

The idea behind this was to help dentists treat more unregistered patients instead of just the regulars that they currently have on their books. You may have noticed the change yourself.

If you have good teeth and go to a dentist outside London, after all your years of visiting, the dentist may have recently told you to return only once a year instead of twice. This is to help spread access to any newer unregistered patients who couldn't previously find a dentist.

Let's see, though, how the system actually works against the untreated patient it was intended to help…

Under the old NHS scheme it was 'fee per item'. When a dentist was required to repair multiple fillings, he was fairly remunerated for each one. Now, I'm not saying that this came without its flaws but check out how the new system compares. With everyone categorised crudely now into bands, the Government has made it such that once the first filling is fixed, the dentist isn't paid to do any more even though more fillings are carried out.

Imagine then, if you were a dedicated dentist wanting to help new patients who needed significant dental care (unlike regular patients), say someone who required six fillings for example – well, by the time you've taken out staff costs, clinical time, equipment use and dental materials for what now amounts to five free fillings (a payment of roughly £50 to the practice if excluding the examination), it's actually cheaper for any practice to say…

"Sorry Mr New Patient but we're fully booked"

Alternatively, under this same banding system, if a patient on the dole came in with a relatively minor problem, say a tiny wear spot on their molar which one might diagnose as tooth grinding, like I explained, the treatment would attract a £300 NHS bite guard. A significant payment to the practice. It is easy to see, therefore, which patient the dentist would welcome in.

Frightening eh?

So, keeping this in mind, although statistically I knew our performance was good and that our lease transfer still had to be sorted, on the clinical side of things, nothing was as important as right here right now. Lumbered with a bad impression, we'd already been pigeonholed for contract closure and were up against governing idiots who, hiding behind fancy terms like 'Vital signs analysis', really just made decisions based on whatever suited them. It was time then to play them at their own game. If this is how the tin gods wanted to judge us, we were just going to have to throw their own superficial impressionist bullshit right back at them and stage everything…

I was scared.

I hadn't slept a wink.

The next morning I arrived inside the practice to see swarms of people already running around like blue arse flies. With rehearsals over, we still had lots to do as everything had to be just right.

The inspection was set for 11.45 am which, in terms of patient traffic, was a quiet time for any London practice. But not at ours – not today.

I'd done all my hard work sorting The Masterplan but I still had one major trick I needed to execute. It was either brilliant or insanely risky depending on how you look at it.

Remember those comedian mates I'd recruited to help flyer the local area, selling the Mega Clean idea to as many as possible?

Well, they were back in the surgery today, preparing for their biggest ever acting roles. I'd paid them to pretend to be patients…

Basically, I'd turned the entire practice into a theatre. Everyone would be smiling, every 'patient' was to say how amazing their treatment was and everyone was going to rave about how much they loved us as dentists. Just to be thorough, I'd even positioned another five comedians outside who were going to ring the reception as often as they could once the inspector had walked past.

Our phones would be going like crazy and the rest of the comedians would be mingling in amongst any real patients. I needed this inspector to believe she'd just visited the busiest, most in-demand, patient-worshipped practice in the country!

There was no way they could take our contract after what we had coming!

With only 30 minutes to go before show time now and nervous for our practice's survival, a single mistake being critical, I had my first big headache. It was Tinfoil Murray, Jack's drunken painting mate…

Bounding into the practice, he was clutching his head, matted in blood.

"What's happened to you?" I said, shocked at the state of him.

"Ahh I know, I know," he smiled, randomly taking bites out of an Easter egg he held in his other hand. "Johnny cut that cyst out of ma heed."

WTF.

Murray was due to act as Sergio's patient.

"How'd it happen?" I asked.

"Ha well…"

Bending over and opening his fingers he revealed a massive gash and explained that it had all begun after I'd seen him late last night.

I'd arrived from IKEA near midnight returning to the surgery in darkness. I'd hoped to offload some Topia Clear Plastic chairs I'd bought for the waiting room when I saw two drunken homeless guys arguing on the pavement outside.

"Hey fuck you," the first shouted. "Gimme my tenna or I'll kill yer!"

"Fuck off," shouted the second. "It's mine."

Shit. I needed to get by them as they argued under the bus shelter. Scuttling along the other side, I was praying that they wouldn't notice me when both of them stopped.

In obscured darkness, the bigger one turned all his attention to me but, laden with Topia Clear Plastic chairs, I just kept my head down.

He stomped towards me.

Fuck.

I braced for something bad. Less than two feet away the grufty man squared up to me when all of a sudden, "HEY MICKEY!!!!" he hailed.

Huh? I looked up.

"Need sum 'elp?" he smiled.

Jeez, it had been Tinfoil Murray all along!

With him now turning to the other guy he'd just been threatening to kill. "Eh Johnny yer cunt, gee up an 'elp Mickey!!"

"Alright, alright," he got up.

It was unbelievable – both being mates – shouting like this was just how they talked.

Anyway, after they'd helped me unload the rest of the Topia Clear Plastic chairs, I bought them both kebabs to say thanks and left them to it. Drinking on into the night, however, it turned out that Murray had decided that there was no better time than four in the morning for his mate Johnny to hack out some cyst (using an old Stanley knife) that had literally been doing his head in for some time.

"You're mad," I said poking it now in reception. "What about infection?"

"Ah dinnae worry," Murray smiled, while Aria, standing next to me, stared at him confused, "we flipped the blade roond so it wa' sterile! Now can yer stitch it up cos we coudnae de that?"

My God.

Looking at it, they'd actually done an OK job but I needed Murray to look less like an A&E problem and more like a dental one. There was no way we could leave him presenting like this.

"Come on," I hurried. "Let's sort it quick."

I rushed him into my surgery. I'd never performed stitches on a head. I'd done plenty in the mouth so I hoped it wouldn't be too different.

Managing to do a reasonable job and clean him up, I passed him onto Sergio's room ready to act his heart out. I brought Margaret, the last of my real patient's, through when Rachel, who had never liked my plan from the start, popped her head around the door.

"She's hea'!"

Shit! The examiner had arrived much earlier than expected. It was time to get serious…

34

GAME FACES

Before I could let this examiner carry out her inspection around the practice, the plan was to keep her in the waiting room for at least five minutes so she could soak up the atmosphere and become spellbound at just how unbelievably busy and happy everyone was.

Like I mentioned, fake patient after fake patient was supposed to come out of each surgery announcing compliments to the reception staff on just how miraculous their dentist was while all the desk phones would be ringing off the hook.

The plan was perfect. I mean – what could go wrong?

Walking over to the sash window in my room facing the main road, I signalled to the comedians hanging about at the bus stop outside to start drop-calling the surgery.

Ring-Ring. Ring-Ring,

They knew what to do.

I wanted to keep myself hidden in my surgery at first as I still had to sort Margaret out who, unlike Tinfoil Murray and the rest I'd paid, was actually an authentic patient. She was having trouble with her loose front tooth and wasn't the easiest to get on with. I had to fix her quick. The examiner coming prematurely had thrown us off kilter which meant that what I really needed to do now was to get my actor in.

"Right," I said to Margaret who was sitting in the dental chair, "how can I help?"

"Well doctor," she pointed. "It's 'mi' front tooth again. It's killing. It's had it this time and really needs to come out. Can you sort it today?"

"Sure," I took a closer look.

Margaret had a partial plastic denture. Her last remaining real tooth was loose and obviously painful, it just needed whipping out. This wouldn't take long.

Quickly numbing her up and leaving her in the chair, I crept off to collect the extraction forceps from the sterilisation room. This was between the other surgeries and the waiting area that connected to reception. Tiptoeing quietly along the corridor and searching silently for the forceps in the drawers, I heard Tiesha pick up one of the ringing desk phones. Being pressured to impress she suddenly started playing her role out way too far!

"Helllllloooo," she began enunciating each and every word. "Would yooooooo like a reservaaaaation?" she said in this weird drawn out verse…

"Cerrrrttttaaaaaaaiiinnnlyyy weee caaann boook thhhaaaattttt foooorrr yoouuuuu."

Fucking hell.

God knows why but, presuming that an entirely different voice would sound great for this examiner, Tiesha was attempting some mega-posh accent.

"Thannnnnkkkkk youuuu," she finished. "Gooood – byyyyyeeee."

Fusing undeniable Jamaican with whatever the fuck it was, she just sounded shite!!

Phone number two rang next when I heard Aria pipe up too,

"Whatttt – is – yourrrrr – daaaaattte – of – birrrrrrth?"

My god!!

She obviously thought she'd better copy Tiesh! Attempting this ridiculous pseudo-posh voice – the two of them just sounded like howling sick cats!!

"Youuuurrrrrr – daaatttte – of – birrrrrthh?"

Why couldn't they just do what I'd said!

Nevertheless, too late to change things, I sneaked back to my surgery, trying to block from my mind the image of this confused examiner stuck watching Bob Marley and the Wailers. No choice now, I had to get on with extracting Margaret's tooth when Shristi, one of the nurses next, burst through my door.

"Mr Michaels, Mr Michaels!" she rushed in.

"What is it?" I asked, my forceps gripping onto Margaret's incisor.

"It's surgery one!" she exclaimed.

"What about it?"

I liked Shristi.

Being Burmese she had come to this country after being impressed as a child when English tourists visited her remote village and handed out free sweets. She thought that any country where people could afford to just give away free sweets like it was nothing must be an amazing place so, years later, she'd made the journey all the way over.

After a few months of being here, she had learned everything I'd taught her from scratch. Still wet behind the ears, however, and struggling to wise-up to the harsh cultural differences, it wasn't long before Shristi was to suffer a broken heart after going on her first ever date. The other nurses had set her up on Match.com only the guy, after taking her for a meal, had changed his mind and, right in front of her, said he'd lost interest. Happening to such a nice girl, it was well harsh and I felt sorry for her.

"Don't worry," I'd hugged Shristi who was crying in my arms the very next day. "He probably wasn't right for you anyway,"

Staring up at me though, teary-eyed and still wholeheartedly convinced that the only man she'd ever dated must have surely been sent from the heavens, in her purest of naïve hearts she snivelled,

"But Mr Michaels… it had to be true love… we were 78% matched."

Poor Shristi.

Right now in my surgery, having been months since, she was no longer like this…

"What is it man?" I asked her just as Margaret's tooth felt ready to pop.

Shristi's answer though left both Margaret and me speechless and made me realise just how much of a bad influence I'd already been on this sweet, innocent girl…

"It's the fucking bastard chair!!" she exclaimed. "It's fucked!!"

"Ooooooo," I had to turn away, blushing in front of Margaret who bolted upright wondering if she'd misheard.

Eeee – English being her second language, Shristi was completely unaware that the words she was using were totally inappropriate. She sounded like Gordon Ramsey.

"Don't worry Shristi," I calmed. "Don't worry, it just needs re-setting. Just switch it off and I'll come through in a sec."

I really needed to stop cursing in front of the staff.

Anyway as she rushed off and I finally extracted Margaret's tooth, I was now ready to make what they call in the industry a 'denture addition'.

Without getting too technical here, after extracting a painful tooth, the normal procedure is to send off the patient's partial denture to the lab so that they can mould-process the extra plastic tooth onto it to replace the gap. It was a fairly simple procedure and only took a day or so to get back. Margaret had had this a few times.

"Right," I started removing my gloves having finished with her, "we'll have your denture back Monday Margaret so see you then OK?" I said, desperate to rush my actor in.

"MONDAY?!" Margaret suddenly shot up.

"Yeah, Monday," I said. "I've just got to send it to the lab to be processed."

Fingering her bleeding hole in the mirror she was clearly not happy with what I'd done. She then dropped the bombshell.

"But it's my daughter's wedding this weekend. I can't have no teeth!"

"What!!!" I exclaimed.

Shit – why didn't she tell me this before – today was Friday!

"Margaret the fastest the lab can return it is Monday!"

"Well this is not on!" she stiffened. "You never told me this!"

OMG

Having just spent the last five minutes yanking at her tooth – what did she think I was doing???

With things about to spiral now even though communication-wise I accepted she might have had a point, there was a knock at my door.

"The examiner's waitin'," Rachel poked her head round again.

"Well am not leavin' here until those teeth are fixed!!" Margaret barked.

Fuck.

Arms folded, remaining defiant in the chair, Margaret was going nowhere but I couldn't bring the examiner into this!!!

"OK OK," I tried calming her at first, no idea what I could do. "Don't worry Margaret we can still sort it."

This was the last thing I needed. Panicking inside and knowing I was completely stuck, my mind raced... suddenly I had an idea but it wasn't going to be pretty...

"Actually Margaret," I made my way to the door, "just hang there I'll be back in a sec."

Dashing into the corridor to grab Rachel,

"Hey," I hissed. "You need to buy me some time with this examiner!"

"What! I can't," she whispered. "She's already suspectin' things an we look well sus!"

"What do you mean?"

It turned out that while the examiner was being kept in the waiting room, my master plan was falling apart. The room was filled with too many actors who were all now hamming it up. This, along with the phones ringing off the hook, meant that no one appeared natural at all.

One comedian, Rachel whispered, had already been busted for nodding to his mate who was sitting opposite. This made the examiner suspicious and start observing his every move. Sitting reading his magazine then and feeling that he better do something to regain the authenticity, in between turning the pages he paused to gently rub his cheek and even mouthed “oooooh”.

Like this represented toothache!!!

“Fine,” I gritted. “I’ll show the examiner around the surgeries but you go to Tesco’s downstairs and buy me this.”

Still in earshot of Margaret, I scribbled on a scrap piece of paper the specific make of what I needed for my idea.

“And when you come back,” I rushed, “keep that examiner in one of the other surgeries, while I fix this.”

“OK,” Rachel shot off.

Jesus.

Leaving Patient Zero in my surgery, I hurried to the waiting room to greet the examiner.

“Hello,” I approached her in our packed out room – a cold 40-something suited lady sitting squarely amongst my crew. “I’m Michael. Thank you for waiting,” I shook her hand.

“Mrs Tate,” she stood.

With short black hair and a dull grey power-suit, report sheet in tow, Mrs Tate looked scary but Rachel was right – the atmosphere in here felt well weird.

I kept my back to the rest of the actors. All knowing me, they were doing their best to act super estranged when, staring at the ceiling and so forth, another one walked in.

“Wow that was the best filling I’ve ever had,” he laboured to Tiesha, having just come from surgery three.

“Oh thannnnk youuuu,” she smiled, “we knoooooow.”

My God…

"Mrs Tate," I needed to get her out of here, "would you like to come through to see our surgeries?"

"Certainly," she broke from staring at Dame Tiesha.

Guiding her down the corridor I cringed to myself at how this was already looking over the top.

"So I'm guessing Rachel showed you our busy day lists?" I tried making small talk.

"Yes," Tate nodded, still documenting her notes. "I've had a glimpse."

"Great."

To help keep up our packed out façade, we'd faked the appointment screens on the computers by inserting hundreds of extra imaginary patient names the night before. It didn't affect the system's real performance and besides Tiesha inventing dubious ones like Munga Morris, at a glance it made us look rammed. We just had to make sure Tate didn't check any of them too closely.

Leading her to outside the first surgery, I prayed that the staff on the other side of the door would all keep normal. I knocked and pressing on the handle, bracing myself, hoping that everything would be ok,

"And here's some of the others on our team," I opened it.

Facing us was Mr Chan, Shristi and the actor in the chair.

Right on cue,

"Hello," Shristi said. "Welcome to the practice."

Brilliant.

Having kitted everyone out in brand new uniforms and ensured that the nurses looked super smart, I'd told them to greet the examiner nicely when she came.

"What shall we say?" they'd asked me late last night.

"I don't know," I'd brushed, a million other things on my mind. "Just say something like 'Hello, welcome to the practice'."

I regretted this now...

Moving to surgery two, I knocked and opened the door.

"Hello," the next nurse reeled, exactly the same as the first. "Welcome to the practice."

My God. This was starting to look well staged. Moving to the door of surgery three...

Please don't be the same, please don't be the same...

I opened it.

"Hello," the third nurse rolled. "Welcome to the practice."

Oh, for fuck sake! Why couldn't someone just say something that didn't sound so scripted!!

Running out of doors now I was freaking that we'd soon be at my surgery where Margaret was still waiting like an angry dog. Thankfully, Rachel arrived and slipped me what I'd asked for.

"Well Mrs Tate," I brisked, hiding the shopping bag behind my back. "I'll just leave you to chat with Sergio here (in Surgery 3) a second while I go and help my patient, Ok?"

"Very well," she nodded, looking perturbed and making notes.

Dashing back to my room in the hope that Sergio could keep Tate occupied, I opened my door to face Margaret who was about to explode.

"I hope you're going to fix my tooth!" she scowled.

"Absolutely," I closed the door quietly behind.

Trying to hide my nerves, I rushed to the back of her chair and keeping out of sight, surreptitiously reached into the bin praying that my idea would work.

What I was about to attempt they don't teach in dental school.

Retrieving Margaret's discarded tooth and spraying it with bleach, I set about with the drill.

"Won't be a minute," I smiled.

Pressing the dental drill as hard as I could against the tooth, I knew that at any moment the examiner would be coming through my door...

Sergio was still talking to her in his room.

"Yes and these are elasticated too," I could hear him.

Jesus, on about his special trousers again, Señor Spandex was doing a shocking job of keeping her distracted while I had Margaret still moaning by my side, "and the wedding photos will be ruined... and my son-in-law's mother will be there."

Yeah, yeah.

Drilling the root as fast as I could now, causing smoke and burning smells to fire from the tooth, I could hear Tate was becoming impatient and was moving to outside my door.

Come on. Come on...

Trying to hold her off, Rachel had resorted to talking about cornices and was doing everything she could...

Boom – the tooth had just sectioned but it wasn't over yet.

Hearing the door handle squeaking (Rachel's way of warning me she was about to bring the examiner in) I reached into the shopping bag to grab the Super Glue that she'd bought. Swiping the denture off the side, I splurged Margaret's human tooth (which I'd just cut down to a crown) straight onto the plastic, *feh feh,* I blew on the glue.

Come on...

No time to properly set, "Right Margaret," I jammed the lot into her gob, "there you go. That'll be the most natural tooth you'll ever have!"

Just then my door swung open.

"Ohh that's perfect!" Margaret held up the mirror. "Looks brilliant!"

"Hello again Mrs Tate," I turned smiling, sweat running down my back.

"Hello," she stood at the entrance.

"Margaret, this is Mrs Tate," I explained. "She's come to see our practice."

"Aww he's a lifesaver!" Margaret beamed. "They all are."

Tate paused not entirely convinced, "Hmm," she said.

Any second now I knew that the glue would be giving way so I needed to edge Tate back into the corridor pronto.

"Well Mrs Tate, I'm sure we must have taken up too much of your time," I moved over to where she was standing, "but if you have anything else you need to discuss," I quickly waved back the others who I saw were prematurely poking their heads out from their rooms, "there's a coffee shop nearby. It serves nice drinks."

"No thank you," Tate finally folded away her notes. "It all seems more or less in order. I think I've seen enough."

"Excellent! Well thanks."

Just then, as we shook hands, Margaret, from behind me, decided to pitch in, "Yeah you should see how he's done my too –"

Clunk – I booted the door shut.

"Well thank you again Mrs Tate," I smiled.

"Yes we'll be in touch," she closed her zipper.

Rachel and I had to fake smile at Tate all the way down the stairs and out of the practice until she finally exited onto the street. The main door closed behind. We all breathed out.

Phew.

I was feeling totally drained but it seemed we'd actually made it. The first half was complete. Now all that was left was court.

I needed a drink.

I needed some sleep.

What I didn't need, was what happened next…

35

SICK OF IT

Monday March 16th
Working Days left on Contract: 11

FUCK! FUCK! FUCK!!

I knew it was too good to be true.

With the weekend passing, today was supposed to be the long awaited morning of our court hearing and we had until only March 31st to sort out our lease. I was due to meet Jack at the courthouse but I was struggling in heavy traffic. Arriving there before me, he phoned with an absolute shocker...

"Aghh. Court's just been cancelled!"

"What!" I shouted, still in the taxi.

We'd scraped through our inspection with the lease being our last obligation. Now the court clerk had announced that Grimston (our landlord) was sick.

"But this is bullshit!" I barked.

"Aghh, that's what I said," Jack's voice echoed now as if making the call from their toilets. "My lawyer reckons it's a scare tactic to price us out."

Our legal bill had already escalated to above £50,000 and whoever lost had to pay for both sides. Given the landlord's ruthlessness, I knew that this had to be a calculated move.

"So when's the next date??" I asked, freaking more about how this would invalidate the only thing that counted: our NHS contract.

"Aghh summertime," Jack said.

"Summer?? You're fucking kidding!" I had to shout over the noise of some hand drier he'd just set off. "Don't you remember our PCT meeting?!"

Hearing no response, only whirring.

"JACK!" I yelled into my phone.

"WHAT?"

"This is serious shit man – the PCT will nail us!"

"Hey you don't have to tell me!" he finally talked.

"Well your lawyer needs to find us a new date ASAP!"

"Aghh I've already told him –"

"Wait I'm getting another call."

<< <<<< Rachel >>>> >>

Switch.

"We gotta problem."

"What is it?!" I said curtly.

"Stuart Farlaine's bin' on the phone. He's bin' spreadin' shit about Mr Chan."

"Who??"

"The PCT's go-to for Complaints!!" she huffed. "When are yer back?"

"Right now, court's just been cancelled."

"Has it?" she quietened. "Ohh shit. OK well I betta' tell yer the rest when yer get hea'.."

Motherfucker!

Wondering how life could get any more fucked up, I ordered the cab driver to do an immediate U-turn. I raced back to the practice and was now standing in the break room listening to Rachel explain what the hell had been going on.

It turned out that this Stuart Farlaine guy, a nearby dental practice owner (who also conflictingly doubled up as one of the PCT's key handlers for Complaints) had received an email from a patient complaining that our lighting was dreary and that she didn't like the way Mr Chan hadn't used the nurse's name when passing instruments.

I mean imagine that. Imagine the dentist saying,

"Yes Shristi. No Shristi. Oh here you go Shristi," every 10 seconds throughout treatment.

What a bullshit complaint!!

Nurses and dentists swap instruments constantly. If they repeated each other's name every time they passed something they would just sound weird!

"Yes, here you go Shristi"

It was ridiculous!

Farlaine, however, who none of us had even met, had, upon receiving the email, decided to handle us completely differently. Instead of accepting the complaint as the bullshit it obviously was and advising the patient on behalf of the PCT to chill their beans, he'd needlessly forwarded it to his other colleagues in the PCT and inserted, from absolutely nowhere, a comment that Mr Chan was dodgy!

What a twat!

Inadvertantly, thinking he was bitching in private, the idiot had cc'd in the patient by mistake so this was how we'd just found out.

I needed to crush this bastard straight away.

Farlaine wasn't part of the main contract committee but I was painfully aware that, in dentistry, reputations are delicate. As an insecure industry, it breeds endless back-stabbing. I knew only too well that it didn't take much to destroy someone's career on the basis of absolutely nothing.

Remember the Uni nurse/drug-rep Trudy who pushed me out to having to work in a prison?

Manipulated idiots always believe, "There's no smoke without fire." Being on the sharp end myself, my counter to this would be, "It's never the fire but always the smoke that kills!"

"Right, give me the phone," I said to Rachel.

I was determined to blast this nob. Mr Chan might not have had the stomach for this but I wasn't about to let it go. Grabbing a piece of paper I quickly scribbled every point that I planned to say.

Fuck this Farlaine guy.

Having had enough of all the times we'd taken shit from snide bastards, I decided that it was time to finally nail a prick like this so he'd never do it again…

(Oh yeah and no Red Bulls or watching *The Godfather* this time…)

Dialling his practice, I asked to speak to him but he was supposedly unavailable until I mentioned who was calling.

"Oh – er certainly," the receptionist flurried. "I'll put him straight through."

Clearly we were hot news.

A nervous voice next came on the line…

"Er hhhello… thank you… thanks for answering."

It was Farlaine muddling his words as if he was the one ringing me.

I stayed silent.

"I'm guessing your manager told you about the mmmishap," he fumbled further, desperate to fill the void.

Deciding I'd rein him in before he started skewing more lies,

"Stuart I'll get to the point," I said coldly. "I've been away from the practice only to hear that you, being a PCT handler of complaints, have been emailing our patient and other PCT staff declaring, without any grounds whatsoever, that Mr Chan is dodgy!"

"Er no, well no – it was just a joke, you know just a private email… a few things I'd heard about him that's all…"

"A few things? Really?" I refused to let up. "Like what?"

"Well er nothing really – just a mmmisunderstanding," he said.

"*'Nothing really?'* Stuart do you know who Clifford Chance are?"

"Who?"

Yeah – this'll get him…

"Stuart, Clifford Chance are one of the biggest law firms in the country," I started driving hard, "and it's where most of Mr Chan's family work as lawyers."

I was lying – none of Chan's family were lawyers.

"So you do realise that by writing shit about him," I bowled on, "without any evidence whatsoever – he and his family are now proceeding to have you massively sued for LIABLE!"

I made sure to emphasise my threat.

"Well err – hhhang hang on a minute," Farlaine was really panicking now. "There's no need to be like that."

But I was on fire.

"Stuart, because of you I'm now going to have to calm Mr Chan and his family down and persuade them not take this any further. So the next time you decide to go bitching about my staff, think again cos I WILL expose you for the liar you really are!"

"Oh please, come on," he begged. "There's no harm done."

This dick, however, knew exactly what harm would be done so I decided I'd finish him off like some seething godfather.

"Just remember Stuart," I fumed, simultaneously feeling that crippling adrenaline beginning to choke me again. "You owe me big-time for this – BYE!"

Boom!!

Slamming the phone down before it properly got to me, I'd managed to make all my points without even breaking into a sweat.

"What do you think of that?" I turned to Rachel, proud about how far I'd come.

"Aye," she nodded. "Harsh... but fair."

Musing a second then with one more thing, "Oh an if yer tryin' to sound posh," she added, "it's 'LIBEL' not 'LI – A – BLE'"

FUCK!!

Putting Farlaine in my pocket, I now had more important things to deal with. What were we going to do about court!??

Down to only 11 working days to go before our contract had to be in order to clear us for renewal, I just couldn't recall if I'd revealed to Mrs Shah and the PCT team our specific court date or if we'd simply guaranteed them resolution sometime before March end.

Either way, too close to call I knew they'd soon be phoning to confirm results.

Somehow, I'd need to make them believe that everything was currently on track but, without an immediate court date, I couldn't risk lying directly. I figured if we could hold them off, at least until we got a new date, we might still be able to blag dispensation, however, I wasn't going to take any chances.

"Right," I gathered everyone in reception. "If anyone phones, say I'm not here and if it sounds like it's someone from the PCT, slip in that I'm out celebrating some lease win or something."

Boom they were on it but being extra cautious,

"Aria,"

"Oui?"

"You just say I'm not here and no more OK?"

"OK," she nodded, probably not sure of anything I'd said – still, fantastic rack.

Sitting in radio silence as we whiled away the hours, I waited desperately for Jack to try to get another court date. One day passed, then two, then three.

His barrister was still getting nowhere and, strangely, there was no contact from the PCT. I even started to wonder if they'd forgotten about us…

The week rolling, it was Friday 20th, however, and less than seven working days before our contract had to be sorted when the call we most feared came in – abruptly!

Night-time, and having just shared some stress-offsetting beers with Sergio, I was walking towards the tube with him when a withheld number started ringing on my phone.

Given the lateness, I assumed it was a mate of mine who would often Skype call me from New Zealand so I pressed answer.

"Hello?" I said.

"Good evening. It's Stuart Farlaine."

What the fuck did he want?!

36

THE STING

Friday March 20th
Working Days Left on Contract: 7

Standing with Sergio on the street, I listened with bated breath.

"I have something very serious I need to discuss," Farlaine continued, sounding a lot more authoritative than the last time we'd spoken.

"Oh?" I quivered.

Shit – I never expected him to be the one dealing with this but I figured the PCT must have somehow found out about court.

"What is it?" I asked nervously.

"Oh, this is so serious I can't even discuss it over the phone," Farlaine lorded it – obviously enjoying himself in his newfound power.

"What??" I freaked. "Well I can come and meet you if you want." I panicked, now certain they knew.

"No I'm busy," he cut in.

Fuck.

I was trying not to lose my mind while bored Sergio became impatient for me to finish the call. Having no idea who I was talking to, "Hey ladies," he started trying to chat up two passers-by.

"This is so serious," Farlaine continued, "I must hand you this directly."

"OK well when then?" I had to turn away from Sergio who was already getting the Vs.

"Tuesday," Farlaine finished. "I'll visit your practice then."

My God.

The call left me frantic. Señor Spandex would have to go cavorting by himself. I needed to get straight back on the phone to Jack.

Dialling him up…

"Aghhhello," Jack croaked, followed by a sound of slurping beer.

"Jack!" I exclaimed. "Stuart Farlaine's been on the phone! They've got us man – the PCT must know about court."

"Well no one's phoned me," Jack responded calmly before taking another guzzle. "But I do have some other news you might not like…"

"Oh?"

"I spoke to the barrister today?"

"What did he say?" I prayed he'd got us a date.

"Aghh, he still hasn't found a cancellation but he's been reading the court bundle submitted by the landlord's side and is worried now because it says I made a few late rent payments years back," Jack dropped this in, casual as fucking always!

"Huh??? And had you??" I could feel myself already pounded to the brink.

"Wellllll," he croaked, "only by a few months but he got his money in the end."

"A few months???!!! JACK!!!!" I exploded. "In court it's your word against his and you're supposed to look the perfect tenant but now he'll prove you're not!!! Oh that's just fucking *brilliant*!!" I finally lost it.

"Aghhh, relax..."

"NO JACK YOU '*RELAX!!*' DO YOU LOVE FUCKING US OR SOMETHING?!!!"

"Aghh we'll be alright."

Feeling on the verge of a heart attack though, I laid into him to get the barrister to get us a date, while all weekend I sweated it.

March 24th

Working Days Left on Contract: 5

Tuesday now and 7.55 pm at the practice – most of the staff had gone home. Alone, waiting in my surgery for Farlaine to arrive, I was watching the clock.

8.01 – No sign of him.

8.05 – Where was he?

8.09 – Fuck me.

Expecting him any second, I was panicking as to how to even broach the subject of asking his PCT boss if he could consider waiving the rules. I should try keeping positive. Surely with everything we'd achieved, we must be able to afford some kind of leniency.

8.12 – Rachel poked her head round my door, "He's hea'."

Here goes...

Venturing down the corridor past the sterilisation room, I turned into the empty waiting room to finally see Dr Farlaine rooted stiff, a briefcase by his side. I'd never met the guy before but he struck me as a cold fucker – 55-ish, heavyset with dark rimmed glasses –

he also randomly looked a bit like Philip Seymour Hoffman, though that's where the similarity ended.

Feigning a smile as I approached, I offered my hand.

"Hi, pleased to meet you," I reached out.

He left me hanging a second before finally shaking it.

"Good evening."

Jesus.

"Is there somewhere we can discuss this in private?" he stood.

"Of course," I turned leading us out.

Walking us down the corridor to take him to our newest surgery, I was bumbling in front, trying to recite what I was going to say.

"Here we are," I opened the door.

We stepped inside the silent room. Farlaine took up a position by the opposite cabinet. Only three feet between us, I watched as he laid his briefcase on the side.

Waiting in the deathly silence, my heart was pounding about what it could be. Farlaine carefully took out an envelope and slowly handed it to me.

"What is it?" I needed some warning.

Dipping his head, he acted as if whatever was on it was too disgusting to voice, "It is a serious allegation regarding you."

"Huh?"

This completely threw me – I thought it was about the contract.

Nervously opening the folded letter, my eyes scattered the page as I tried frantically to read all the words at the same time.

It was a letter about me that had been sent straight to the GDC:

General Dental Council
37 Wimpole Street
London
W1G 8DQ

Date: March 19th.

To whom it may concern,
I was treated by Michael Sydney at Epple Park Dental clinic a few weeks ago where I was disgusted to see him behaving very strangely. I am thus led to believe he is currently operating under the influence of narcotics. This is very serious and must be investigated.

Fuck.

Having finally read it, I stood there trying to act calm while Farlaine studied my response. I was unable to stop the betraying paper cackling a shimmer in my unsteady hand. It was hard hiding my fear. I didn't take drugs but that wouldn't make a difference now.

"Look I know dentistry can be stressful," Farlaine piped up, clocking my panic, "and I know we all have different ways of dealing with the pressure."

"But I don't take drugs," I murmured, looking up at him.

"Hey," he held up his hands. "I'm sure you don't but is there any reason why a patient might think this?"

"I don't know," I trembled, my mind racing over the last week. "We do see over 200 patients a day so maybe someone could have taken me wrong… I'm not sure."

Farlaine relaxed against the cabinet a moment.

"Look don't worry," he began warming to me, "I know these things happen. It's just that the GDC have referred it onto the PCT to investigate so I'm only here to send you for the test."

My God – the timing of this couldn't have been any worse.

Regardless of the fact that the results would be negative, my bigger worry was the gossip that this would cause in the PCT. Farlaine told me the results would take ten days. I knew that the break room idiots would have the last critical days of our contract to spin defamation into fact – I could just picture their bitching...

"Well he must be on drugs – after all he was sent for a test..."

"Yeah we can't be seen condoning this – burn him."

This was a disaster.

When it comes to healthcare and the suggestion of drugs, higher management back away like you wouldn't believe. In honour of arse covering, they punish first then find out later and as for the accused, truth means shit. In fact, the PCT and the GDC have been known to overreact to such an absurd extent that they even struck off a dentist for farting!

I could see, however, that things were stacking up against us. The lack of any court date, the failure to deal with the lease, the bribe, Jack being struck off and now the possible consequences of the letter that Farlaine had just presented to me eliminated any chance of that far-reaching dispensation I'd been hoping for.

Fuck!!

Finishing up, Farlaine eventually provided me with the details of where to go for the test. I saw him out of the door. He'd left me strangely thankful for his compassion.

March 25th

Working Days Left on Contract: 4.5

The next afternoon sitting in hospital waiting for a disapproving occupational nurse to sample my blood, I couldn't stop mulling over the event.

It was the details I didn't like. Something about this letter just didn't add up…

In my whole dental career I'd only ever had a few complaints – all very minor and only ever reported to the practice reception – things like running late or a patient's filling hurting. All standard stuff and the kind that every dentist gets. This, however, was different.

The letter was anonymous, defamatory and inflammatory as hell and had been sent directly to the GDC. This had never happened to any of my colleagues nor do patients even think about complaining in this way. Being an NHS practice, patients only ever complain to the practice or NHS Choices, which is where they're directed to first. All this occurs before anything gets escalated to the GDC.

Strangely though, this letter had been sent straight to them.

Also, the wording was odd – 'narcotics' and 'Thus, this must be investigated' – these are the words only a doctor would use when signing off referrals…

Motherfucker – it just hit me.

It wouldn't take much of a gambling man to say Farlaine had set me up!!!

Bastard – I bet this was why he couldn't tell me what the issue was over the phone or even say it to my face. And I'd just thought he was being dramatic!

Farlaine would have realised it would be impossible for him to look authentic when reading out the words of an accusation letter if he'd made it up. This must have been the reason that he relaxed once he'd seen that I believed it! Safe then to play out the rest of his role, he could even add a sprinkle of empathy… It would make for a perfect crime.

Doubling as one of the PCT's key representatives for handling complaints, Farlaine must have been shitting his pants after we'd caught him out for smearing Mr Chan's reputation. Who else would know how to play this better than Farlaine?

By bringing a drugs allegation against me only days after I'd threatened him meant that he could get his revenge by anonymously causing me maximum indefensible damage. He would know that this would fire up both the GDC and the PCT tearoom scandal machines and my name would become shit. Now, I was the subject of the smoke without fire and should I ever want to expose the bastard for who he really was, I would be pissing into the wind as he'd have burned me first. Who then would favour trusting the young dentist who'd just got off a drugs charge?

Fucker.

Checking his Facebook page, I was sickened how obvious it all was.

Plastered all over it was how he went to church and was a devout follower… Now I know a few religious people and some are ok but the ones who feel the need to advertise it, more often than not, use religion to purge their sins on Sunday so that they can continue committing clandestine nastiness whenever they see fit. I can't bare that sort.

Reading further, Farlaine even laboured how he was a 'charitable giver'.

You tell me of anyone who is genuinely nice but has to brag about it... they never do... they're just nice... whereas this self-branding prick, having already revealed himself trying to needlessly screw over Mr Chan, knew exactly what he was up to.

Bastard Bastard Bastard.

The best way to counter a sniper like this would be to go on holiday and send more anonymous letters to the GDC and PCT accusing myself. This way, sitting abroad while similar allegations rolled in and declared I was high on specific days I wasn't even in the country (passport stamped) everyone would soon wake up to hunt for the original culprit. After all who would be crazy enough to accuse themselves?

If only I'd had more time.

None though so this option out, here was the bigger dilemma it created...

Today was Wednesday 25th. Running out of days to fix our contract, the question now was should we sit tight right up to March 31st in the hope that we'd get a cancellation court date or, with our reputation now mud, do we just come clean to the PCT about our lease??

Telling them carried the risk of making us look even worse, however, the PCT may appreciate the honesty and, with the advanced warning, could perhaps extend lenient arrangements for our contract renewal before it was too late...

Fuck.

Both plans could backfire big-time but it was impossible to know which to go with.

Maybe I should ask Mrs Shah? Then again, this could be dangerous too. After all, times had changed...

Although Shah had helped me with minor things in the past, I still didn't know her that well and I was aware that there had been recent job threats to her department. She probably shared office space with Farlaine and it was likely that they were friends. Also I couldn't be sure how close she was to the top contract boss... If I gave away too much about our worsening crisis with the lease, would she decide to burn us this time just to score brownie points with him... especially in the light of my drug test issue??

Hmm, this was tough but I couldn't just sit on the fence....

37

THE CAT

March 25th

Working Days Left on Contract: 4

Fuck it.

After giving the nurse my blood for testing, I dialled Mrs Shah from the hospital car park.

Ring-Ring. Ring-Ring.

I waited for her to pick up. I needed to tread carefully to find out what the hell I should do.

"Hello?" she picked up. "Mrs Shah speaking."

"Oh hi, it's Michael Sydney here."

"Hello," she quietened. "It sounds like you've been having trouble."

"You mean the drug test?" I blurted. "Yeah, just so you know it's all lies by the way. I haven't taken any."

My God, hearing myself talk I sounded so weak.

"Anyway, I was just calling," I continued, gutted at how gossip really did travel fast, "to see if there was any way we could perhaps meet privately or something?"

"Privately?" she hesitated. "Er, this isn't something I would normally do…"

Shit – this did sound a bit weird but I was desperate to get her on her own. Thankfully she agreed.

We arranged to meet in a coffee shop that same evening. It was supposedly her favourite. Arriving first, I stepped inside. I was surprised to see the place she'd chosen was really quirky. Taking a massive hot chocolate recommended by the hipster behind the till, I was soon sitting amongst bohemian style candles, incense sticks and mini Buddha's making it almost easy to forget this was about to be the most consequential meeting of them all.

Sipping my drink a few minutes I felt nervous about what I should say.

"Hey Sapphire," I soon heard Mrs Shah follow in, already talking to the girl on the till, "Soy latte please."

Looking pretty fit in her work suit and wet through from the rain, "You're here!" she turned, spotting me as I approached to say hello.

"Hi yeah."

Jesus, I was not sure whether to hug her or shake her by the hand. Having stepped too close, in the end I just waved right at her face. It was awkward and feeling half casual, half I don't know what, I even took her bags as if this was some sort of date.

Having directed her to the two high-backed chairs in the middle, I watched as she finally brought her coffee over to where I was sitting.

"So you found it ok then?" she said.

"Yeah it's a cool place," I bumbled.

We sipped on our drinks a minute.

"Tell me," I couldn't resist, "Is anything dodgy going on in the PCT?"

"Err… No." she firmed, my question making her defensive. "Everything's normal. Why would you ask?"

Damn, feeling this was tight-lipped compared with the last time we'd spoken, maybe Shah believed the drug gossip or was worried she'd better not risk being open with me anymore.

Hmm. Without me revealing our situation, how could I find out what to do?

Another five minutes of me making awkward chitchat followed while I wondered how to safely get her to open up. Out of nowhere, however, the coffee shop cat, I didn't even know they had, suddenly leapt up onto the back of my chair…

"Ha, I've never seen her do that before?" Mrs Shah exclaimed.

"Oh yeah?" I said, equally shocked at the purring cat now perching right by my neck.

"Ha yeah she must really like you," Mrs Shah continued gazing in awe!

My God – was Shah really buzzing off this??

Looking down I noticed she was wearing a Ganesh bangle and had a hippy thumb ring on. Suddenly it struck me what to do.

With the cat being mystique black 'n' all, maybe Mrs Shah thought this was some kind of spiritual sign… Yeah, fuck it. If believing in nine-armed elephants was what it would take to get this woman onside – I'd better go all the way.

"Yeah it's a cute kitty eh?" I started nuzzling the back of my head right into its belly.

"Ha she really likes you!" she watched us in delight.

Man, I just couldn't believe this Dr Dolittle stuff was impressing her!

"Of course," I rubbed on. "Maybe it sees something in me."

Cringe.

I was trying my best to act relaxed praying this thing wouldn't scratch my eyes out. A few more minutes passed when I realised Shah's leg had half-rested against mine…

WTF.

"You been busy then?" she continued, sipping on her coffee.

Was this on purpose?

I mean, I know our chairs were close but I could feel the heat of her skin building. She had to be feeling this! It was so sexy.

"Yeah," I kept my leg perfectly still. "We've been busy."

This was bizarre.

Maybe I was reading too much into it. Despite all the pressure I was under and the surrealism of the cat on top of my chair, the idiot part of my brain started debating as to whether this could turn into some scene out of *Basic Instinct.* I glanced momentarily at her blouse.

Yeah I bet Mrs Shah would be amazing in bed.

Remaining still, I could feel myself getting a semi-on. Oh now it works!

Stop it. Stupid thought.

"Look," she'd almost finished her coffee, her leg still touching against mine, "I've got to tell you that your practice is in serious trouble."

"Oh?" I nodded still somewhat dreamy with my semi-on.

"Clive blocked you on the contract."

"What???"

Yeah this woke me up.

"After you asked him for help with the tender that time," she said, "he phoned us demanding that we never let you win."

"Fucking bastard!"

With my hard-on shrinking, I remembered how he'd agreed to help me.

"What about now?" I asked confused. "Has Farlaine set me up on this drug charge?"

"I wouldn't know about that," her leg was still against mine.

"All I know though is that your place is creating serious enemies and there's some big changes going down but, as long as you win at court, there's nothing they can do..."

Hearing this, both my heart and my semi-on sank.

"Well that's the problem," I began opening to her now. "Our court date has just been cancelled. I only came here to see if the PCT would give us more time."

"What? No!" Shah turned worried. "You've got to get the lease! This boss is doing everything to finish you."

"But why?" I said dry mouthed, my quarter-on now well and truly dead.

"It's your performance! It exposes him and his golfing cronies as incompetent!"

"Huh? But I don't understand..."

Clearly I was naïve about the bigger picture. She started to fill me in...

Our PCT was responsible for the performance of 30 NHS practices in the borough, Clive's being one. Out of the 30, 29 had been consistently failing to meet NHS targets. Up to now, they could blame this on demographics saying that the patients were more difficult to treat compared with other boroughs.

Government pressure was building and desperate to fix it, the PCT had been trying everything – even blasting cash on some marketing guru from a drinks company. This, however, had flopped big time.

Besides the one practice on target, our practice had shot ahead displaying a huge surge in performance which was verified by the inspection. Displaying such success, this had proved that the 'demographics excuse' was wrong and it not only exposed the PCT for its failings but exposed all the other practices for their mismanagement too, thus making everyone look bad. The boss and loads of practice principals all now wanted us eradicated.

"But this is crazy," I slumped, struggling to comprehend. "We can't take our performance back – the UDAs have already been submitted and with this drug stuff…"

"Look, I'm sure the drugs thing will be fine," she said. "Just do whatever it takes to win your lease."

As she stood up to leave, she leaned in close and kissed me on the cheek.

"Why are you helping me?" I had to ask.

"I don't know," she shrugged, her light perfume smelling beautiful, "I didn't like the way Clive treated you that time when he introduced you to me only to shout at you to get out. Plus for some reason you strangely remind me of my ex. He was a musician, kind of free."

Just then we both heard a noise and turned to see the cat had leapt down onto the seat of my chair – bastard – it had obviously just been waiting to use the cushion I'd been sitting on the entire time.

Where was all my mystique now?!

After saying goodbye, I caught the tube back to the practice feeling ready to give up. At the surgery everyone had gone home. Everyone except Tiesha who was still hanging back, using the computer to book some reggae gigs. She came over to talk.

"Me nah you're upset man. Wagwan?"

"Tiesh, we're fucked man," I wasn't bothered anymore to withhold how everything was against us.

"Pff," she immediately scoffed. "You white folks don't get it do you?"

"Huh?" this wasn't the reaction I expected. "What you on about?"

"Well y'always stressin' cos you don't know how to enjoy life!"

"Bullshit man," I said not in the mood. "We're fucked – really."

Tiesha though bound on,

"Nah. You won't be – just see it as fate's way of making room for somethin' betta."

"Oh yeah??" I mocked. "So how's this landlord making things better? With stress and bankruptcy?"

"I don't know? I don't make the rules," she shrugged, "but whatever 'appens as long as you keep tryin', I bet somewhere you'll be glad!"

"You're talking shit!"

Switching the lights off, I started to lock up. Tiesha followed me out to the main door when she stopped to add something more,

"Hey yo?" it appeared she was about to say something profound.

"What?" I waited…

"Gimmi twenty pound!"

Unbelievable.

I let her take £30 out of my wallet before she danced off to do her nails. As I finished locking the door I noticed a missed call and an answerphone message was waiting on my mobile.

"Aghh, good news," I listened. It was Jack. "The lawyer's still worried about the rent bollocks but next week, Monday 30th he's found us a cancellation at a different courthouse. He won't be able to make it because of the short notice, but he's made his colleague available to us."

BOOM.

It was back on but our last chance and no room for mistakes – it was Jack against the landlord. This would be down to whoever performed the best. I just had to pray then that going up against one of the sharpest operators I'd ever come across, Jack would be anyone but himself.

Beyond all my control, however, would he listen?

Would he fuck…

38

JUDGEMENT DAY

March 30th

Working Days Left on Contract: 1

Literally down to the final day and hours on our contract. Screw this up and it was over.

The PCT wouldn't give us our vital renewal. Without the NHS contract, Jack's place would be worth zero. All the staff would have to lose their jobs.

In a nutshell, every one of us would be fucked.

Nervous as hell, I arrived outside Bow County Court; it was 8.45am and with the last chance to save ourselves I met Jack on the steps only to find that things had already started to head south.

I couldn't believe it!

He told me that, just the day before, Sunday afternoon, his house had been ransacked and his whole Samurai collection, worth tens of thousands, was gone.

It was shocking!

It seems that, despite him having fitted reinforced doors and barred windows to make his home like Fort Knox, the burglars had broken in by lifting tiles up off the roof!

Jack was still in the midst of the aftermath of having to deal with repairs.

I helped him up into the courthouse entrance and took his crutch so he could pass through the security's metal detector. Just then, Tinfoil Murray called Jack's phone.

"YEAHHHH MURRAY," Jack retrieved his ringing mobile from the guard, "I'VE BEEN BURRRGLED."

Shit.

Supposed to be looking innocent, Jack waded ahead of me right into the middle of the marble library-like foyer, to continue his deaf shout.

"AGHH, THEY TOOK EVERYTHING!" he blasted in the hub of lingering court staff. "THEY TOOK MY SAMURAI SWORDS, MY CS GAS…"

"Jack!!!" I gritted, rushing through to catch him. "Shut the fuck up!"

But waving me back, oblivious to stares, "AGHH, GOD KNOWS HOW THEY NEW IT WAS CS GAS," he shouted, "I'D HAD IT SPRAYED BLACK…"

Unbelievable!

Impossible to silence him, I shuddered at him splitting the foyer's muted ambience like some firecracker. Next I saw our young replacement barrister who was hoping for a pre-hearing talk.

"Morning gentlemen," he approached.

"Hi. Jack's just finishing," I nodded.

"OK, well I'll just explain how it's all going to go down…"

Doing my best to concentrate I continued to signal to Dr Deaf to get off his phone.

"I trust you've refreshed your memory from your witness statement?" the barrister asked Jack once he finally hobbled over to join us.

"Aghh, how could I?" Jack barked, "I've been dealing with this!"

Oh for fuck sake – the barrister's face said it all.

Both sides must submit a witness statement on which they will be cross-examined in court. Knowing how Jack was about to be grilled on something he'd written ages ago,

"Man, you're supposed to have read it!" I snapped.

"Aghh I've got nothing to hide."

"Well how you gonna explain the rent?!!!"

"Five minutes gentlemen," the usher passed through.

"I've paid the rent!" Jack resisted. "It's the bribe we're here for!"

I wanted to kill him.

"Jack," the barrister interjected, "this legal team will try to pick you apart on every last detail!"

"Yeah man," I couldn't help myself. "Listen to him!"

Leaving us abhorred at his complete indifference,

"Looook!" Jack brushed us both off. "This isn't the first time I've been to court so relaaaaaax!"

He was shocking.

However, swanning in next was the landlord.

"Hello Jack," he sauntered across to us.

"Arright, Victor."

I'd never actually met the landlord face to face. A tall slick suit, a slim gold watch and gold tie matching the year-round tan, the real type that only comes with wealth. This was Victor Grimston. Our bastard of a landlord emanated power. He was surrounded by a whole legal entourage and, as if this wasn't intimidating enough, they had loads of papers and bundles of documents that none of us seemed to have.

"The very best of luck," Grimmer's teased, his team sniggering by his side.

Twats.

"Aghh thanks but I don't think we'll need it," Jack remained polite.

I watched them almost ice-skate off to their side, certain that they had something in the bag.

"Are they any good?" I turned to our young barrister, who now looked ill-white.

"That middle one's a QC."

"So what does that mean?" I delved, not liking the fact that our guy looked scared.

"It means we have to do our best," he began fumbling with some last minute checks.

Great.

I was worried about our barrister's competence; I'd read somewhere that the darker the wig, the more experienced the lawyer. Our guy's wig looked like a spring lamb compared with team-landlord's QC who was wearing *Fifty Shades of Domination.* This was not good.

"Gentleman we're now ready," the usher announced. "If everyone could please enter through the double doors," he began guiding everyone into Courtroom One.

Shit.

This was it. It was time to get serious.

Hanging back a second while all the others bustled through, I turned to Jack who was still sitting quietly on a bench.

"Hey man," I bent down, "are you alright?" I asked, ignoring passing gloats from Grimston and his team.

"Yeaah," Jack muttered.

I was worried knowing that our futures rested entirely on Jack's performance.

"Listen," I felt compelled to say, "just make sure you give it some about the bribe and whatever happens, try to look upstanding, OK?"

"Aghh I am upstanding!!" Jack grumbled.

"Yeah I see that," I passed him his crutch.

"All rise."

Hearing the usher, I hurried Jack to his feet so that we could catch up with everyone inside.

"Please be seated," announced the usher once the gowned judge had walked in.

It began.

First on the stand was the landlord. Before anything could get underway, however, he was asked to explain why he'd missed the previous court date. He still hadn't provided a doctor's note to support his apparent sickness.

"Oh your honour," Grimmers started, clearly well versed in the art of schmoozing, "I'm so terribly sorry," he was hamming it up, "I'd suffered an intractable bout of gout and was literally crawling on my hands and knees, so ill I could barely get to the telephone."

What a slime ball. The judge appeared to be accepting his account but then, Jack shouted,

"THEY CAN TEST FOR THAT!"

Ha! I'd forgotten about Jack's degree in pharmacology.

"Oh err well err." Grimston was thrown off course, "... thankfully your honour," he quickly recovered, "I've since made a full recovery and with no lasting symptoms any test wouldn't be possible, but thank you," he finished somewhat relieved.

"YOU DON'T NEED SYMPTOMS!" Jack yelled again from the pews, "THE TEST IS VALID FOR FOUR WEEKS!"

Ha!

The landlord was squirming when his QC dived to his rescue,

"Yes well, if MR BROCKS could please understand that he is forbidden to speak unless explicitly permitted!!" old Fifty Shades scowled over. "And as much as we'd love to confirm this explanation with such tests, given all the trauma my client's suffered and being afraid of needles, he couldn't possibly face more pain."

"IT'S A URINE TEST!" Jack shouted, even our own barrister was not able to stop him.

Amazing! Grimmers was livid. Jack was formally warned though that he must remain silent unless specifically told otherwise. The judge accepted the weak excuse and we moved on with the case we were really here for.

As we progressed, Grimmers appeared to be gaining the upper hand. Our guy was rubbish!

Fending questions from our barrister about the lease, Grimmers first plied the court with a well-rehearsed sob story about how he'd struggled during the months Jack hadn't paid rent. Then, with everyone on side, he exaggerated how losing his previous court case (which had ruled that Jack's rent could not be increased for a further five years) had driven him to the point of near bankruptcy.

It was gutting.

The judge's face was showing sympathy, the landlord was clearly doing a good job of making us look bad. Had it not been for the fact that I knew this tyrant owned over 60 London properties and the very reason for the ruling was that he'd tried hiking Jack's rent way beyond market value in the first place, maybe I'd have felt sorry for him too.

The judge was obviously waning in his favour while our barrister hadn't exactly smashed it to anything like OJ Simpson's standard. Next on the stand was Jack, who in complete contrast to the landlord, was a sight to behold...

Suffering good days and bad, Jack's balance today was definitely bad. With zero finesse, causing everyone to gasp, Jack grunted and painfully struggled his way up to the stand. Finally he stepped up wobbling until he could grip both sides of the box for support. Even the judge looked dismayed.

"Sir, are you OK?" he asked. "Do you need any assistance?"

"I'm fine," Jack firmed, as if to say get on with it.

Jack never was one for sympathy.

With that, the QC for the landlord stood poised to fire his bullets.

"Mr Brocks in your witness statement you said..."

Oh, here we go.

It was obvious that the QC and his team had scrutinised every line of Jack's prewritten witness statement and were going to destroy him on every inconsistency they could. Opening to a highlighted section of his bundle,

"... you said here," the QC read, "you've always been a flawless tenant who's honoured all lease agreements, namely..."

Shit! I waited for him to throw up some inconsistency in Jack's statement.

Once Jack conceded, he'd be forced into an inescapable trap and the QC would then be able to follow with,

"Ah, well, because you said X Y Z, you must be lying about ABC."

I knew Jack wouldn't see any of this coming, then again, I'd forgotten who we were dealing with here. Our Dr Crazy was more used to talking through people, not with people, so this is how it went…

"Mr Brocks," the barrister started. "In your witness statement you said you've always been a flawless tenant who's honoured all lease agreements, namely…"

"LOOK!" Jack cut him straight off. "I DON'T KNOW WHAT I SAID. ALL I KNOW IS THAT BASTARD THERE," he pointed to the landlord, "TRIED TO BRIBE ME SIXTY-EIGHT GRAND!"

Ha! Jack at his best, this was a killer line.

"Mr Brocks no!!" the QC jumped. "In your witness statement you said you've honoured all lease agreements, namely…"

"LOOOOOOKKK!!!" Jack stopped him again. "Like I've told you. I might have, I might not – I CAAAANNN'T REALLY REMEMBER! ALL I KNOW IS THAT BASTARD THERE TRIED TO BRIBE ME SIXTY-EIGHT GRAND!!"

Ha.

Without realising it, Jack was smashing the QC. He was legendary. The QC was finding him as difficult as I did and was stumped. For all their fancy tactics, they'd probably never come across anyone like this. The landlord was screwing!!

Next came the cross-examination about the past year, which Jack would have to deal with. Jack was completely out of my reach now but I was worried that I might have stressed the importance of him mentioning the bribe (while we were back in the foyer) a little too much. It was here and now, however, when we most needed him not to come out with anything stupid or to slip up with any exaggeration that would give rise to disbelief, we watched as our case nosedived.

"Mr Brocks," the QC recomposed himself with a new line of questioning. "When did you first approach the landlord about changing the lease?"

"Agghhhhh, I'm not too sure..." Jack dithered. "Some time in summer."

"Very well," he took note, "and when did you decide to start court proceedings against my client?"

"Agghhhhh..." Jack wavered again. "I'm not too sure. Maybe winter some time."

"OK," the QC narrowed now. "So this meal you talked of, where you were allegedly bribed by my client, when was this?"

"JULY 14TH!!!" Jack yelled specifically.

Fuck.

Watching Jack nodding over to me now, loyal like a trooper, I wanted to cry.

I mean, I know I'd just pressured him to talk up the bribe but I never wanted this!

"I see," the QC smiled to a volley of smirks from his team.

"So just to reiterate," he made sure he'd cement it, "You wanted to change the lease when?"

"Aghhhh like I said," Jack repeated, "some time in summer."

"And this decision about these court proceedings...?"

"Aghhhh maybe winter some time."

“But, this very convenient meal you mention,” the QC baited, “where, in Mayfair a considerably long time ago, you were allegedly bribed by my client, this was when?”

“JULY 14TH!!!!” Jack shouted again.

Fucking hell.

“You sure?”

“Yep.” Jack nodded.

Shit.

The QC was straining not to laugh. Jack had fallen right into his trap and had given him everything he needed for the kill.

About to bring the case to a close and with no hard evidence about the bribe, it was down to whoever’s story seemed believable. Even our own barrister had his head in his hands.

Everything we’d worked for was about to collapse.

“Your Honour,” the QC firmed approaching his final summing up. “Why is it that Mr Brocks seems to be very vague about important details such as when he wanted the lease changing, when he filed court proceedings and any details surrounding that… yet, when it comes to this very convenient meal story and a bribe, which allegedly occurred even further back, he can somehow remember the date exactly??”

“Yes Mr Brocks,” the judge joined, “I’m afraid I must agree here. Why is it you can conveniently remember this date so well?”

Everyone stared at Jack now who was standing like a rabbit in the headlights. The silence was excruciating.

“… Mr Brocks?” the judge prompted, the whole courtroom, including me, having written him off, “you may speak…”

"AGHH, COS IT WAS MY BIRTHDAY" Jack bellowed.

Ha WTF!

It was a miracle!

After losing the football bet, the landlord had taken Jack to his members' club in Mayfair as forfeit. What none of us knew, not even me, was that, by pure chance, this had all happened on Jack's birthday!

"YEP, SEEM TO REMEMBER IT EVERY YEAR," Jack added sarcastically. "DUNNO WHY!!!"

No advocate's skill could cast doubt on this irrefutable answer!

"Err no," the QC jutted. "Er," but it was too late.

It had been touch and go but everyone now realised that Jack was no liar. The case was won!!

Breathing a sigh of relief, we listened to the judge's deliberations.

The final outcome was that the landlord had to immediately sign over the lease and pay both sets of legal fees plus an additional 7% interest on what Jack would have earned had the lease been transferred when it should have been. This meant that, on top of all the costs, the landlord would, effectively, have a debt of £100,000 to pay.

This certainly was justice.

Rushing out into the foyer, leaving Jack to be debriefed on logistics, I dialled Mrs Shah at the PCT.

"We did it, we did it!!!" I exclaimed.

"Ha. That's brilliant!" she hailed.

The lease being transferred into my name meant that, not only could the bank release the purchase money enabling me to buy the business but the PCT now had to renew our contract and Jack could finally retire. It was more than I could have wished for. I felt like all my

Christmases had come at once when Mrs Shah added to my euphoria with one more thing,

"You'll never guess what," she was bursting to tell me while I was still on the phone with her. "The PCT boss has quit!"

"What!!"

"Yeah I don't think he wanted to wait 'till the borough's year-end underperformances were exposed."

"You're kidding?!!"

"No, and here's the best bit," she said. "The board are already talking about redistributing the total shortfalls from all the other practices to anyone overperforming; your place being the only contender."

"What! That's amazing!!"

"Ha well, one thing's for sure," she returned with a laugh, "I don't think Clive will be happy!! His practice was one that wasn't exactly on target."

Man – this felt like one of the best days of my life!!

Crashing out of the double doors, Jack, having finally finished with logistics, stumbled towards me.

"We did it, we did it!!" I hailed to him. "And I've just been told that the PCT might increase the contract!"

"Aghh you can keep that," he smiled, happy to be retiring.

Seconds on, the landlord walked past.

"Well done," he gritted.

"Aghh it was only fair," Jack smiled as if this was all just another day.

For me though, well... I couldn't believe it. Up ahead I saw big Tony, Jack's driver, waving from the main security entrance having parked on double yellows (as usual).

"Man, I just can't believe we won!!!!!" I repeated to Jack.

We started heading towards Tony but Jack, pausing a second, then turned to me with something I'll never forget…

"Michael… Michael," he tapped my elbow, "when are you going to realise that things always have a way of working themselves out. You've just got to learn to trust."

Walking off happily, he left me standing a second.

What he said might not have been consequential to him but it stuck in my mind and off the back of it, I would discover one of the biggest life lessons of all…

Over the following six months the sale went through and with the redistribution of all 28 practices' shortfalls, I was awarded a record uplift on the contract.

During this period, I started to have flashbacks to all the times I'd stressed. Right from the start – the beauty salon horrors, being fired from prison, London, Clive's betrayal, losing the tender, failing at auction, the landlord, even suffering his critical delay in our lease transfer which upset the PCT – suddenly it hit me how every single event and setback I landed was essential and had one hidden and very unique link.

It has become my firm belief that (unless it is death or terminal illness) all bad situations (and mostly these are outside our control) land on us for a reason… a reason that is waiting to offer us a hidden benefit or pathway that we will not be able to see at the time.

Look again at any single event, big or small, that you pick from this story.

If I'd not had my reputation screwed by the drug-rep Trudy and then been fired from the prison, I probably would never have moved to London.

Had I not worked in the beauty salon, I would have had no idea how effective marketing could be and would, without such knowledge, have been at a serious disadvantage when taking on Jack's business, especially in our cut throat capital.

If conditions while working for Clive hadn't caused me to become so frustrated, I would never have stripped naked, got fired and have to subsequently search for another job.

I would not have noticed the advertisement for the tender and would never have attempted bidding for an NHS contract (a bid which gave me the opportunity to impress the PCT). And, significantly, I would never have been introduced to Jack. Had I not met Jack, I probably would never have had the opportunity to buy such a goldmine of a practice.

Had the landlord not been so obstructive and fought us every step of the way to enforce his bribe and make the transfer of the business so impossible, unsettling the PCT and making them impose conditions, I never would have had to ramp up our performance to such an extreme level to satisfy their demands.

Had I not ramped up the business and over-performed, I never would have been awarded a record uplift on the NHS contract, and on and on this goes…

Bad situations occur and often persist for many of us throughout our lives.

For example, we may be in a job or town we hate, have a relationship that we know is unfulfilling and going nowhere, we may have been dealt a heavy blow to our finances, been dumped by a partner we loved or embarked upon a career we were not suited to.

The situations may be big or small but if there's anything I've learned from my struggles it is that there is usually a choice and that the outcome relies on whether we react or not.

We can remain in the unwanted situation and tolerate its effects.

In the immediate term this often presents the easiest thing to do. At best, however, this will leave us exactly where we are, unfulfilled, unhappy and with no improvement.

Alternatively, we may react out of each setback thrust upon us (and for the more severe situations this sometimes takes fighting with everything we've got) and if we take this road, we'll notice something unique follows.

By focusing our efforts on reacting out of the bad situation, and I mean really focusing our efforts, the bad situation will not only be tackled but it will elevate us to a position beyond our original expectation.

The road may be a rocky one but, in a bizarre way, taking action actually turns the situation into a gift. However, it is only on looking back that we can understand how and why.

I'm not trying to paint the stars here, far from it, but look at situations that have occurred in your own life that you did not welcome at the time, but that you reacted out of.

Do you not now see that those situations were the steppingstones required to give you the chance to make the changes that were strangely needed to improve your life?

Armed with this insight into what bad situations really offer, we can react and free ourselves thus allowing life to magically grow into the exciting and colourful joy it should be!!

So friends, in the spirit of non-worriers and people like Jack, my parting rhyme should you ever feel you're a little off track…

"Don't waste a second longer
stressing away from bliss
But, instead, welcome life's rollercoaster
you otherwise might miss!"

Happy living…

PS. Don't ever do dentistry; it's absolutely horrific ;-)

END CREDITS

Following the record overshoot of Michael's practice's performance, the PCT redistributed the total shortfalls of the 28 practices' underperformance to him.

As a result he was awarded a record-breaking uplift from a contract of £340,000 to £1.25 million, which at the time was the biggest singly awarded NHS contract for a practice in the UK.

Using the extra turnover Michael was able to escape the landlord and move to much larger and more elite premises. Although this didn't come without its own problems, the relocation attracted a private income that actually surpassed what was being produced for the NHS.

This resulted in his business delivering a record service, both private and NHS, which produced annual profits of £750,000 from a turnover of £2.5 million.

Within one year Michael quit dentistry and sold his practice as the highest-grossing, most rapidly expanding expensive surgery in the country. Following the twelve months of extreme change, he had managed to walk away with just under £3 million.

Him and Jack still remain close friends to this day.

In 2013 the PCTs, for their failings around the country, were abolished. In their place Care Quality

Commissions were brought in to inspect practices, while other restructuring resulted in Area Teams which continued handling the NHS's hugely failing UDA system.

The 'non-profit' making General Dental Council still operates in its multi-storey central London location. Even now, it carries on driving the highest charges it can and works to generate even more complaints against dentists to justify its own importance.

With regards to what happened to the rest of Michael's team, Tiesha came upfront about her situation with the Government and managed to gain residency. She left nursing and is striving to make headway in the reggae world under a stage name.

Mr Chan, helped on by all the extra patients, triple work efficiency and formula one support, quadrupled his wage and was able to retire early and move back to Hong Kong.

Aria 'the note masher' moved on to Amsterdam.

Rachel became a hygienist. Shristi, who according to her profile remains 78% matched, eventually married Mr 'I do' while lastly, Sergio, who still sports an entire wardrobe of skin-tight elasticated shirts and trousers, is just waiting for the fashion day he will finally be right.

THE END

AUTHOR'S MESSAGE

Firstly, I would like to give a massive thank you to you for reading this book.

I know that releasing this book could derail any future dental career, but it has already broken my neck, as I wrote all 76,000 words lying flat on my bed. Nevertheless, if you loved reading this as much as I did telling it, or you've found my story to be a big help in any way, posting your review on Amazon would be greatly appreciated.

Secondly, as a bonus follow on to sharing more fun, to hear interviews from some of the real characters or be part of the bigger party before it really kicks off, come and join us at:

HangoutWithMikey.com

See you on the flipside....
M

I

THE DARKER TRUTH BEHIND THE SCENES

As I mentioned at the beginning of this book (and this is only for those interested), in the interests of story form some characters and events have been transposed or simplified. In reality, our situation was far worse.

After completion of the court case, I signed with Neil's bank but, to raise the necessary purchase loan for the business, I had had to put up my parents' house as security.

Months after locking myself into the practice acquisition, the PCT announced that they wanted to phase out any practices that couldn't offer disabled access (ours couldn't). Furthermore, the ruthless landlord, to whom I was now beholden, had secretly gained planning permission to turn our practice into flats.

Nowhere else to operate from and with location restrictions imposed by the PCT, I was out of options and facing certain bankruptcy. During this time, I couldn't sleep a wink. I don't think my parents had any idea how close I actually came to causing them to lose their house, the same house I had been born in.

I was devastated when I saw the advertisement billboard showing that our landlord was actually auctioning off our very own practice premises for residential conversion along with the rest of his building stack, which already contained flats.

The guide price was £4.5 million. This was ultimately purchased by a consortium.

Having only a short time left on the lease, I figured the only escape from such a dire trap was to do whatever it took to grow the business. This way, if any other building did come along, I would have more money which would surely give me a better chance.

Attending a PCT meeting around the same time, it was announced that out of the 30 practices they were contracting to, one was slightly ahead of target (ours), one was on target while 28 were severely behind. Keeping this in mind I watched from the back as all the failing principals, losing their minds, were pointlessly complaining and joining the demographics argument that it wasn't their fault that they couldn't find enough patients. Looking at things differently, I, instead, figured that if I hired even more staff and went over target as much as I could, the PCT, needing to clear its own government targets of new patients, would somehow have to transfer their entire shortfall to me.

Over the next two months, taking on loads of dentists and nurses for contracts that didn't exist, I marketed like crazy with the comedians. It was a big risk but I gauged that I would have to afford to do this for only a month or two.

Six months on however, I'd reached a dangerous point where, on top of the main loan, I'd borrowed an extra £200,000 high-interest cash just to pay for all the marketing and staff I'd recruited in order to provide endless NHS work for the new patients I wasn't even being paid to treat. Time dragging on, things had escalated so badly I was either going to be made bankrupt and cause my parents to lose their house or somehow bounce back with enough money to finally escape.

It was a horrible time and losing myself even deeper down the rabbit hole, I was gambling way beyond my chips. The only consolation I had was to keep reminding myself that once I was made bankrupt, what difference did it make how much debt I'd accrued, after all, the dreadful outcome would still be the same.

I had never been under so much stress.

Thankfully, two months further still, my risk paid off and the PCT, having scrutinised our practice performance for over half a year, redistributed their entire shortfall of all the failing practices to me, more than tripling our contract. It was a record uplift but I was not out of the woods yet.

During such a crucial time, the new consortium (that had bought the building at auction) threatened to action the landlord-only break clause that had been written into our infamously bad lease. Keeping silent, I prayed that they wouldn't kick us out as we still had nowhere else to operate from. Added to this, pressures were rising from the PCT about our lack of disabled access.

When their new inspectors visited (new because staff there changed all the time), despite me bringing my actors in again, the PCT (their boss, hitherto mentioned, being fictitious) did not like to discover that, having awarded us the biggest contract, we were mixed amongst residential flats and still operating from such a small, non-dental like place.

Only making matters worse, the landlord consortium did, in the end, serve us their termination notice on what was the very last day of service.

I was away when this happened and it was arguable whether they'd served the notice within the legally specified time. Hitting us at the worst possible moment, however, they argued that they'd dropped off the letter by the entrance downstairs and had thus complied with the terms of the lease.

Despite being open until 9pm, we hadn't received anything until the next morning when a patient handed our receptionist the letter having apparently found it on the steps. This meant that the service date could not be proved either way.

Still being haunted by our lease and its imminent termination, my only chance of hanging on was to take the consortium to court and stand up to these bastards the same way that Jack had taught me throughout. Stringing along the court date, like the previous landlord had done to us, I was able to keep our lease in a holding pattern. This gave us a few more precious weeks. We still, however, had nowhere to go. All I could do was hope.

Literally weeks later and out of nowhere, a nearby ground floor premises became available. Even here we had to fight against complications and compete against publicly listed companies. Against all odds, and having to ply yet more tricks with the representing estate agent, I managed to sign the lease and move everything but still it was down to the wire.

While moving all the equipment across and plumbing everything in, having risked legally binding myself to a seven-year lease, I was conscious that I still didn't have planning permission. In the event, I had to appeal for approval just before our doors opened.

Adding to the pandemonium, none of the telephone lines were ready and our original landline number, which we needed in order to receive the hundreds of daily bookings from patients, still had to be transferred. On the day of opening I had to rush to three separate Maplin electronic stores and buy every single phone extension they had.

Camouflaging these with foliage, I cheekily sneaked the Sellotaped connecting cables over the back walls of restaurants and all the flats that stood in between the old practice and the new. At least then, the receptionists could take bookings and our performance could keep afloat.

Just as the whole operation was being finalised, I was able to drop the court case and accept the eviction. Ironically, being evicted by the consortium protected me from severe liabilities that attached to the unusually onerous lease. Had I not been evicted, I would have had to bring the structure of the 100-year-old subsiding building back to its original state of repair before I left. This would have cost me thousands. Thankfully the severance, prompted by their side, allowed me to relocate free of all dilapidation costs.

On moving, I was able to clean up the practice and because of the significantly bigger private income that the new premises attracted, I could make it absolutely top notch, both in service and in profit.

By this point, I was responsible for 28 employees (I'd started off with three). Finally, I was free to sell it for the record figure and quit.

I can confidently say that the period between being thwarted with the tender right up to the sale of the practice, was the most stressful time of my life.

With regards to simplifying the rest of the events in this book, a few other minor transpositions have been made. For example Mrs Shah's character represented a daisy chain of different people, both male and female, who were passing me information from inside and outside the PCT. In addition to occasional fused characters, a couple of scenes also had to be linked via narrative license, however, most situations occurred pretty much in the order I've described, even down to the meeting where I had to take advantage of the random coffee shop cat jumping on my chair. More importantly, there were some saga's that were actually left out…

Mark Twain once said, "A lie can travel halfway around the world while the truth is still putting on its shoes" and this would be true for me.

During my vocational training year (VT), apart from the problems caused by the nurse (doubling as a drug-rep) Trudy, who was telling practices not to touch me with a bargepole, I found myself up against a religious type (separate to Farlaine and the anonymous drugs accusation) who almost derailed my career too. As a key VT advisor, it was widely known that the person, who I shall not name, was an ex-alcoholic and had since become a church pastor, portraying a holier than thou image.

Doubling as a mentor to new graduates, he was employed to meet us weekly and ask how we were getting on. I told him that, having just qualified, I didn't really understand what all the dental snobbishness and prestige was about. After all, I was good at the job but no matter how frequently I listened to dentists dressing it up, scraping decay out of rotten mouths wasn't exactly thrilling.

I told him I was considering changing careers.

As it turns out, he was just that sort of dentist. As I saw it, he was a man who was obviously desperate to win back his own status in society.

Being a prominent dental advisor and a church pastor put him into the elevated position he craved. Listening to someone who didn't fawn over what, to him was beyond great, clearly made him take offence.

Without my knowledge, he created heat for me diverting it from himself. He visited, individually, other members of my VT group telling them that he was worried about me and thought I might kill myself. He asked the students if they knew anything. Of course, this being complete lies, none of them did. Conveniently, he never thought to share any of these precious concerns with me.

I had no idea this was even going on and only found out months later at the VT ball when graduates from other universities and practices, people I hadn't even met, were asking my mates who I was, me being the guy who was 'going to kill himself'.

When I challenged him about this, he backtracked (in a similar vein to Farlaine with Mr Chan) saying that he was just concerned about me (yeah – secretly spreading absolute lies that I was going to kill myself – I'm sure he was really concerned).

For the first time in my life, however, I realised how, regardless of truth, reputations can be destroyed and the impacts are lasting. I threatened to sue. As a result I was soon called to the more senior county VT advisor (his boss) who held a high position in the echelons of society.

In my opinion, he was just as bad. I hadn't been signed off with the VT's vital 'licence to practise' by this point and during the interview with him it became apparent that the purpose of our meeting was really just a shake down to scare me into not kicking up a fuss.

He started by saying that he'd had complaints from patients that I was "drilling someone's tooth while I was staring at the ceiling" ... Once again this was news to me. He then said another patient had complained saying that I "changed the radio half way through treatment".

Carrying on, he then badgered me as to whether I had asked the patient if he liked the radio station we'd been listening to and whether I'd given him the option of changing to another station.

This weird exchange continued and it appeared that he really wanted to sound out if I was going to cause them a fuss about the made up rumours. I soon sensed his undertone and had to reassure him and everyone that I was willing to kowtow. Just like with the drug test I was later set up for, however, the damage was done.

After working in prison and the beauty salon, I moved down to London and applied to Clive's.

On my CV I left out the parts about my working in a beauty salon but thankfully, for the main reference, my VT boss, my first boss who hasn't been mentioned in the story, valued me as a good worker.

As my primary reference he supported me despite the lies the VT head had spread. I set up and provided the prison email as I've described but, luckily, being secondary, it was never relied upon.

Pretty much everything else in the book – having to fake-play the drums, the revelation when I lost the tender, nearly all the shenanigans with Jack, the anaphylaxis, the inspection right the way through to the court case and Jack being burgled, plus every other chaotic thing in between – has been described as closely as possible.

For any worrying animal rights activists, I did, some readers may be relieved to know, take a minor liberty with the dead pigeons. No pigeons died in the telling of this event. Instead, once I'd taken over the practice, I'd asked Jack if he had anything I could use to deal with them. Being an ex-pharmacologist he had some random poison. I never used it in the end as, with nets, they just went away. I felt the poison did deserve a mention though, as related to this, for months, Jack had been complaining that he was ill.

It transpired that, while the poison was stored in his garage, which was directly underneath his bedroom, the top had been left partly off. The stuff was very dangerous and over time low concentrations of it had been evaporating through the floorboards and were slowly poisoning him.

No doubt this, along with his cerebellum damage from the scuba diving accident, hadn't done him or his balance any good.

Still, being the most charismatic and successful man I've ever met, both in fulfilment and adventure, Jack taught me so much about the zest for life and makes for such an exciting bloke to be with.

Besides being arrested for firing his magnum in the back garden, in the 90s, his life was threatened by a bouncer. Jack had been seeing the bouncer's girlfriend. As a reaction to the threat, Jack started to bring his loaded magnum into work. The bouncer never turned up in the end. I didn't know where to fit this into the book but it just makes me laugh how times have changed and stories like Jack's, in our grey humourless society, would cause people to lose their minds.

Looking over everything, I see now, that when I set out on this journey, I started with the same naivety any youth would but I was launched onto a very steep learning curve.

What astonished me most were the seemingly innocuous bastards I came up against. The VT dental advisor, the prison manager, the dentist Farlaine – all charlatans who opened my eyes to the reality of how many people holding higher positions, more often than not, have managed to climb there by fronting a completely false image.

Running a business in London eventually hardened me to such sharks but besides them and the likes of the financial adviser Neil, I found the most ruthless to be the landlord.

After all the years he'd been friendly with Jack, he had no qualms about imposing his bribe on what should have been a simple transaction. This shocked and abhorred me.

I could understand it if it had simply been about money or gaining some selfish benefit. For the first time in my life though, even when the landlord had every chance to drop the case and it was obvious he was actually going to be worse off, I realised his trapping actions were that of an evil man who simply enjoyed squashing people for the sake of flexing his might.

Following the court case win and with the landlord putting me under even more pressure, me being at serious risk of losing my parents' home, I began to have murderous thoughts about someone for the first and only time in my life.

Whether I'd have acted on them if he'd kept on pushing me is debatable. I doubt I would but it certainly wasn't cool.

With regards to the others, I have to say that Clive wasn't so bad. At times he could act a little pretentious but he was actually a decent dentist and before Jack, he had taught me an awful lot.

I was just disappointed when I discovered he'd screwed me on the tender, although to be fair, he did have every right to as I did strip naked at his Christmas do.

II

WHAT LIES AHEAD...

Since leaving dentistry, there is one thing I can be certain of. Although I came out of it uniquely well compared with my other colleagues and everything might sound easy and appealing from this side of the fence, I would never wish to go through such stress again.

On top of the growing pressures that now come with the profession, our own governing body (the General Dental Council) has started to work against decent dentists. This only represents the tip of the iceberg for a career that has shot to having the highest suicide rate in the UK. To me, it feels like all sensibility has been lost while our healthcare's ever-poisoning hunger for complaints is escalating way out of control.

Consider the press stunt the GDC pulled in 2014 where they used our money to nationally tout for the public to complain against us. It's worrying signs like these that show that they have clearly lost sight of their real purpose which is to root out and stop dodgy dentists.

Instead, they now beaver hard to advance their hidden primary interest which is not to contribute to a better healthcare service but to generate more complaints, boost their own importance and drive for the highest fees they can by cleverly using scaremongering tactics on both public and dentists alike. All actions of course, executed with complete plausible deniability.

To me, the other dismal players in all this, and perhaps somewhat the victims, have been the PCT's.

Operating as regional bodies for the NHS their purpose was to progress NHS dental care and other healthcare services such as GPs. Conducting themselves completely contrary to the way highly successful service industries do, they allowed themselves, unfortunately, to become complaint driven instead of service driven.

Just like the GDC, the PCT's reactions reached such ridiculousness that when they received even the slightest complaint, no matter how skewed or lacking in credibility, unable to react with measured insight or any sort of intelligence, they panicked by slamming down on the accused dentist almost as ruthlessly as the GDC.

It's not because the PCT's were staffed by bad people. It's because, unlike the GDC, they were stymied between pressures from central government (which are shaped disproportionately by complaints) and the hostility that their self-protecting policies created against the very healthcare professionals that they were supposed to support.

Forming an environment of engineered panic and misery, it's no accident that the staff turnover in these places was rapid. Furthermore, when it came to relationship building, they acted like scared chickens having just got hold of the farmer's axe.

When I was set up for the drug test for example, it was horrible to realise that as a professional, I was immediately treated as guilty until proven innocent from such a vague and anonymous complaint.

When the hospital lab sent me their all-clear results, I forwarded these onto the PCT to exonerate my name.

This, I was told, couldn't be regarded as even interim proof that I wasn't taking drugs and that it would only be resolved once they had the results sent directly from the lab.

Healthcare relies heavily on professionals being treated as professionals. The system has removed the benefit of the doubt for those who serve it.

This policy is not just restricted to dentists, it occurs, to an even greater extent, in medicine. Is it any wonder, then, that the relationship between healthcare workers and the NHS has become so fragmented and devoid of trust?

In 2013, as a result of their failings, the PCT's were closed around the country but in their place and picking up the baton of over-looked problems where PCT's left off, Area Teams were formed to continue the NHS's hugely failing UDA system while Care Quality Commissions were brought in to inspect practices.

Like the failing PCT's, the Government, regardless of all the rejigging of the applecart, still encourages the ever-worsening and remaining bad apple – the heavy hammer weighted to crash down on healthcare professionals who become the subject of complaints.

This undermines professionals at every stage ruining what could collaboratively be achieved.

In dentistry, yes I know everyone can gripe about our current UDA system and, further afield, how targets in other areas of healthcare, such as GP services, are derived, and yes, inevitably every system will have its flaws.

But the deeper and more insidious problem, unfortunately, and the one that no one in the mainstream is addressing, is the fact that the core of mutual trust between healthcare professionals and NHS management, under the direction of the government, is taking a nosedive.

If we wish to have a country that can offer a progressive National Health Service, something which I'm proud of and truly believe should remain, the weighting between professional respect and sensible responses to complaints must be brought back into balance.

If the weighting goes too far towards the professional where they are given blind trust, we end up with situations like Harold Shipman who did literally get away with murder for a time. Obviously this is not good.

However, when it goes too far the other way, which is how things are now, where decent professionals are being undermined at every opportunity, not only do the professionals suffer but the patients lose out as well. If you think about it, what other business or service would function successfully if its inherent nature was to split apart its own team's trust?

The NHS is one of the biggest employers we have, however, already the warning signs are upon us.

In recent years nearly all my professional friends, who are dedicated dentists or medical surgeons, are pulling away from working in the ever-worsening NHS environment that is now geared up to slam them.

The ones who stay have become conditioned to treat defensively instead of caringly. In hospitals, pretty much every junior surgeon I know now feels too scared to learn and progress as this inevitably involves mistakes – mistakes that in the past would have been understood as part of the learning curve but are deemed now as disciplinary mistreatments.

For now, the seeds of this problem are only bubbling under the surface. However, in a few years' time when all the well-trained consultants, buffering this inevitable shortfall, retire, we simply won't have the skills to deliver our best.

Added to this just look at the mass exodus of top doctors escaping to Australia and New Zealand. As a direct result of government attacks on them, applications to elope have shot up in recent months from 25 per day to, sometimes, 300. That's over a 1000% increase!!

Even if some of these numbers are spikes, that's still reaching 300 per day!!

What some of the general public forget is that while medicine might be a vocation it isn't another word for crusade. As you would expect in any other career or job, everyone has their breaking point and doctors are human just like the rest of us. When conditions are made impossible and all respect is bled, they leave.

So perhaps it can now be seen why, at some point, many decent professionals, the ones we should intelligently be nurturing, switch from wanting to give it their best to fighting back at the system and eventually saying, "Fuck you".

Well folks, besides the rule I learnt standing side by side with Jack which, incidentally, I've found to be so exact that I almost welcome the chaos, my closing message to you all is to have fun in life, never lose your sense of humour and hopefully I'll see you around.

Oh yeah, brush your teeth some of them stink...

To continue the fun join us at:
HangoutWithMikey.com

+

If you could please leave a review on Amazon. that would be fab!! :)

xoxo,

Tiesh